MADNESS IN ITS PLACE

This fascinating study presents a unique social history of psychiatry in the twentieth century. It brings together the memories and narratives of over sixty patients and workers who lived, or were employed, in Severalls Psychiatric Hospital, Essex, England. Personal accounts are contextualised both in relation to wider developments and issues in twentieth-century mental health, and in relation to policies and changes in the hospital itself.

Organised around the theme of space and place, and drawing upon both quantitative as well as qualitative material, chapters deal with key areas such as gender divisions, power relations, patterns of admission and discharge, treatments, and the daily lives and routines of patients and nurses of both sexes.

Madness in its Place provides an unusual and very accessible account of trends and changes in the history of psychiatry during the twentieth century, while at the same time offering a lively narrative of the daily lives of those who worked and lived in a typical psychiatric hospital. It is valuable reading for anybody with an interest in mental health, hospitals and hospitalisation, and social policy.

Diana Gittins is a writer and poet who studied Sociology and Social History at the University of Essex. She was awarded a Hawthornden Fellowship in 1993 and has worked as a consultant in Women's Studies at the Open University. Her publications include *Fair Sex: Family Size and Structure, 1900–39* (1982) and *The Family in Question: Changing Households and Familiar Ideologies* (1993).

MADNESS IN ITS PLACE

Narratives of Severalls Hospital, 1913–1997

Diana Gittins

London and New York

First published 1998
by Routledge
11 New Fetter Lane, London EC4P 4EE

Simultaneously published in the USA and Canada
by Routledge
29 West 35th Street, New York, NY 10001

Typeset in Sabon and Helvetica by
Florencetype Ltd, Stoodleigh, Devon

Printed and bound in Great Britain by
Biddles Ltd, Guildford and King's Lynn

British Library Cataloguing in Publication Data
A catalogue record for this book is available from the British
Library

Library of Congress Cataloging in Publication Data
Gittins, Diana.
Madness in its place: narratives of Severalls Hospital,
1913–1997/Diana Gittins.
Includes bibliographical references and index.
1. Severalls Hospital (Essex, England – History.
2. Psychiatric hospitals – England – Essex – History
– twentieth century. 3. Psychiatry – History
– twentieth century. I. Title.
RC450.G72S484 1998
362.2'1'094267–dc21 97–39489
CIP

ISBN 0–415–16786–8 (hbk)
ISBN 0–415–18388–X (pbk)

I am! Yet what I am who cares, or knows?
My friends forsake me like a memory lost.
   I am the self-consumer of my woes;
     They rise and vanish, an oblivious host,
     Shadows of life, whose very soul is lost.
     And yet I am – I live – though I am toss'd

Into the nothingness of scorn and noise,
   Into the living sea of waking dream,
     Where there is neither sense of life, nor joys,
     But the huge shipwreck of my own esteem
     And all that's dear. Even those I loved the best
Are strange – nay, they are stranger than the rest.

I long for scenes where man has never trod –
For scenes where woman never smiled or wept –
   There to abide with my Creator, God,
     And sleep as I in childhood sweetly slept,
Full of high thoughts, unborn. So let me lie, –
   The grass below; above, the vaulted sky.

John Clare (1793–1864)

In memory of my mother
Lloyd Pierce Butler
(1922–1984)
who died in Severalls

CONTENTS

CONTENTS

ILLUSTRATIONS

TABLES

ACKNOWLEDGEMENTS

I would first and foremost like to thank the North East Essex Mental Health NHS Trust who funded this project and generously gave me access to their information, records and photographs. Christopher Bridge, Chief Executive of the Trust, has been particularly helpful and encouraging throughout, and I would like to thank him for all his support. I would also like to thank the University of Essex for appointing me as Research Fellow in the Sociology Department, and gratefully acknowledge a small grant from the Sociology Department's Fuller Bequest that enabled me to research Dr Russell Barton's archives.

Joan Busfield, Felicity Edholm and Paul Thompson – but especially Joan Busfield – have given me a great deal of time, encouragement and constructive criticism; all good friends, I would like to thank them warmly for their sustained, and sustaining, support. One of the most rewarding aspects of this project has been getting to know Dr Russell Barton, who kindly gave me many interviews as well as access to his private letters and records, and who became a good friend in the process. I would also like to thank Marion Haberhauer for her skilful and speedy work in transcribing many of the tapes, Maureen Bragg, who made me feel very welcome when I first arrived at Severalls and performed many much appreciated jobs for me there, and Brenda Corti and Mary Girling who have given me no end of support of all kinds throughout the project.

My greatest debt, however, is to all those people who gave me so much of their time, memories and accounts of their lives and work at Severalls Hospital, and who often made me welcome in their homes. I am especially grateful to those people who had been patients in Severalls and were willing to share with me their often painful, albeit moving and invaluable, memories of such difficult times. Without their generosity and courage, this book could not have been written.

It has been my hope to present as wide-ranging a view as possible of the very mixed, and often contradictory, history of Severalls Hospital over the past eighty-four years. I have tried, in the process, to offer as balanced an account as I can, letting people who lived, worked and were confined there speak in their own words of their own memories and impressions. Given the vagaries of all our memories and the even more slippery processes of selection, editing and interpretation on my part, no doubt I have presented material some will consider inaccurate or inappropriate. If so, I apologise, but I hope readers will understand the spirit of the project: to try and better understand the ways in which people at all levels acted, interacted, reacted and remembered some of the intricate threads and strands that made Severalls Hospital the unique tapestry of lives and experiences it was.

Part of 'An Anatomy of Migraine' from *Archaic Figure* by Amy Clampitt is reproduced by permission of Faber & Faber Ltd. Figure 1.1 is reproduced by courtesy of Essex County Newspapers; Figure 2.1, 3.2, 6.5 and 7.2 by courtesy of the Russell Barton archive, University of Essex; Figure 6.3 as a gift from Julian Taylor, and the remainder by permission of the North East Essex Mental Health NHS Trust.

1

INTRODUCTION
Space, time and madness

A few weeks after Severalls, Essex County Council's second lunatic asylum, opened its doors in May 1913, the first radio signal was beamed across the world from the Eiffel Tower. A symbol and portent of impending collapse of earlier notions of space and time, it established world time and would also make the earth a 'global village'. In that same year, Henry Ford began the first assembly-line production of cars, heralding both mass-production on a huge scale and a revolution in transport. Just over one year later, the First World War would shatter old beliefs about madness and psychiatry, religion, nation, gender. Prior to this, of course, myriad changes had already come about and were still in process, but the rate of change varied enormously, and though the industrial world had long been ruled by the invariant measure of clocks, it could still be said that in some areas of the world, particularly remote areas, different ways of experiencing time still existed.

Rural Essex at this time still operated in ways that had changed only slowly over the past century; the majority of patients who filled Severalls' wards, at least until well into the twentieth century, came from rural areas and agricultural work where their lives were dominated by time that was as much determined by seasons, moons, frosts, rains, planting and harvesting cycles as by clocks. The rural population was still travel-ling by foot, bicycle, horse and cart. Towns such as Colchester, Chelmsford, Clacton and Harwich, which were also part of Severalls' huge catch-ment area[1] were different, and those who worked in the manufacturing industries and shops would be used to a rigid clock-dominated way of life and work. Temporalities shift and vary according to people's lives and experiences.

The world was rapidly speeding up, becoming a smaller and increasingly more accessible place, but the rate and the pace at which it did so varied enormously from country to country, region to region, hamlet to town, and town to city. Such changes meant a more extended reaching-out to other cultures, other places, a process begun with colonisation and one which accelerated dramatically during the course of the First World War,

1

to a large extent as a result of the new 'world time' and the revolutions in communication and transportation.

While on the one hand new developments reached outwards, parallel developments resulted in an increasing tendency to look *inwards*, to seek to understand and analyse the invisible interior. Rutherford's work on the atomic nucleus was a looking-within which would in time have, literally, earth-shattering repercussions. The discovery of X-rays by Roentgen in 1895 meant, among other things, that for the first time the interior of the human body could be scrutinised. The writings of Joyce, Proust, Woolf and Richardson were all both exploring a more interior world of the individual and challenging old notions of temporality, linearity and realism. Much of this had been influenced by Freud's theory of psychoanalysis, another prime example of a quest for the unseen, the unknown, the invisible darkness, a quest that was in many ways represented in Conrad's *Heart of Darkness* and, of course, acted out in reality in colonial quests, expeditions and adventures generally.

Freud's theory challenged prevailing ideas of psychiatry, dominated by the ideas of genetics and a 'faulty-machine' model, by claiming that much, if not all, mental illness can be seen as a result of childhood trauma. This model was to become known as a 'functional' model and the two models, or discourses, would vie uneasily for dominance throughout the twentieth century. Freud's ideas were to have, of course, much wider influence on the world, and on the arts and literature in particular. The famous Armory show in New York in 1913 brought together art by Picasso, Matisse, Brancusi, Braque, Klee, de Chirico and Kandinsky, all of whom were challenging old realist ideas of perspective, space, realism and dimension and were much influenced by the idea of the unconscious. Yet these were, at least initially, metropolitan developments, changes at the core that were, in time, to reverberate through peripheries, but which in 1913, in rural Essex, were probably noted by only a small handful of local middle-class professionals. Most probably the walls of small agricultural workers' cottages in Great Horkesley or Boxted or Elmstead Market would display an old sampler proclaiming 'Bless this House'.

As the new atonal music of Schoenberg, Bartok and Berg was blowing apart old ordered patterns of narrative in music in concert halls in New York and Paris and Berlin, agricultural workers in north-east Essex would still be singing folk songs going back a hundred years or more, dancing to melodic tunes played on a fiddle at a Harvest Home in the local barn. Indeed, the farm workers and patients who worked on Severalls' two farms were still celebrating Harvest Homes after the Second World War. In 1913, when D.H. Lawrence's *Sons and Lovers* was first published, challenging Victorian ideas of morality, sexuality and secrecy, illegitimacy and pre-marital sexual relations were still considered shameful among the Essex population at virtually all class levels, and remained grounds for certifying wayward daughters as 'morally insane' for many years to come. Many such young women were brought by their families to Severalls and left there, their very existence denied by their kin, for thirty, forty or fifty years. Many of them died in Severalls, some very recently.

Chaos was increasingly seen by philosophers, artists and writers as characteristic of the new, modern world, a view to which, at least until 1914, probably the majority of the population, going on about their work and lives, trying to make ends meet and survive, gave little thought. Unemployment and poverty were rising in Essex. Times were hard. In 1911 30 per cent of the entire population of Essex was classified as paupers. Though people might marvel at a new steam threshing machine, theories of chaos or modernism were almost certainly not burning issues to the thousands of people who would soon come through Severalls' gates both as patients and as workers. Yet modernism was at its peak in 1913. Not easy to define, it is generally taken to encompass, along with fears of chaos, parallel beliefs in, and a veneration of, objective science, rationality and the possibility of universal laws and morality: 'Generally perceived as positivistic, technocratic, and rationalistic, universal, modernism has been identified with the belief in linear progress, absolute truths, the rational planning of ideal social orders, and the standardisation of knowledge and production.'[2]

Integral to the belief in rationality and the potential of scientific progress was medical practice and discourse. Psychiatrists desperately wanted to be part of the strengthening trend towards medicine-as-science, yet during the course of the nineteenth century they had worked and practised almost exclusively as 'alienists' within asylums. As such they were more custodians than doctors and were regarded by the rest of the medical profession as poor cousins, Cinderellas of medicine. The track record of cure in psychiatry was very poor indeed; some treatments, such as bromides, paraldehyde, continuous baths and physical restraint by straitjackets, helped to alleviate, sedate and control, but at this point there were no more real 'cures' in evidence than there had been a hundred years previously, or indeed, a thousand years previously.

A PLACE FOR MADNESS

Severalls Hospital was constituted as a specific set of buildings in time and space. Between 1913 and 1997, the years of its opening and closing, although there were additions and alterations,[3] the infrastructure of the hospital remained very much as it was built, covering a specific area and space. Severalls as a material place therefore continued in apparently the same way over time. Yet between those years many things changed and altered within the hospital's routines, staffing, population, rules, divisions,

Figure 1.1 Aerial photograph of Severalls, 1978
Source: Picture by courtesy of Essex County Newspapers

regulations, administration and management. To try and account for the history of the hospital thus demands consideration of both space and time, and the interstices and intersections between them.

Space, as Foucault argues, is a metaphor for a site of power which usually constrains but can also liberate. The way in which space is organised constrains, limits and divides can, and frequently did, oppress and repress. Class, gender and categorising of illness were literally built into the hospital infrastructure and thus operated as primary determinants of power relations and a way of life. Through these, Severalls' inhabitants' notions of identity and self were to a great extent constructed, or re-constructed (indeed, *de*-constructed in the older sense of the term), imprinted and defined.[4] It thus formed a representation of the world that was, or some thought should be, a mental hospital and all those who lived and worked inside it. It was, in a sense, a 'realised myth'[5]: a myth of what an elite group wanted to represent as madness, and madness contained and controlled.

Material space, however, is not the only space, and try though authorities may to define, delimit and contain mental illness within material confines, there still remains another space: the space of imagination, vision, madness, or what Bachelard calls 'poetic space'.[6] Patients I interviewed often described their experiences of visions/delusion/epileptic fits as if they were quite distinct landscapes they inhabited at times, landscapes for which, and in which, the lines and grey routines of the hospital were but hazy, one-dimensional unrealities. One woman, who has been in and out of Severalls since the 1960s, described her experiences of manic-depression to me:

It was like – like being put into a glass case, and gradually the lid was lowered, the sound was blocked out. Then the glass was scoured, so you could see less and less through it. And somehow the temperature was dropped. The worst of it is, when it starts, when the glass case is first on you, the lid being put over, and the first scratches on the side, you know what's happening and you know how it's going to develop. That is the worst part. When I get to smashing windows, I'm getting better. That's coming out of the glass. But this knowing how it's going to develop, knowing you're powerless to stop it, is the worst part of all. People keep saying, 'Oh – it was so bad seeing you in the hospital and – you know, this, that or the other was going on', and I can't, can't get over to them that by then it was actually better. It was the weeks and months before, when it's closing down . . .

I've been on walks when I could see the black beast, which is my name for it. But I could actually see it. I'd turn my head, I'd see it behind me. I'd hear it and smell it. I can't really say what it looked

5

like, except it always had claws, which would land on me or grab me, or whatever. I can smell it and hear it as well as see it. In fact, the smell is – the first symptom, always. I start smelling things that aren't there. Usually burning.

And then you come out, and the rooms are small, and there's all these self-contained little human beings, apart from the one or two really close to you, all the others are all sort of wrapped up in poly-thene, little layers of it. You can't get, you can't get hold of them. There's no way to make contact with them. It's a reverse of – for me, when I'm going into the illness, there's the glass case which gets more and more scratched, but when I'm coming out, everyone else is in a glass case.

Colour was more intense, and blacks and reds and blues in partic-ular – very very strong. And coming out, there doesn't seem to be that. And coming, actually, I was last in in 1990, and it's only this summer [1995] that colours and people are beginning to take what I feel is a more natural – place. When I come out everything's small, even trains are small. And everything's sort of – everyone is, as I say, sort of wrapped up, so you can't see their – their physical colours or their mental colours, without a great deal of difficulty. And then over the next few years, the first thing I – there are two things I notice first. Birdsong. And the colour of the grass. And I know when I, when I feel those two things, that I'm coming to the end of the bout.

When I'm clean out of my head? Oh. I don't think I can explain it in clear, verbal, logical language. It's – it's – being in a room – I'll have to do it by describing some of the visions . . . Sitting in a room, and suddenly not being in that room, but being on a completely unsolid snowscape with – sort of birds swooping down. And suddenly the snowscape isn't unsolid, it's black and grey and slushy, with bits of orange. You know the plastic orange sort of netting that's put round a manhole sometimes? Well, bits of these orange plastic netting sticking up and tripping.

And then suddenly – small children appear, that they've – no faces, and where they should have eyes and nose and ears and mouths, there's just worms coming out. And – I'm just getting sicker and sicker, but I know I can't vomit. And I just start running and running and hitting anyone who gets in the way, and smashing any windows that get in the way. And if the nurses or anyone tried to stop me, I know the one thing I was ever saying was, 'Let me go! Let me go! Let me go!' Because I just wanted to run and get away from it all, and the only way I could get away from it all was to kill myself and to run and run and run and run, until I could do it. And all the time, these things were running with me.

This place is a special place, a landscape shared and experienced by few, although feared and generally stigmatised by the majority. Listening to the powerful, often beautiful and colourful descriptions by these people, and the often profound insights arising from discussing them, made me understand why and how such visions have been linked with shamanic powers in other cultures and how in the 1960s, so-called 'anti-psychiatrists', such as R.D. Laing, revived the idea of schizophrenia as visionary and positive.[7]

The material space of wards was designed to facilitate containment and control of people during such experiences when, as the above patient makes clear, violence can become an inherent part of the extreme pressures within an interior landscape. Locked wards, side rooms with judas holes, padded rooms, half-padded rooms, enclosed airing courts, were all sub-spaces of control. Sometimes even these needed to be reinforced by mechanical restraint or physical restraint; the woman above gives an account of being held down by seven nurses during one of her bouts of going 'out of her head'. Interestingly, she never experienced this as anything but helpful. Over time, chemical means of restraint have grown to dominate and replace other means of control.

Severalls was conceived and built on the basis of old nineteenth-century architectural ideals and practices laid down by nineteenth-century ideals of madness and psychiatry; in just over a year a world war was to test many of these ideas and practices and would, indeed, fill many beds with shell-shocked soldiers. Gender barriers, so meticulously set up, crashed down, albeit temporarily, as male nurses vanished *en masse* from wards to vanish for good on the battlefields of the First World War. Women, defined by Victorians as weak and helpless, worked in the fields of the hospital farm, worked in the male wards on the male side of the hospital, worked in the engineering factories in Colchester. Time was blown apart during those years, and with it many long-standing ideas and traditions.

But there are, and were, many times, just as there are many spaces, and the time experienced by artists, musicians and writers in Paris was not those of women and men working as laundry maids, nurses, porters and attendants in Severalls. Nor were the workers' times the same as doctors' times or patients' times. Nurses were bound by strict time-keeping regimes; night nurses had to punch in 'tell-tale clocks' on their rounds. Virtually all staff except the professionals had to clock in and out. Patients' time appeared to relate to an endless daily routine of meals, medications and exercise in which months, years, even decades rarely bore much relevance and were almost impossible for them to remember. Yet for many patients, just as there was a 'mad space' or 'poetic space', so there could also be, linked to that space, a different sense of time. A man who spent much time in and out of Severalls since the late 1960s, shared his experiences of past lives and visiting other planets with me. It is worth pointing out that new age shops are now full of books on 'past-lives therapy' and past-life experiences written by those who have not been classified as mentally ill.

According to what I've visualised – visions of things – I don't die this time, I've worked out enough. My millionth life and I've worked out enough to stay alive now. So, it's pretty good – a good prospect, isn't it? And people are thinking more along those lines now, that maybe we don't have to die if we treat ourselves in the right ways.

I can remember some of the other lives. Yeah, I've had so many in so many different countries. Well, most of all I've been an American Indian, 'cause I like their way of life more than anyone else's way of life. And Tibetan, I might have been a Tibetan, I'm not sure about that, but I think I understand them pretty well. At school I used to draw a lot of Viking battleships and felt as if I'd been a Viking as well, and I felt I knew all about their boats and the things they wore and things like that.

They're either visions or hallucinations, you see. They may be true and they may be false. But I tend to think they're true. I'd think, yeah, I definitely have. Well, I know I have. You know, I think some people are newcomers to earth and they don't know how to behave. Some people have got more experience 'cause they've lived other lives, many other lives for a long time, had long lives. I think I don't quite understand people on this planet. They don't seem very normal to me, not very normal at all, some of them.

Well, you might think what I'm saying is a load of rubbish, but I am, well, I'm pretty sure I came from Jupiter at one time. I visualised coming down in an automatic spacecraft. Down to earth. Yeah. Blue, purple, mauve and white colours. I don't remember any other colours – it was all like as if it was tranquillised. Everything was sort of destroyed, so we had to get off the planet in the spacecraft really. Don't know – it was a huge planet, but there'd been storms, you know, I think we had storms when we were leaving, yes. Swirling winds round the planets. But that I don't remember – only that, I've read. That part I've read about, 'cause I can't really connect that with why we left. That might have come a lot later.

I just thought when we left that we'd be tranquillised for ever more. Everything had this sort of starey feel about it, look about it

– sparkling and things destroyed with no vegetation left at all. Roads and dome buildings – and not all that many of those – quite thinly spread around. I remember white domes, sort of like that, buildings where we lived, but I can't remember any industry.[8]

Inpatients were organised by a strict routine, a routine so rigid and regular that those who lived there for years often withdrew into muteness, passivity, an inner world, of, perhaps, memories and dreams, but equally likely to have been one of nightmares bounded by a need to forget. And yet, as with so much, contradictions abound. It seems that for some, particularly women, the fact that they *could* withdraw from the outside world, from family time and body time dominated by endless pregnancies, poverty, abuse, meant that life in Severalls could provide a time of peace and a possibility of *asylum*, in the original sense of the word. One woman, when I asked what had helped her most to recover from mental illness, said:

Getting lost into the lovely grounds. There was plenty of places to look and come to terms with one's feelings, whereas the new mental hospitals they just haven't got the facilities. They've got tiny gardens which are locked often. You don't have the space. It was an *asylum*, so that in the grounds, you know, you were safe. It was an asylum, and yet you were free.

Architecture, the philosopher Karsten Harries has argued, functions not just as a domestication of space, but also as a deep defence against 'the terror of time'.[9] How, for instance, did the organisation of space of the place itself affect daily routines, work tasks, a sense of past, present and future? In what ways did the design of the buildings impose patterns of interactions and power relations? How did the passing of time in the wider world, historical events such as war, depression (economic), the NHS and welfare state, technological innovations such as radio, TV, computers and cars affect both the place itself and the regime and routines within it?

THE IDEAL OF AN ASYLUM

Since the early nineteenth century the ideal for asylums was one of fresh air and a rural setting that offered patients peace and quiet. In effect this meant most asylums were situated in fairly isolated locations:

From 1815 onwards it became fashionable to emphasise the importance of healthy, airy sites, a pure water supply and enough space

Figure 1.2 Ward and grounds, *circa* 1955
Source: North East Essex Mental Health NHS Trust

to permit recreation. The actual choice of a site for an individual asylum was increasingly determined by its proximity to county towns, the ease with which the site could be reached using public transport and the need for it to be at the centre of the catchment area to be served by the asylum. Asylums built in the latter part of the century were of increasingly large size.[10]

Such ideals were still very much in fashion and in force at the time when it was first decided to build a new county asylum near Colchester. Part of the history of Severalls Hospital during the course of the twentieth century, and indeed a central part of the history of mental health during this period, concerns changes in this ideal, the reasons for the changes, and the effects of the implementation of such changes on hospital patients, staff, buildings and conditions.

The original ideal was one carefully stipulated and outlined by a small group of officials: first, the Commissioners in Lunacy[11] until 1913, then the Board of Control[12] until 1959. Both of these agencies were appointed and run by central government. The Lunacy Act of 1845 made it compul-

sory for counties and boroughs to provide pauper lunatic asylums. At
that time a system was also instigated to control all such projects and
implement inspection and design standards by which local authorities had
to abide. Separation of different patient types, for instance, was a principle
laid down by John Conolly in his book *The Construction of Government
and Lunatic Asylums* (1847). While various asylum architects subsequently
modified some of Conolly's ideas, nevertheless fundamental principles of
divisions, first, by gender, and second, by patient types, remained central
to the construction of all asylums. Equally important was the orientation
of the asylum so as to maximise sunlight and views of rural landscapes,
both deemed fundamental to the well-being, if not cure, of patients. Patients
I interviewed clearly still valued such ideals. This woman, for instance,
compared Severalls with the new acute unit, The Lakes, attached to
Colchester General Hospital:

> The grounds at Severalls, they were safe, they were – there were
> places where you might catch the odd glimpse of beauty. I mean,
> there was more than the odd glimpse then, but when you're in that
> state, you only see the odd glimpse. No, The Lakes is all wrong.
> Wrong. I don't care what they say about those big wards – there
> was *light* in them. A lot of light. You go to The Lakes now, it's
> almost like being in an air raid shelter, except you don't feel safe
> – or I don't. When The Lakes was being designed, plans were
> brought into Birchwood, the day hospital, for staff and patients to
> look at and make their comments, and I think nearly all the patients
> said, 'It's too claustrophobic. There's not enough light.'

Mental hospitals are designed by a few people in relation both to financial constraints and what is thought to be good for mental patients by
the medical profession, politicians and administrators at that particular
point in time. Light and fresh air have not been fashionable cures, or
therapies, for many decades. Before Severalls was built, it was the
Commissioners in Lunacy who laid down specific laws for the construction
of *all* asylums. From the 1850s the Commissioners in Lunacy produced,
and regularly updated, a pamphlet entitled *Suggestions and Instructions
with Reference to Lunatic Asylums*. This laid down

> a firm set of constructional criteria and space standards to be
> addressed by the architect – with precise particulars of the drawings,
> building schedule, estimates of cost, specification and service system
> details ... On the document's inner cover there was a sharp
> reminder for the more adventurous: 'Elaboration of design for
> merely architectural effect will not be sanctioned, and decorative

stonework or other expensive material introduced for that purpose
will prejudice the approval of the plans for the Home Secretary'.[13]

A final revision to this document was made by the Board of Control in
1911, specifying that no estate of less than 50 acres would be a suitable
site, and that the site 'should be elevated, undulating in its surface, cheerful
in its position, and having a general fall to the south or south-east', while
the overall form 'should be such as to afford an uninterrupted view of
surrounding country and free access of sun, and air'.[14]

PUTTING THE IDEAL INTO PRACTICE

By the early twentieth century, at the time the Severalls site was being
chosen, and early plans drawn up, the themes and plans of asylum architecture had become more extended, largely because of the ever-increasing
numbers that had to be accommodated. The original Essex County Asylum
at Brentwood, for instance, was designed initially for 300 patients on an
86-acre site. By the time it opened in 1853, the number of patients had
already expanded to 450. In 1891 it had 1,350 patients and it was just
this severe overcrowding at Brentwood that made a second county asylum
an urgent and pressing need for the county.

The first inkling that Colchester might be the site of the second county
asylum was reported in the local press in October, 1902:

> foreshadowing the necessity for building a second lunatic asylum
> for Essex, nothing is said as to the cost . . . the new building must,
> in the opinion of the committee [the Committee of Visitors from the
> Commissioners in Lunacy], accommodate not less than 500 adults,
> in addition to 100 idiot children . . . it is evident that an undertaking
> of great magnitude and cost is contemplated. It will be seen that the
> Committee propose that the new asylum should be designed to
> specially provide for patients from the Northern and North-eastern
> districts of Essex . . . Under these circumstances the well-meant
> suggestions made by Alderman Kemble, that the committee should
> buy up a big hotel at Southend, does not seem to be exactly prac-
> ticable. As a matter of fact, I believe that Colchester holds the
> field, or, in other words, contains the most eligible site for the new
> building, in the Corporation Severalls.[15]

And, indeed, such was to be the case. In 1903 Colchester Corporation
offered to sell 295 acres of the Severalls[16] Estate, which it had owned since
the middle of the nineteenth century.[17] The price was £10,000. After the land
had been sold, however, a number of debates and conflicts arose over, in

particular, water supply and provision of electricity to the site. There had also been an old infectious diseases hospital on the site which needed to be removed. Most of the conflicts focused, then as now, on financial issues; who should bear the costs of providing mains sewerage and water were particularly acrimonious areas of debate. In the end it was agreed that Colchester Borough Council would provide the mains sewer and half the cost of the water mains, while the hospital would generate its own electricity.

Essex County Council architects, Whitmore and Town, drew up the plans in 1906; certain amendments were made subsequently. In 1909[18] the tender accepted for building the new asylum by Essex County Council was rejected by the Home Secretary on the grounds that, of the twenty-two tenders offered, the one chosen was not the lowest.[19] Cheapest is best has long been an implicit policy of central government, it would seem, when it comes to allocation of resources for the mentally ill. The committee resigned in protest, but advertisements were nevertheless made for a fresh contract, much to the disgust of the local media at the time, which made broad hints about corruption. Newspaper reports drew attention to the high numbers of unemployed in Colchester and their very great distress: 'What Archbishop Tillotson said of the Athanasian creed we may all well say of the proposed Asylum which is not likely to do our town any good when it is completed, and is doing us a good deal of harm while it is uncompleted.'[20]

Finally the tender of £188,350 put forward by W. King of Westminster was accepted in March 1909. By September of that year the number of paupers in Essex was 31.7 per 1,000 population, an 11 per cent increase over the previous ten years, and that figure excluded tramps and pauper lunatics.[21] And the number of pauper lunatics rose rapidly from the first half of the nineteenth century up until the 1930s. In 1847, for instance, there were 5,247 pauper patients in 21 county and borough asylums in the publicly placed sector in England and Wales.[22] By 1914, the year after Severalls opened, there were over 138,000 patients. By 1990/91, six years before Severalls closed, there were only 48,700.[23]

Since by far the great majority of patients in county asylums were paupers, the swelling numbers of paupers needed the hospital both as a source of employment and as a potential refuge. The links between poverty and mental illness were particularly marked because of their shared location within the poor law system. As Busfield states:

> Public asylums were first and foremost poor law institutions and it was the character of the poor law that largely determined their nature. It affected the numbers, flow and characteristics of the inmates to be found within them; it affected the size and scale of the institutions; it affected the resources available to them, including the numbers, qualifications and attitudes of the medical men and the attendants who worked within them.[24]

13

Table 1.1 Average number of resident patients, Severalls, 1913–1974

Year	Number	Year	Number
1913	719*	1947	1782
1914	1234	1948	1766
1915	1386	1949	1742
1916	1796	1950	1721
1917	1900	1951	1719
1918	1784	1952	1726
1919	n/a	1953	1738
1920	1388	1954	1781
1921	1434	1955	1771
1922	1477	1956	1757
1923	1573	1957	1809
1924	1621	1958	1769
1925	1615*	1959	1675
1926	n/a	1960	1511
1927	1739*	1961	1413
1928	1735	1962	1345
1929	1809	1963	1412
1930	1821*	1964	1313
1931	1895*	1965	1267
1932	2044	1966	1203
1933	1987	1967	1188
1934	2086	1968	1127
1935	2173	1969	1096
1936	2222	1970	1072*
1937	2155*	1971	933
...		1972	953
1945	1965*	1973	919
1946	1920	1974	852

Source: Medical superintendent's reports, Severalls House Committee, 1913–1960.
*based on incomplete records for that year

A temporary railway line was built to run from North Station up Clay Lane (now Turner Road) to carry building materials to the asylum site, about a mile away. At this time, and for many years to come, however, there was no public transportation available beyond North Station. Mile End Road was a country lane, and although in 1904 three electric tram lines were set up in Colchester, all stopped at North Station.[25] Not until 1929 was a bus route established that went to Nayland.

By June 1910 the main structure of the asylum, the main building, was nearing completion and almost fully roofed. It measured some 1,500 feet from east to west, and about 800 feet north to south, covering some 14 acres of ground. The western boundary was laid out and planted with trees and shrubs and a large cricket ground on the southern side was being prepared. Designed to hold 2,000 patients eventually, at this point there was accommodation for only 1,500.

The hospital was originally designed to separate what were then seen as different categories of patient in relation to their illness:

> In the planning of the ward blocks, a key function that the architect had to allow for was the suitable and convenient categorisation of different types of patient. At the most fundamental level there would be bi-axial symmetry ... the separation of the plan into two almost identical halves, one for female patients and the other for male. A ready identifier of this primary division would be the allocation of the laundry complex and drying court to the women's side, and the workshops area to the men's side ... The more detailed levels of classification would, by the 1890s, be providing quite separate ward blocks and related exercise ('airing') courts to respond to five main groups of patients. One recommended allocation was: 25% Sick and Infirm; 20% Recent and Acute; 15% Epileptics; 40% Working and Quiet Chronic.[26]

As Busfield[27] points out, however, classifications were more a matter of convenient categories for management than of medical diagnosis, and were primarily grouped 'along lines envisaged by the poor law – by age, sex, social class, curability, quietness and amenability'.[28] The estate was completely surrounded by oak palings 6 feet high, and wards had small gardens, or 'airing-courts' all of which were enclosed by ha-has and iron railings. At the time the land was purchased, the estate included the rather aptly named Cuckoo Farm (the name pre-dated the siting of the asylum there), and this began to be farmed in 1904, under the management of a Mr Fairhead.

In June 1910 the foundation stone was laid by Sir Thomas Barrett Lennard, chairman of the Visitors of the Essex and Colchester Lunatic Asylum.[29] By this time the water tower and chimney shaft, which rose nearly 100 feet above ground level,[30] were clearly visible from the top of North Hill and from Balkerne Hill, reminders of an area beyond the town, beyond 'civilisation' and 'reason', an area little known or understood, though much feared, where each and every individual might, if they were not careful or if luck failed them, end up. On the periphery, after initial press coverage about its opening, Severalls was rarely mentioned in the media again between 1913 and 1960.[31] Yet there it stood on the horizon, a concrete reminder to all in the Colchester vicinity.

All wards in the main building were connected to each other via communicating corridors, or coverways as they were first called. One nurse, who was born in 1918 and began working at Severalls in 1936, remembered:

> You know the corridors? There were lots of little ladies scrubbing the corridors. They would be scrubbing the corridors with sack

aprons on their knees. Have they got windows in the corridors there now? Well, there never used to be any windows. There were the holes, but no glass in them. Open to the elements! And we'd come off duty and all you'd hear was a screaming – the bats would be coming up and down the corridors! Yes! They'd be flying up and down the corridors! When we came off duty we'd put our capes over our heads and we'd be screaming!

The windows in the corridors were not fitted with frames and glazed until 1950; there were 234 window frames in the corridors. In later years nurses bicycled up and down the corridors, and indeed there was a story told by several people I interviewed about a patient bicycling down the corridors. Here one man who came from Hong Kong as a student nurse and rose into management, tells his version of the story:

I can still remember one particular lady, one of the biggest things that – and it must have gone down in the folklore of this hospital. One of the incidents was that we had this patient went missing from what was then the locked female ward – Osyth Ward – and somebody who tended to be extremely violent. And if you happen to find her you need at least ten staff to pin her down, and she's capable of lashing out and inflicting. And we look for her all over the place. And we're getting more worried. We tell the police. We said, 'Be careful with her! This lady, this person, is very violent. Approach with caution!'

The next thing, we heard this bell. Clink-clink, clink-clink! coming along. And this particular lady come along riding on a bicycle, absolutely starkers, and laughing and smiling to everybody, waving at them – and had a whale of a time! In fact, when she eventually stopped, we had no problem getting her back to the ward. She just come – she had her fun.

Severalls generated its own electricity from the start and this must have seemed very modern indeed to those who came to stay and live there, many of whom came from homes which would not have electricity at all until the 1940s. Artificial light changes daily rhythms and their variability by season; it enables rigid daily routines to be enforced year-round in an invariant manner. Such time-tables were a result of hospital needs and hospital times, not patients' needs or times. The boilers for the hospital were supplied by Paxman's of Colchester, a local engineering firm. There was a recreation hall 120 feet long by 60 feet wide, which came to be well known locally and much loved by staff in particular. During the

16

Figure 1.3 Staff New Year's dance in the main hall, 1950s
Source: North East Essex Mental Health NHS Trust

Second World War, a man who worked there then said it was the first place American soldiers asked for on arrival to Colchester during the war, as it was famous for being the largest dance hall for miles around.

Numerous workshops existed in the main building for upholsterers, tailors, cobblers, painters, carpenters, plumbers, glaziers, electricians on the male side. On the female side was a huge kitchen and bakehouse, a large laundry, and workshops for needlewomen.

Central and vital to the whole structure was the division between the female and male sides. The hospital, as stipulated by the Commissioners in Lunacy for all asylums, was designed in such a way that female and male patients would not meet except under carefully controlled and supervised circumstances. This was enforced and reinforced through separation, locked doors, ha-has and iron railings.[32] Since 1853 the design of asylums had moved away from highly centralised, prison-type plans to larger ones incorporating Conolly's ideals of light, landscape and, by the early twentieth century, the 'villa system'.

Severalls could be said to resemble the human brain: the left side, the left hemisphere was the female side, while the right hemisphere was the male side. The two were divided, and linked, by a central corridor of power, a kind of *corpus callosum*, bifurcating what were, in many ways, two completely separate hospitals. In the corridor of power, the *corpus callosum*, were the offices of the medical superintendent, the secretary and clerk, the

17

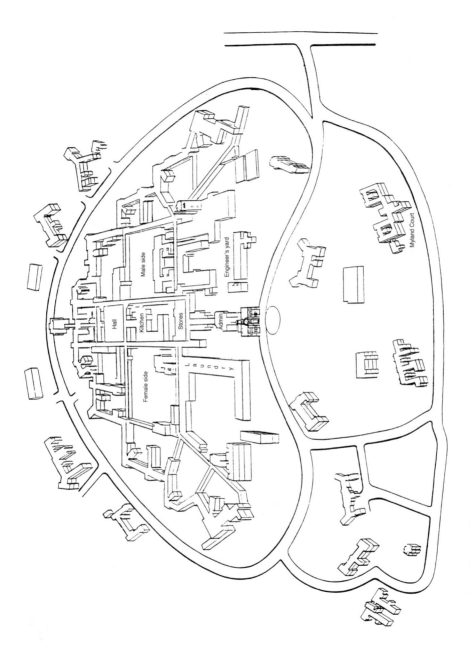

Male side

Engineer's yard

Hall

Kitchen

Stores

Admin

Laundry

Female side

Myland Court

Figure 1.4 Plan of Severalls, post-1930

administrative and clerical staff, matron and the chief inspector. The committee meeting room was here as were the visiting rooms. This was the public face of the asylum, graced as it was with a grand and imposing facade.

It was all designed in such a way that 'the receiving and dispatch rooms are conveniently spaced so that male and female patients will not come in contact with each other.'[33] The rationale for such rigid separation by gender was partly rooted in prevailing ideas as to the necessity of separating the sexes in *all* institutions – schools, factories, prisons, workhouses – and partly rooted in ideas about genetics, a belief that mental illness was a result of brain disease, usually caused by 'faulty genes'. The possibility of reproducing yet more diseased brains, therefore, was to be discouraged at all costs. As Rogers and Pilgrim remark with regard to the early twentieth century:

> The segregation of madness from society, and between the sexes within the asylums to minimise the inheritance of purported faulty genes, had been a convergent policy in Europe and North America. This measure was then amplified to include sterilisation of patients in Denmark and the US, and extended further in the 1930s in Germany when the German Medical Association proposed a policy of involuntary euthanasia for 'life devoid of meaning' . . . people with learning difficulties, physical disabilities and . . . mentally ill.[34]

Severalls, like other asylums of the time, was not only divided first and foremost by gender, but also by social class and by category of illness. Division by class was most noticeable *between* different institutions at the beginning of the twentieth century; wealthy middle-class patients tended to be sent to private asylums such as Ticehurst.[35] Less affluent middle-class patients did come to county asylums such as Severalls as fee-paying private patients. They were kept quite separate from the rest of the hospital. Until the 1960s Myland Villa East and West were used, at least partially, for private patients. Here conditions were more secluded, more spacious and more comfortable. A woman who worked as a nurse at Severalls in 1936 remembered Myland Court:

> I did quite a variety of wards, but one that stands out in my mind was the private villa, for paying guests only. It was a lovely change from some of the wards I had been working on. There were carpets, very nice furniture, mostly private rooms, and the food was quite good in comparison to the other wards. There was a parrot on a perch which we tried to teach swear words – no luck though. One old lady was a real terror. Some days she decided to stay in bed for the day, and had us waiting on her hand and foot. And if we

didn't please her she would hit out at us with her walking stick. Sometimes she could be very sweet. There was a Lady So-and-so in there and, oh, there were lots of business people's wives. Oh, the difference in the surroundings! And the food – you had a sort of a lid to put on over the plate to keep the food warm, you know, not sort of dash around with three or four plates and dish them out. Every week we took some patients out for a ride in a taxi round the countryside. We enjoyed that, but I don't think the patients noticed anything different going on.

Records of private patients admitted between 1913 and 1918 (153 patients in total) show that the majority came from Essex (62 per cent), while 14 per cent came from the Home Counties and 13 per cent from London. Only 72 of the people who had their relatives certified gave their occupations (largely reflecting the fact that those not giving occupations were women), but of these the majority seem to have come from the lower middle class (18 per cent were clerks, 18 per cent were shopkeepers, 10 per cent were builders) while some 25 per cent came from the professional middle classes (accountants, architects, solicitors, managers, doctors and civil servants). Not surprisingly in an army town, 10 per cent were army officers or soldiers, but, surprisingly, considering the preponderance of agriculture in Essex, only 6 per cent were farmers or nurserymen. A mere 3 per cent were of independent means, suggesting those with ample wealth went elsewhere. A few private letters that have survived indicate severe troubles with paying the fees and repeated requests to waive fee increases and save the relative the ignominy of being reclassified as a pauper. Here are some extracts from a correspondence between a woman about her husband in the private ward at Severalls, and Dr Turnbull, the medical superintendent. They are all from 1915:

It is now twelve months since I removed my husband to Severalls and I am thankful for the great kindness he has received from one and all who has [sic] helped to make things as right as possible ... I am now faced with the problem – how can I continue this payment? I am reduced to £65 per annum to support my husband and partly support myself ...

I am thankful for your suggestion about my husband wearing his private clothes. Were it otherwise, the shame would be great for me. If my husband [sic] an ordinary county patient would it be perceptible to him in any way – would he know of the change? ...

I do not want my husband to be a burden on the rates. Will you pardon me for saying – my father has been a large rate payer in

the county for 32 years and is a very old and much respected
Freemason, and also my uncle ... of Chelmsford ... my brother
at Witham. The family are no aliens in the county. I only mention
these matters that you may know who are my family connections.

The Committee agreed to reduce her husband's fees and let him continue
as a private patient.

FEARS OF POLLUTION

While buildings undoubtedly determine and affect much of social interaction, social interaction itself can subtly alter and change the uses of the
buildings. Within broad divisions other quite marked sub-divisions often
developed and reinforced existing ideas and ideals about hierarchy, status
and pollution. Denise Jodelet, for instance, in her book, *Madness and
Social Representation*, shows how categories that were carefully planned
and laid out by officials so that mental patients in a colony in France
(Ainay-le-Château) should live with, and become an integral part of, local
families, were subtly and not so subtly undermined and redefined by the
families themselves who, afraid of 'pollution' by patients, developed their
own boundaries within the household relating to meals, partitions, use of
water, laundry and washing. Dishes used by patients were invariably
washed separately from those of the family: 'what is feared is the direct
contact of the patient with the water reserved for the use of the foster
parents'.[36] She argues this shows the 'pollutant power of illness, a magic
force transmitted by contact with living secretions, becomes in the patient
a sign of otherness proper to his nature as a bearer of an insanity where
impurity threatens the integrity of others'.[37] Jodelet concludes that when
a community feels threatened from within, as this one did, a collective
representation develops that adheres to a body of representations of the
'others' in their midst as a way of affirming the receiving group's own
unity and identity.

Fears of the polluting powers of the mad and of madness, and, in particular, the polluting potential of fluids and water in relation to them were
inherent in much of the design of Severalls, most notably in that wettest
of places, the laundry.[38]

Men's and women's dirty laundry was received, and their clean laundry
dispatched, from quite separate places. Patients' laundry was dealt with
separately from that of nursing staff. The laundry area was divided between
the main rooms, where patients' and nurses' clothes were washed, dried
and ironed, albeit on different days, the foul laundry, where soiled linen
and sanitary towels were soaked and washed, and the officers' laundry,
which dealt exclusively with the clothes and linen of doctors, the medical

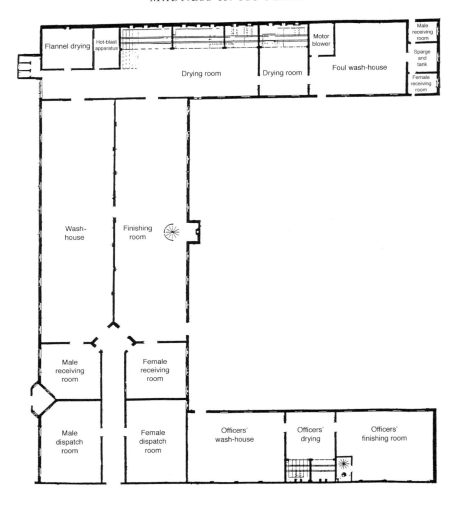

Figure 1.5 Plan of Severalls laundry, 1913
Source: North East Essex Mental Health NHS Trust

superintendent and senior nursing staff. A woman who was born in 1910 and came to work in the Severalls laundry in 1928 explained how, although patients worked in the laundry with laundry staff, they never did so on the days when *staff* laundry was being washed; indeed, all machines and surfaces had to be scrubbed particularly thoroughly on the day patients' laundry was finished, before staff laundry could be started. She attributes this to class distinctions, which were undoubtedly central, but they could also be seen as indicating fears of the contaminating potential of madness itself:

There was always this class distinction. It went through the whole system. Just like the Army. The laundry. Everything – in, in the system. So those that had been there a long while, they were the senior maids. Then there was those that had been there a couple of years, they were the ordinary maids, and we were the beginners. And – that was Thursday, and that used to go through, and that was paid out [i.e. given back] on the Friday. That always had to be done, and that was passed then through to the senior maids that did the staff. And that was – the machines were all done, and they were kept special for the staff laundry. Just for staff laundry. Yes. They did that. They didn't have no patients on that day. No patients touching their laundry! Not with the nurses' uniforms or staff things. Well – because you don't know – they used to do all sorts [the patients] and touching themselves – you know what I mean [i.e. masturbating]. So their hands were – we never had no gloves or anything. They had to keep washing their hands theirselves. But patients never touched the staff laundry.

And we got that all through from the Thursday, early morning Thursday, right through the day, and that was paid out Friday after-noon. Male and female, they were separate. The male – the male came in on a different day. The general laundry came in on a Monday. It might have been, perhaps, on a Wednesday when the – the male – the day before the female. And again, that was all kept on its own. All their shirts, everything. No patients touched the nurses' stuff.

The doctors? Well, there was – attached to the laundry there was what they called the 'Officers' Laundry', and two ladies lived at Horkesley – Lily and Florrie – and they were there for years, and they ran that. They were sisters. They were senior. Senior maids. They'd been there ever since Severalls opened. And so they did that and everything – they, they did have a patient in there. I think they had two. They did some of the heavy work, pushing things, but they didn't touch anything. And all the matron's work was done there, all her uniforms and stuff. Everything was ironed by Florrie or Lily, and the – what they called the assistant matron's things. And then they had the – what they called the sisters, and they came, they came. There was the nurses, there were probationers, then there was the nurses, then there was the fully trained nurse, there was a staff nurse, and then there was a charge nurse. And then came the sisters, and then assistant matrons – there were several of them – and Matron Cuthbert, on her own, she was the

23

top dog. And she had a little dog and all, a little Scotch terrier – and that used to bark, so we knew when she was coming! So – and their work was all done separately. There was a little laundry all on its own. And that went right through the system, right through.

Men were generally seen as less subject to being polluted than women: men ran the foul laundry. Yet one man who came to work as an attendant (male nurse) in the 1930s told me how his mother pleaded with him not to take the job, for fear he would 'catch the mania'. Another man said that he 'reckoned if I hadn't 'a worked in a mental hospital I'd've been daft as a coot'. Even a medical superintendent in the 1960s tried to cover for a fairly serious *faux pas* at a formal occasion by saying 'I have to apologise, Chancellor, I've been dealing with the mad for so long and I don't know who's staff and who's mad and I get it all mixed up!' There was an implicit understanding running through many of the interviews that contact with 'mad' patients over time did affect your own sense of reason and 'sanity', although most often this message was conveyed by means of jokes.[39] A woman who came to work as a nurse in the 1930s remembered how, before she came, there was suspicion of those who tended the 'mad':

> I remember coming to see my mother in hospital, in the General Hospital, and there were two people visiting somebody, and my mother said, 'They're wardens up at Severalls' or 'up at the asylum'. And I thought, 'Mmm, they don't *look* any different to anybody else!'

Though officially opened in 1910, Severalls did not begin receiving patients until 1913. On 20 May 1913, 200 invited visitors came to inspect it. Tea was provided, although it is interesting to note that one of the ungrateful worthies apparently removed a billiard cloth from Ward 13 during this ceremony. Thus began a long tradition of petty pilfering. The asylum was then opened for general inspection by the public for three days, during which time 5,700 visitors came. No thefts were reported. On 27 May the first patients arrived. After this date a long silence began. Like a family secret, everybody knew it was there, indeed, they could see it in the distance, but those who did not work there knew little about what went on inside. Until the Second World War, recruitment of nursing staff, when possible, was made from people who lived outside the area: areas of high unemployment such as Yorkshire, Lancashire, Wales and Ireland were favourite recruiting grounds. The fact that it was contained, locked away, removed from everyday life, seems to have reassured the local population that they were safe to go about their lives and business without fear. Except, of course, for their own secret fears of irrationality and madness.

PLACE AND SOCIAL CHANGE

From 1913, the infrastructure of Severalls was up and running. Much was to change between that time and 1997, but the buildings remained much as they were – and they were built to last. Government policies changed, medical practice changed, people's attitudes, patterns of poverty and unemployment also changed. Some of those changes had important effects on the structure of the hospital, or at least the routines and practice within it. Doors, locks, railings and fences could be, and eventually were, removed. They can also, of course, be put back, as has been the case in recent years with secure and semi-secure wards/houses. Wards and rooms have been used differently over time: in 1923, for instance, the dormitory in Ward D was converted into a weaving room, but in 1931, when pressure of ever-greater numbers of patients was reaching a peak, it was converted back to a dormitory once more. Patterns of economic change – unemployment, government policies and various political and economic crises (two world wars, the depression in the 1930s, the recession/depression and fiscal crisis of the state from the late 1970s) have affected the use of wards, space and policies of admission and discharge.

As poverty and unemployment rose from the late 1920s, so did patient admissions to Severalls. The number of female patients, however, rose more dramatically than did those of males, suggesting that women experienced poverty more severely than did men. Indeed, the early Liberal reforms and the National Insurance Act of 1911 did not cover dependent wives or daughters, nor did it cover domestic servants. There was no safety net for those who had not been in full-time employment or had been deserted by their husbands.

Overcrowding became increasingly severe and resulted eventually in government funding for a series of new buildings. In 1930 a new nurses'

Table 1.2 Total population of Severalls, male and female patients, 1927–1937

Year	Males	Females	Total
1927	742	996	1738
1928	724	1050	1774
1929	723	1094	1817
1930	725	1104	1829
1931	743	1170	1913
1932	781	1221	2002
1933	798	1215	2013
1934	875	1268	2143
1935	920	1292	2212
1936	911	1309	2220
1937	867	1270	2137

Source: Medical superintendent's reports, Severalls Hospital

home opened, an annexe to Chestnut Villa was built, and a second farm, Whitehouse Farm, was bought. In 1932 an annexe was added to Ward 2, building began on two new 'temporary' villas (both still there in 1997, one the staff social club, the other, now derelict Tamarisk Villa). In 1933 a new dormitory was opened for the isolation hospital, where patients with infectious diseases such as typhoid, scarlet fever and dysentery were treated. In 1934 the new male observation villa, Myland Villa, opened, Myland Lodge became occupied by patients, Eden Villa (female), South Villa (male) and Orchard Villa (female) opened. In 1935 it was agreed to build a new block for sisters, complete with lecture room, and in that year the female temporary villa was completed. Extensive building and purchase of staff housing in surrounding roads was also carried out during the 1930s.[40]

The 1930s was, ironically, a heyday for Severalls, at least in relation to new buildings. Because employment was scarce, it was also a time when female nursing staff, usually very difficult to find and keep, were in relative abundance. The proportion of trained nurses, female and male, was high at this time, and, although overcrowding was acute, particularly on the female side, conditions at Severalls at this time were probably much better than during the war years, and possibly also better than during the early 1950s.

After the 1930s building boom, however, no more major construction work was to take place again. One reason for this was that Essex County Council had planned to build a third mental hospital at Margaretting, and indeed the foundations were laid by 1939. The start of the war, however, put a stop to all building and building plans, and they were never resumed after the war. Between 1938 and 1945 patient numbers declined, and although these rose slightly again in the mid-1950s, numbers declined again sharply from the end of the 1950s and have continued to do so ever since.[41] The reasons for this are much contended: psychiatrists have argued the national decline was a result of the new neuroleptic drugs that came into use in the 1950s, but evidence from Severalls shows the decline there began beforehand.[42] Severalls records indicate a severe labour shortage, but one of *female nursing staff* from the Second World War, a shortage so severe that several wards had to be closed down, and remained closed, for years. Whatever the reasons, the order of the day from the 1940s onwards was maintenance, refurbishment, containment and, at times, changing use of premises.

From the early 1960s, however, talk of closing down all mental hospitals altogether gained momentum. Enoch Powell, Minister of Health in 1961, referred to mental hospitals as 'doomed institutions' that must disappear. Initially perhaps such rhetoric can be seen more as a political football bounced back and forth from time to time. As the fiscal crisis of the state grew deeper, overlaid with years of Conservative government and

26

monetarist policies after 1979, so the rhetoric became one of 'community care', implemented by a new managerialism, and a philosophy in which place and space became more fragmented and the old idea of a self-contained, isolated hospital community fell away, dispersed and scattered along with the erstwhile inhabitants and workers, to different buildings, towns, houses and offices joined together by faxes, e-mail, telephones and cars rather than bricks and mortar.[43]

Some of the history of the changing use of space in mental hospitals in recent years can be related to the increasing use of pharmacological means as a primary source of restraint and control. Politically and economically, this has had the overwhelming advantage of being cheap, cheaper than running large hospitals with large numbers of staff. In 1961 the total volume of prescriptions was £32 million in England and Wales, while by 1973 it was £45 million for England alone.[44] The space of control as a result has increasingly gone *into the patient's body itself*, instead of the body being restrained by outside forces. For patients this often means a loss of visions/delusions. One ex-patient told me of a friend, diagnosed as schizophrenic, who had had visions of angels. The drugs she was given resulted in her 'losing her angels', whom she had experienced as benevolent and protective, and from then she lost all interest in living. Many, of course, lose visions/delusions that are terrifying, malevolent and painful.

The pharmacological revolution has resulted in a major shift in the use of space, essentially transforming the control of hospital space, and control *by* hospital space, into control of patient body space by chemical means. One central result of this has been that patients can now be dispersed away from hospitals and yet remain, on the whole, controlled and restrained. Euphemistically this has been called 'care in the community', but it is important to bear in mind, first, that the hospital itself was very much a community in the first place, while control of patients by chemical means in a more dispersed space may mean many are simply confined pharmacologically to small bedsitting rooms, nursing homes and flats where chances of interaction with a wider community are constrained both by poverty and by side-effects of medication. In Clacton, for instance, where a great many ex-patients from Severalls have been accommodated and rehabilitated, and where facilities are particularly good, with two day centres, the spatial distribution of patients and day centres is nonetheless focused to a large extent on one particular area of the town. Patients generally socialise with other patients. There is a sense of a ghetto, a 'transinstitutionalisation',[45] with many features of institutional living reproduced and relived in a somewhat more dispersed way than in the actual hospital.

It should be remembered that for many people who came into Severalls it became their home, albeit a home run along very different, very rigid schedules and routines. For some, notwithstanding, it may well have been a far easier and pleasanter home, time and life than the ones they had left behind. Changes in the divorce laws and marriage laws, and more comprehensive provision of social welfare and social security have meant many people in recent years have been able to change their own home time and home life enough to make their homes a more viable option than institutions, although, of course, not all people *have* homes, and homelessness is on the increase.

2

AT THE GATE

I am the way into the doleful city,
I am the way into eternal grief,
I am the way to a forsaken race ...
Abandon every hope, all you who enter.
(Dante, *The Divine Comedy*, vol I, canto III)

Hark! Hark! The lark at heaven's gate sings
Shakespeare, *Cymbeline*

A gate marks a boundary between two worlds: familiar and strange, outside and inside, seen and unseen, mad and sane. Like a port, it is a liminal place, a threshold, a place of entries and exits, a dividing-line that marks some kind of change: of place, time, power, status or rights. In western culture over the past two hundred years one of the most feared gates, along with that of the workhouse, has been that of the asylum, the loony bin, the nuthouse. Naughty children were taunted with the threat of being taken by the men in the white coats or, as was commonly said in Colchester, 'going on the number 5 bus'. A refuge for displaced persons, it was a place most definitely to be avoided. And yet, ironically, it was also a haven for some, a place of prosperity and security for many, a source of much-valued employment when jobs were scarce, a place where working-class men in particular found regular, pensionable work that also provided excellent sports facilities and tied accommodation. It was a place where whole networks and generations of kin worked in a web that spanned almost the entire twentieth century. Until it was taken down in 1962, the gate at Severalls,[1] like other gates at other mental hospitals, meant different things to different people, but always marked the boundary between two distinct communities and signalled the cutting-off point between a whole range of different rules, regulations, behaviours, divisions and separations.

A 'community', of course, is notoriously difficult, probably impossible, to define. Perhaps it is better to use Goffman's concept of a 'total institution'[2] although this does not convey the sense that most people at Severalls had of living and/or working in a place quite separate and distinct from the rest of the world, and in which they had a definite feeling of *belonging*. This is the sense in which I refer to Severalls as a community, where the idea of belonging was as important as, and operated in conjunction with, spatial boundaries and distinct rules, laws and regulations. The densely interwoven network of kinship connections reinforced this sense. Nevertheless, *within* Severalls a number of other quite distinct groups, or communities, existed, all of which were clearly marked by boundaries, locks and a greater or lesser sense of belonging.

BOARDS AND BOUNDARIES

The most basic boundary was between staff and patients, although arguably division by gender was even stronger, while certainly class divisions also figured prominently. A woman who worked at Severalls in the 1920s gave an account of how the material fences (the 'boards') round the hospital affected nurses' experiences at the time:

> A lot of the nurses were courting the soldiers, and them soldiers used to walk them – there was no transport, no buses running up there, the trams stopped at North Station. Nothing further. You had to walk the rest of the way. And them soldiers used to leave the dances with the girls, the nurses, and they had to leave fairly early. The dances used to start about seven in the town, and if they were off duty – they had two days a week off duty – and sometimes that was cancelled if there was any shortage on the wards. And so they used to go out and come back with a soldier, and they used to come right up with them to the boards.
>
> All along was 6-foot boards. And the other side was a 6-foot ditch, so patients couldn't climb over. And that ditch mostly had water in it. And all along them boards, from the beginning of Severalls' grounds to the Gate, which was locked – big gates, always locked – there was boards, and there was all these couples. Well my boyfriend, he lived at Boxted, and he used to come into town – I used to be at the dances, you see, as well, and he used to say, 'What a sight!' because he used to bike by it, he lived out at Boxted. He said, 'There's nothing but couples necking,' he'd say, 'all the way along the boards', until about a few minutes to ten, when they'd got to go in.
>
> What they had to do when they went out, they had to put the keys in. You untook, you untook them off your uniform and you

took your keys – there was a ring, and you had to go through the lodge where Mr Dixon – he was one of the men there – give him your keys, and your keys had a number, and he put it on a hook with a number, and off you went. Well, when they – if they come in just before ten, or on ten, he was pretty liberal for a few minutes, they used to say their numbers to get their keys – they were all right. Those that didn't when that got – I think he used to give them till about quarter past, quarter of an hour's grace – he shouldn't, but, you know, he used to be sorry for them in a lot of ways.

And so he, he used to have to shut it down and they couldn't get they keys. They couldn't get in. And he wasn't allowed to let them through. He was there. He was there all night. But he wasn't allowed to let them in. He used to shut the door and on to his little gangway. The big gates were all locked, so they had to get over the boards. The soldier used to heave them over and they used to have to be careful they didn't fall in the ditch, but some of them did.

The whole structure and organisation of the hospital was hierarchical and bureaucratic; the medical superintendent, like a feudal lord, ruled over all other groups in the estate and had his own office, office staff and a – large and extensive – house on the edge of the estate. The psychiatrists he worked with were all carefully graded by seniority, although this was to change with the 1959 Act and, indeed, became a cause of great bitterness and rancour between the medical superintendent and the consultants in the 1960s. From 1971 the position of medical superintendent was abolished and medical matters were decided by a committee of psychiatric consultants, ruled by a chairman. This would shift again into a managerial system from the 1980s.

Prior to the 1960s, however, the medical profession within the hospital lived a separate and privileged, albeit rather isolated, life, having little to do with other employees or patients (except for the few who worked as their servants), once their ward rounds and meetings were over. Similarly, nurses and attendants were organised along hierarchical divisions of seniority which were marked both by uniform and eating arrangements in the mess-rooms. Such divisions were clearly demarcated until the 1960s; the medical superintendent's secretary and junior secretary, for instance, ate in the assistant matrons' dining room with seven or eight sisters, where they were waited on by maids. The matron had her own flat and office with her own maids in the main building, while the deputy matron had a flat at Myland Court. A man who worked as a clerk from 1940 remembered the eating arrangements on the male side then:

31

That was the *sub*-officers' mess! You see – *class*. There was one for the nurses, you see, but the artisans had their own sort of mess-room in the engineer's yard, there was a sort of room there. But they brought their own food, they didn't have it catered for. But we did. And we had a room on our own called – people like path lab technicians, the laundry manager, storekeepers, ourselves – anyway, that was for us and there was a billiard table in there as well. The stuff was brought to us on the table in tureens and things like that, but we did, as it were, help ourselves from that point on. We didn't have to wash up afterwards either!

The storekeeper – he didn't mess with us, he had his own place off the kitchen. Because he was presumably a grade above everybody else and couldn't be seen – he'd eat alone! Nurses had a separate mess-room of their own – the male ones – and the females had of course a separate one on the female side. The doctors – they'd be eating upstairs. The doctors ate on their own, above the superintendent's office. The engineer lived on the place, so he'd go home, the same way that the clerk and steward would go home at lunch-time.

It was not until the 1960s that a canteen was opened for use by all staff, although the doctors continued to eat separately.

Because of the way the hospital was organised on hierarchical lines bounded by locked doors, with wards effectively ruled by the charge nurse, wards could differ markedly in their regimes. Charge nurses often made it quite difficult for psychiatrists to see patients on their own. Within each ward, each corridor, each half of the hospital and each professional or occupational group there were clear boundaries laid down in rule-books, traditions and architectural barriers. Separation was central to the whole running and philosophy of the hospital, although from time to time such a Victorian set of beliefs and practices was challenged. In effect, it worked quite well and smoothly, if the premises of inequality, division and hierarchy were accepted. It meant, however, that there were regimes within regimes – some benevolent, some cruel, some strict, some lax.

Arguably it was during the Second World War that such barriers became increasingly unworkable, partly because of severe and chronic staffing shortages, partly because so much of the war was a civilian war where ideals of popular participation, redistribution of power and, to some extent and for some groups, redistribution of income was becoming increasingly important, partly because mental hospitals became part of the general hospital system from the implementation of the NHS in 1948, when they, as all other hospitals, were transferred to become part of newly created

Regional Hospital Boards. At this time the Local Health Committee took over statutory duties formerly carried out by public assistance committees, and had to appoint a mental health sub-committee.

Labour's landslide victory after the war spelled the beginning of an era of hope, new ideals and practices of universal healthcare, a more equitable education system, a period of full employment and a welfare state dedicated to ideals of equal opportunity. Change to a more therapeutic and less custodial method of treating and dealing with the mentally ill had long been an ideal of some reformers, but was increasingly accepted by psychiatrists, politicians and administrators from the end of the war. Ultimately this would mean change in relation to hierarchy, divisions, boundaries, keys and gates within the hospital itself: the 1959 Mental Health Act brought a range of new policies into effect, most notably the abolition of certification.

In 1968 the Seebohm Committee set up a new managerial framework for local authority social services which led to the development of separate health and social services empires. It also signalled the increasing bifurcation between, on the one hand, a bio-medical model of psychiatry in the tradition of general medicine and general nursing, with a great reliance on drugs and somatic treatments, and, on the other hand, a social model that saw mental illness as primarily related to social problems. Though these two models go back much earlier in time, and have coexisted, from the 1970s in particular there has been a growing tension between them, partly as the result of the growing power and influence of the nursing profession. Since the 1970s, social workers and community psychiatric nurses have become increasingly important, in parallel with managerialism, in the mental health service which has meant a different approach to gate-keeping in the treatment of mental illness. As one of the executive directors of Severalls said in relation to a new system of community psychiatric teams in the 1990s:

> Anyone who wanted to come into our service for any care had to come through that gate, in the community team. If you want to get into admission, or you want to get into day care, or you want to get anywhere, you come – you are referred – to the community team, and they gate-keep that.

Whoever guards the gate holds enormous power over all those who hope, or are forced, to enter or to leave. Yet the embodied gatekeeper who sat in the gatekeeper's lodge until 1960 was himself a pawn of far more powerful gatekeepers who determined the fate of all those who entered and left: from charge nurses to psychiatrists, and ultimately the legal system and government policies, there was a hierarchy of gatekeepers who set the conditions for entries and exits. Gatekeepers come and go, and the laws for admissions and discharges changed. Gates open and gates close. Wards and gates were opened in the 1960s; new smaller units built, or converted, since then are increasingly locked once more. Gates and gatekeepers still exist, albeit in different forms, to define, diagnose, treat, rehabilitate – or turn away – the desperate, dangerous, confused.

PATIENTS' ENTRIES AND EXITS: CERTIFICATION, SECTIONING

Under the laws of certification that defined English mental health policy from 1890 until 1959, the process of certification was for many an irretrievable transition. Certification, like marriage, was incredibly easy to get into. Also like marriage, at least until recent years, it was extremely difficult to get out of. Even if lucky enough to be discharged from a mental hospital, the stigma attached to once having been in was enormous. To pass through the gates of Severalls Hospital as a patient, especially in the early years to 1930, but also to a great extent until 1959, meant possible incarceration for years, even for life. Although many did leave, a substantial number did not, often hampered by a legal system that made de-certification difficult. Certainly a number of people who were certified and spent much of their lives in Severalls were certified originally for quite minor reasons. Many staff, for instance, remembered one patient who was certified as a young man in the early months of Severalls' opening:

We had one patient here who was brought to Severalls from Chelmsford, he will always tell you, by these two men dressed in long black coats with tall black hats on. They brought him to Severalls from the court, and he knew the name of the magistrate in the court, and he knew the name of one of these men who brought him in. And he never forgot it. And you only ever had to say to him, to mention one of these two names to him and he would go absolutely – he would sort of, you know – he would just explode and swear about them!

And he did this right up to the end of his life. But he was one of the patients who was held in great regard by all the staff in this hospital, and when he died the church was full. He'd had some problem with a girl, I think, and he was committed here, and he stayed here. Everybody knew him. Yeah. He used to work in the kitchen – the cooks used to pick him up and sit him on the hotplate! But they all used to look after him, he was looked after in every way.

Denis Hooton, who was secretary of Severalls from 1956, and then group secretary of the St Helena Group of Hospitals from 1963, gave this account:

> When I moved to our house in Severalls in 1956 the chief male nurse looked around and he said, 'Do you want the patient who's worked here for years?' I said, 'Yes, keep him.' Because there was a lot of ground at the back. I said, 'Yes, he'll work in our garden.' Well, he proved to be a lovely fellow. My daughter grew up with him. And I'll tell you, his story is typical. He came back from the war in 1918 to find his wife had had a baby by some other man. He went in a pub and he found this man, and he had a fight. And the police took him away and he got certified. That kept him in. Now he couldn't get out, because he needed a relative to vouch for him financially, otherwise he would have fallen on the rates, you see. Never ever till he died. No, he sort of made a home with us. He went in the town and did what he liked. Once in, they couldn't get out though. And when he died four sons turned up. One of them had visited periodically, the others not. I said to one of them, 'Didn't you ever come and see your father?' 'No,' he said, 'Mum told us he was mad.'

English mental health policy has always been concerned with regulating individual conduct and expressing that regulation through the law. The law in turn has been administered and enforced by central and local government officials. Until 1959 mental health policy was determined by the Lunacy Act of 1890, although important modifications were made to it in the 1930 Mental Treatment Act. The 1890 Act, as Jones points out, 'was a reflection of legal determination to take control of a process which concerned the liberty of the subject – a desire to draw a firm legal boundary between the sane majority and the insane minority'.[3]

Mental health policy was very much part of the poor law system. Procedures for certifying private and pauper patients were different.[4] The overwhelming majority of patients at Severalls, as in other county mental hospitals, were paupers. In 1929 the Local Government Act abolished the poor law as such and replaced it with 'public assistance committees', which served very similar functions to the old poor law. Pauper lunatics needed a 'summary reception order', for which a poor-law relieving officer or policeman was responsible and had to notify a magistrate and obtain one medical certificate and a justice's order which certified the individual for fourteen days. The ease with which one could get out of either depended to a great extent on social class. A private patient could be discharged on direction of the person who signed the original petition for a reception order. A pauper lunatic, however, could be discharged only on direction of the poor-law authority, although the medical superintendent had a right of veto.

Shame of the stigma attached was an important reason why few relatives reclaimed their kin from certification. Poverty was another reason for not taking back relatives: to take on an extra mouth to feed, an extra dependant, would have spelled disaster for many households. The stigma of illegitimacy was another reason why kin failed to claim back female relatives. Men might leave their wives in hospital deliberately because they were having a relationship with another woman, although it could also work the other way round. Russell Barton argued that many families 'did a flit' once their relatives were certified, so that they would not be liable to pay any fees for them. Thus many patients were left without home or kin, entirely dependent on the hospital. Others, he maintained, had relatives certified for financial or personal reasons:

And of course, ladies also got rid of their husbands. They got control of the money and pushed them into hospital quite often. The doctors would certify people that became a nuisance. And that was the key to it – if they were a nuisance to the duly authorised officers to the Act – the older Act[5] – then they would advise the GP to get a psychiatrist in to certify them, that was the purpose. And the GP would get in a doctor who would certify them. And that was – it was only £3 in those days, but so what? 'That's my job.' The fact that it's the poor woman's life.

I remember a woman had a fire in her place in Clacton. She came into Severalls – and two days later there was a guy round, who was a pushy fellow in his forties, saying, 'Look, she's never going to go home, everyone knows she's a nutter, and I can get a good price for this – for this – this plot, this good site.' I was a little suspicious about it. The woman could have – could go home, and did go home, but not to that place that was burned out. But she collected the insurance on it and didn't take an immediate offer. And things – the treachery, you know.

Another case – a family moved in with their mother, who was rather ill, and they found her an awful nuisance because she was incontinent at times. I prescribed Haradol – 5 mg two or three times a day. And they *pretended* they'd misread it, because next time I went in she was drooling, and she'd got one of these disorders of movements, and they eventually got rid of the old trout. They were living in her cottage and they took it over after so many years – I

> think it's twelve or twenty-one by, by prescriptive rights. And they got an attorney in to advise them.

Another way in which patients occasionally gained freedom before the 1959 Mental Health Act was to escape and hide. A patient who escaped and was not recaptured after fourteen days, was free 'by discharge of the law'.[6]

The results of this complicated, but water-tight, system were, first and foremost, that mental health policy became largely custodial. Jones argues that this contributed to a decline in standards of care and treatment,[7] although it would seem equally pertinent that mental health care and mental hospitals in particular remained notoriously underfunded throughout the twentieth century. Because certification was both a painful process and one from which it was hard to get free, potential patients resisted it and relatives were often, though by no means always, reluctant to invoke it. Nevertheless, scrutiny of existing records reveals a fairly substantial rate of discharge, even before 1930.

Although a number of patients were discharged each year, and, of course, some died, there was a surplus of admissions over discharges, which resulted in an increasing accumulation of long-stay patients.

An obvious result was increased overcrowding. In 1890 there were 86,067 people detained under the lunacy laws in Britain; by the end of 1920, in just thirty years, the figure had reached 120,344.[8] During the 1920s, as discussed earlier, the numbers at Severalls grew steadily. Overcrowding led to poor conditions, poor staff-to-patient ratios and some of the worst effects of institutionalisation generally. There were a number of outcries and protests about the state of the asylums during the 1920s. Most important of these was the publication by Montagu Lomax in 1921 of his indictment of asylums, *The Experiences of an Asylum Doctor*. This caused considerable consternation generally, and in the government

Table 2.1 Admissions and discharges for selected years, Severalls, 1920–1955

Year	Admissions (numbers)	Discharges (numbers)
1920	256	97
1923	328	152
1929	234	135
1931	360	173
1945	505	354
1949	629	545
1951	741	597
1953	825	639
1955	934	725

Source: Management Committee minutes, Severalls Hospital

Figure 2.1 Patient at Clacton, *circa* 1960
Source: Russell Barton archive

particularly. It is difficult to know to what extent the horrendous conditions described by Lomax at Prestwich Asylum applied to Severalls.

Unlike the older asylums, Severalls was in new buildings still presumably in pristine condition, and had an extensive estate and farm (the second farm, Whitehouse Farm, was bought in 1930). Committee minutes suggest ongoing attempts to instigate a caring and liberal regime for patients in the 1920s: about two-thirds of the patients attended the Annual Fete for Patients each year; motorcoach day trips to Clacton began, taking on average 200 patients (out of about 1,600) each summer for a day by the sea; there was always a Christmas dance and party, and in June there was a Sports Day, as a woman who worked at Severalls in the laundry in the 1920s remembered:

> We had a Sports Day – they knocked all that out during the war, but in my time, that was quite a day. That was in June and they'd got a big sports field there, and that was all laid out with marquees and things. That was a Saturday, and we worked in the morning and we had to stay all day, and we were told that we had – well, they didn't tell you you'd got to, but as near as that – to look after our laundry patients and see that they enjoyed the day – the races and the things. And we all got ourselves done up – we took our

black stockings off and put light lisle ones on, and we had white shoes and we had all clean uniform, and we made sure we had a white apron, not a bleached one! And that was another step in the class distinction – maids didn't have white aprons – until we boiled them white! And of course we were in the right place to do it!

The patients were in the field and we used to go out and we used to enjoy it with them. And they were all there, the nurses and all, all in their uniforms – but they kept the male patients one end of the field. The sexual impulse was rather frequent with some of them – but it's natural, they were young people, some of them. They weren't all old people.

And Sports Day was good. The patients used to go into one of the big marquees where tea was all set out, and we waited on them – and the nurses – we all waited on them, and served it all, see they had everything they wanted. Sixty patients or more from the needle-room and the laundry. And the nurses looked after their ward, kept them together. And they had a good day.

Well, after about a fortnight, Dr Turnbull, in return, he was always very grateful, he used to thank the staff for what they did for the Sports Day – how we all, you know, came together and did what we could and made a good day for the patients. And he used to give us what they called the 'strawberry tea'. And that was a garden party. It was music and different amusements and all that. And that was for staff only. And it did include the domestic staff. We were included. On the sports field, and a big marquee again. And we waited on the nurses – they had their tea first – and we waited on them. And they waited on us, the domestic staff. They were good in that respect. And the doctors came, yes, they came to that, and talked to us.

In 1921 the Board of Control was pleased to note that patients now got porridge and two hot breakfasts a week instead of bread and margarine, and that their milk was now unskimmed. Handicrafts were introduced in 1922, in 1923 a library was set up and fifty-two pictures were hung in wards. Two gramophones, thirty-six records and fifty needles were purchased. Lantern lectures were given once a fortnight (interestingly, replacing evening religious services) and a football team for male patients was established. By 1927 there were gymnastic classes for a few women patients.

Yet during the same period there was an ongoing problem with rats eating women patients' clothing in the wards; patients wore regulation uniforms; some worked as servants, cleaners, farm hands, assistants in the laundry, kitchen and gardens, but the majority had little to do except walk in circles round the airing courts at prescribed times of day. Some had parole of the grounds, most did not. Staffing shortages on the female side, an endemic problem from the time Severalls opened, meant early bedtimes and overreliance on sedatives for women patients. Numbers were increasing each year.

As early as 1923 what was to become, and remain, a major problem for the rest of the twentieth century, was already noted as problematic: nearly 50 per cent of recent admissions, the medical superintendent noted with dismay, were over 65 years of age. By the end of the 1920s patient numbers had risen substantially; these were not just the elderly, but were overwhelmingly women. Dr Turnbull noted 'female patients continued to be admitted in large numbers, and there was great difficulty in providing further accommodation.'[9] Unemployment by the late 1920s, especially in Colchester, was high. Unmarried women, widows, deserted wives, domestic servants had no state protection and no pensions, although longevity was increasing. Poverty among the elderly, and particularly among elderly women, was rife. With no pension and often with no family to provide shelter or food, the mental hospital and the workhouse were the only option for many, and the conditions at Severalls were arguably better and preferable to those of the workhouse. Undoubtedly Severalls saved many lives simply by providing warmth, food and shelter.

As a result of complaints and indictments such as those of Lomax in the early 1920s, a Royal Commission was set up to investigate lunacy and mental disorder. The Macmillan Report, 1926, was the result. In this the medical view of mental illness gained sway over the legal view. The importance of prevention in mental illness was stressed, and it expressed concern both about false detention and stigmatisation. All these issues were taken up in the Mental Treatment Act of 1930, which introduced care in mental hospitals without compulsion. Patients could now be admitted on a voluntary basis and could discharge themselves if they gave seventy-two hours' notice.[10] Denis Hooton, who was working as a clerk at Springfield Hospital when the 1930 Act came into force, remembered how nobody in his office could fathom how anyone could possibly *volunteer* to go into an asylum. Slowly but surely, however, people did.

Nationally, 38 per cent of all admissions in 1938 were voluntary.[11] At Severalls, however, the proportion of voluntary patients remained lower than the national average until 1959. In 1932, for instance, 6 per cent of all admissions were voluntary. This rose steadily to 22 per cent in 1935. In 1945 it had doubled to 44 per cent, yet by 1950 it had dropped to 17 per cent and even by 1959 it stood at only 32 per cent of all admissions. The Commissioners of the Board of Control, in their annual report on Severalls in 1959, remarked that it was not a hospital 'approved for the purpose of Section 20 of the Lunacy Act, with the result that the proportion of patients admitted under certification is higher than we usually find'.[12]

One effect of voluntary admissions was that increasingly patients came in and out of the hospital on what would later be called a 'revolving door' basis. One woman, for instance, was certified in 1935, at the age of 28, diagnosed as suffering from *dementia praecox* (schizophrenia): her certificate claimed she was mentally unstable, excitable, noisy, continually singing and insisted that two of her brothers, both killed in the war, were still alive. The doctor injected her with insulin a few weeks after her admission (this is the first instance I could find of insulin being used at Severalls), which made her very ill. Three months later, however, she was doing occupational therapy and showed a marked improvement. The following month she was discharged on trial, then discharged completely as 'recovered'. She resumed her duties of caring for her father and brother, her mother having moved out some time ago.

Three years later, however, she was readmitted on a voluntary basis feeling depressed and emotional. She told the doctor she 'hears God telling her she is lost and wicked'. Three months later she became mute, but the following year discharged herself. A year later she returned, with delusions that she was the Devil and a heathen and that the wireless was influencing her. Case notes report her as 'defective in habits: masturbates'. Again she became mute and stayed in for over two years, but was discharged in 1941 as 'relieved'. Six years later she came back once more on a voluntary basis; she was depressed, tearful, and thought she might be the Devil. By this time she had married and had three very young children. She was only in for a month before being discharged. In 1951 she returned, once again as a voluntary patient, because she was depressed. She was given an intensive course of ECT and left after just one week. She then came back the following month, again depressed, and had another course of ECT. Four weeks later she left and apparently never came back again.

Once a person had been admitted as a voluntary patient, however, it was not always so easy as it might have seemed at first to be discharged. The labelling process of simply being a patient in a mental hospital, whatever your legal status, meant that everyone else saw you as by definition mad, and therefore unable to make rational choices or decisions for yourself. The following account gives a good idea of this dilemma:

> After five years in the WAAF during the war, I could not settle, I tramped the roads by day and slept in haystacks and sheds by night, as an escape from a problem to which a more suicidal nature might have sought the solution in a gas oven. An unlucky choice of haystacks in the small hours of the sixth day brought a pair of

wildly yapping terriers down on me, shortly followed by a heavily built farmer. The dogs, better mannered than their master, contented themselves with prowling continuously round me at a distance of a few feet, merely snarling occasionally, as soon as they had brought me to a halt, but the farmer stood in my path swearing and threatening, until I was obliged to caution him for his language. Thereupon, he produced a rattletrap car, driven by an inexpert yokel, in which I was rather uncertainly conveyed to the nearest police station.

Here the situation, which up to then had appealed chiefly to my sense of humour, became suddenly all too serious. The police doctor, summoned by the sergeant in charge, was in no mood to deal sympathetically with a female vagrant who had been the cause of his being dragged from his bed at three o'clock in the morning. After a summary examination, I was given the alternatives of allowing the sergeant to put me on the first train back to London (at my own expense) or of becoming a voluntary patient in the nearest mental hospital, failing which, he warned me, I should be certified insane.

Why, I argued, should I be forced to return to an environment that had become intolerable to me, when my present way of living was causing trouble to nobody? And why, indeed, if I was considered capable of travelling back to London alone, should I be incarcerated in a mental hospital? My experiences had taught me the worthlessness of the 'voluntary' system and I knew that, having once entered the portals of any mental hospital, there was no predicting to where I might eventually be consigned.[13]

One man, who came to Severalls as a cadet nurse at the age of 16 in 1954, gave an account that illustrated just how easy it was for the authorities to change a patient's status, should they wish to:

I've seen the medical superintendent in action and I remember later, just before the Mental Health Act changed – because this hospital was a dumping ground for a lot of people at one time – anybody they didn't want, they'd dump at Severalls. But I can remember this chap being transferred from Goodmayes – Brentwood had refused to have him because he'd attacked nurses, so they put him in Severalls and we had him in Ward 3.

We still had certification then, but this chap was a voluntary patient, and this chap would say, 'You can't touch me, I'm a voluntary patient!' And he attacked one of the staff. And I remember Dr Duncan going in to say to him, 'I want to talk to you – you can't behave like that!' And there were some abusive words – a lot of violent words and threats and everything. So Dr Duncan turned round and went out of the room and returned with two others. The chap then became very abusive and threatening. They turned and went out of the room. Dr Duncan returned and said, 'You've just been certified. Now you're certified, we're transferring you back to Goodmayes.' These two gentlemen – one was a doctor and the other was a JP. 'I'm not going *any*where!' And Dr Duncan just said, 'Mr Smith and Mr Brown,[14] will you come in?' Because they still had the old assistants who'd been here a long time on the staff, and some were quite tall and hefty, and they were good to have around sometimes. And these two walked through the door, and he said, 'You are going to be transferred, and Mr Smith and Mr Brown will make sure you go.'

Once in, even on the basis of voluntary status, the chances of getting out were not good. The pattern of a surplus of admissions over discharges and deaths, however, changed quite dramatically from the Second World War. For various reasons, more people were being admitted while at the same time more were being discharged after the Second World War. New somatic treatments were being introduced, though the effectiveness of these at this time is open to question. Perhaps more important, people seemed more willing to seek treatment earlier and to seek treatment for less serious conditions. This was made possible to a great extent by the early out-patient clinics, which the 1930 Act had encouraged. As early as 1926, however, a new outpatient clinic block was opened at Essex County Hospital in which a psychiatric clinic was set up under Dr Turnbull; the clinic opened for two hours once a week. In 1934 an outpatient clinic was established at Chelmsford, which ran for one afternoon a week, and in 1947 outpatient clinics were set up in Clacton and Braintree. Each consultant at Severalls ran one of the clinics.

Nevertheless, although terminology was to some extent changed by the 1930 Mental Treatment Act, and responsibility for administration devolved to the local authorities (although policy was still formulated and initiated by central government), mental health policy still remained defined essentially by the lunacy laws of 1890. Certification continued after 1930 'as a penal sanction on the insane, which associated them with the criminal and the socially suspect. Certification also acted as a social barometer which created a personal stigma for those mental patients discharged from the hospitals.'[15] The process of certification itself made people feel as if they were criminals being punished, as the following account by a man who was first certified and put into Severalls in 1954 bears witness:

I worked as a clerk until I was called up for National Service, and that was when I was 18. I passed the medical A1, Grade 1, and I was stationed, told to go to Claygate for my square-bashing, and I spent about a week there and I was taken ill. Then I went to RAF Horton where I was invalided out by the MO, but my father was an Air Force officer and I met my father there in the RAF, and he was talking to the MO at RAF Horton, and he sent me, without any hesitation, to Severalls.

So I was transferred by RAF ambulance to Severalls and there I was put into Male Hospital Villa – that's the name the villa was called then – and I was put into a bed. I was – I could walk, and I didn't feel all that ill. They didn't say what it was. They didn't say what it was. And I didn't feel ill. Well, I passed my medical A1, Grade 1 and I didn't think anything was wrong with me. And I was under lock and key, lock and key, not to go out of the grounds at all, not even outside, for a long, long time. I don't know how long.

I still, to this day here, I have no idea *why* I was put into Severalls. When I was first admitted to hospital, the staff nurse said, 'You're here at the Queen's Pleasure,' whatever he meant by that. I'd done nothing criminal or anything like that. I'd never been in prison. I never felt ill. I was never mental. It made me feel envious of other people living outside. Locked up wrongly. It felt as though I'd done something criminal. It made me feel as though I was a criminal, and I hadn't done anything wrong at all. I've never understood it. I've never understood it. Why I should be locked up like that. Punishment. Punishment.

The sense of being criminalised and being punished for not having done anything wrong at all is evocative of Kafka's *The Trial*. The ways in which the whole process was defined in, and carried out by, the law made such feelings inevitable. In the early days patients were often, if not always, brought in handcuffed by the police. Physical restraint, in any case, became less and less necessary with the development of somatic treatments, particularly the new psychotropic drugs that were developed in the early 1950s. Insulin coma therapy, electroconvulsive therapy (ECT) and psychosurgery were all developed in the late 1930s and led to an increasingly strong belief among many psychiatrists that mental illness could, in fact, be cured rather than just managed and controlled. There had also, however, been a long traditional belief in the value of 'moral treatment'[16] dating back to the early nineteenth century, and in the twentieth century, but particularly from the 1940s onwards, there was a growing movement for social rehabilitation of mental patients. Increasingly the message was that mental illness, and treatment in a mental hospital, was not a matter of a life sentence (or at least, shouldn't be), but that it could be, and should be, a short-term place for treatment, rehabilitation and cure. The whole elaborate hospital system, however, including hierarchy, bureaucracy and a spatial design that encouraged regimentation and institutionalisation rather than rehabilitation, combined with well-entrenched prejudice at all levels of society, and most important, chronic underfunding, meant that such ideals were not easy to implement.

There was increased movement towards 'open-door' policies from the 1940s. New treatments, new ideas about social rehabilitation, increasing despair with the whole infrastructure of Victorian mental hospitals and their regimes, in conjunction with new attitudes to health, the NHS and a period of greater optimism for change led to a number of pressures to overhaul the whole mental health system. More and more it was believed that treatment should be early rather than later, voluntary and short-stay instead of enforced and custodial. In 1954 the Percy Commission was appointed and the eventual outcome was the Mental Health Act of 1959.

The Mental Health Act repealed all previous lunacy and mental health acts, and defined mental illness as a medical condition. Tribunals were set up as watchdogs in cases of compulsory detention (sectioning). Patients could now be admitted without any formalities, although three types of compulsory admission remained.[17] Informal patients could now discharge themselves whenever they chose. Informal patients, however, could be sectioned, and this was often a fear of patients once they were in hospital. Admission to hospital, while still not a pleasant procedure, may have become generally somewhat less traumatic than it had been under the old certification process; although people could still be forcibly detained, there was sometimes an element of choice afforded to those who were suffering. The following account is by a woman who was a patient at Severalls off and on from the 1960s, and she is talking about another woman (my mother) who had also been in and out of various hospitals for many years. They were both diagnosed as manic-depressives:

> There was one wonderful day I remember long, long before she died. All her friends were very concerned about her. It was a Sunday, and I happened to go to post a letter, and she was outside what's now the baker's, with various people trying to get her to go home or to come with them, or what have you. And they'd had the doctor down and he said he could do nothing. They had an ambulance down, and they'd gone away. And a couple of police cars were there. And in desperation, someone turned to me and said, 'Well, you have a go.'
>
> So I tried. I wasn't getting anywhere and, I mean, she desperately needed to be in care. And she was rabbiting on to me and I had

a brainwave. I jumped in the police car and I said, 'Look, Lloyd, I can't hear you when you're out there,' so she got in the police car and the police promptly took off. And Dr Sanderson from Rowhedge was meeting us, and he met us up at Greenstead roundabout, and took one look and said, 'Yes! She has to go in!' And so then there were two police cars and Dr Sanderson. And we got her to – well, we got a bit along the bypass – and she wanted to dance! So the policewoman who was – there was a policeman driving and a police-woman next to him – and she got really worried. And I said, 'Lloyd, we can't dance here – it's too crowded! Shall we sing?'

So we drove up to Myland Court singing our heads off, and a charge nurse came out and sort of looked in the car, recognised me as well – 'God! Which one? Or is it both?' She wouldn't get out of the car, so we had a bit of talking and so on. The police were marvellous, they really were. And Dr Sanderson – I could have kissed him. He said, 'Well, what were you singing just now, Lloyd?' And she couldn't remember. And he said, 'I'm going to go down this passage singing "Onward, Christian Soldiers" – do any of the rest of you know it?' So there was the two police, Dr Sanderson, Lloyd and me sort of marching down the corridor! It ended up with being such a gentle admission for her. It was lovely. I thought, 'Oh, why didn't anyone admit me like that?' And later, she did say one day, 'I felt very safe when you took me to hospital. It was fun!'

In 1983 a further Mental Health Act retained three main forms of compulsory admission from the 1959 Act, but modified these somewhat.[18] The result is that people can now admit themselves, be referred by a GP or, indeed, be compulsorily detained. It altered the principles of the 1959 Act and improved administration. Existing professional roles were 'formally codified, especially in relation to compulsory detention of patients. Mental nurses were given "holding powers" to forcibly detain 'informal' patients'.[19] One woman, who had been in and out of Severalls for many years from the 1960s, was sectioned for the first time in the 1990s:

This last year was the longest I've ever been – I was *sectioned* this last time. That had never happened to me in all my life! And I said to the doctor, 'Look, I'd like to know why I was sectioned!' 'Well,' he said, 'you should have taken them to a tribunal', which I was going to do. Then somebody said, 'Oh, you don't want a tribunal,' you know, 'it would be too much for you. Just let it go.' You know? But it's sort of a stain on one's character to be sectioned,

46

and it was this young girl who did it, she'd just qualified, a young nurse. It was awful. I felt so humiliated.

The irony now is that so many cuts in hospital beds have been made, even people who have been ill for years and know they need help in the context of a mental hospital are not always able to be admitted. One man, who had been in and out of Severalls since the late 1960s, and who had been rehabilitated in Clacton, told me how much better a service he found it there, and how much happier he was than he had been at Severalls. Still taking a considerable amount of medication for what has been diagnosed as schizophrenia, I asked him if he gets warning signals when he begins to get ill again:

> Yeah. I start thinking about space and time. Things like that. Well, I can't sleep, that's when I get ill and I start thinking about going back in time and how things started, and I get confused by it all, and not being able to get off the subject, and it takes over my life. That is one of them anyway. I start thinking about evil in people and their negative ways and the amount of things on television that are, you know, pretty disgusting. Violence, I mean. And then I *want* to go in. They say, 'Well, you're not really ill enough', and then I get too ill and I *don't* want to go in, 'cause I think they're going to do some damage to me.
>
> You have to be *really* ill to get in now. So many people – it's only a small unit, you know. Well, Severalls Hospital had about 1,000 patients, I believe, but this place can only hold about 25! If that. So – I'm just on me own, really. And then I cut myself off from people completely. I feel really fearful – and evil. I think everybody's evil and things like that. So feel *really* scared. I suffer it. And then they say, 'Come in,' and I say, 'No.' I'm afraid of what's going to happen to me, from my past experiences. Even in Peter Bruff[20] they don't know what to give me – well, they do give me a depot injection. That's three quick jabs in the backside, to calm me down, but then I've usually been off medication when this happens.

STAFF ENTRIES AND EXITS

Staff, unlike patients, moved in and out frequently, although a surprisingly large number worked there all their lives, as did, very often, their children and their children's children. Severalls was a way of life, a different way of life from that outside the gates. Some loved that difference, others could not tolerate it. For some staff, their first visit to Severalls was like entering another world. A woman who began work in 1941 as a junior secretary gave this account:

> When I walked up the drive when I came for the interview, it was a lovely sunny day, and it was like walking into a lovely park. The grounds were so beautifully kept. Well, we had several gardeners and lots of patients helping, so of course it had to be, and that was the standard of everything in those days: it had to be just so. And where there are now conifers on the left-hand side, to the best of my recollection they were gardens – and then they grassed it over. There were herbaceous borders interspersed with rose trees. It was a lovely approach, it really was, and it was a marvellous place for psychiatric patients who could appreciate it, but I'm not sure that many could in those days. They weren't allowed out on the drive, you see, they were enclosed with the railings.

Patients have also mentioned the beauty of the grounds and how they found them healing and comforting. Administrative workers and estate workers in particular seem to have very fond, often idyllic, memories of their work in Severalls and what they described as it being 'like a family'.

To work at Severalls, however, many in the outside community believed, tarred you with the same brush as the patients, suggested you might be likely to 'catch the mania', or were at least to be regarded with suspicion, associated not only with madness but, to some extent perhaps, with death. A woman who came to work in the administrative office in the late 1950s when she was 15 years old, remembered how:

> We had to do deaths. I can remember I had to do the deaths with the medical records as well, and I can remember the first person I saw was an older man who'd lost his wife and he was crying and I was crying and I was telling him what to do, but I felt so sorry for him. Gradually I got so that I didn't cry with them. The undertakers, though, were friendly, because I mean we all got on a bus didn't we, everyone did. But the undertakers used to say, 'Well, we're going' – if they'd come for a body, they'd say, 'do you girls want a lift?' And we all used to pile in the hearse! It saved us our bus fare! Fourpence return, that was a lot of money, and we all used to stop at North Hill and pile out.

Not everyone, particularly young women at that time, would have been happy to be seen piling out of a hearse in the middle of town. It suggests

Figure 2.2 Male patients working in the gardens, 1950s
Source: North East Essex Mental Health NHS Trust

that employees may well have felt, at least at some level, both their own stigmatisation by the outside community and a pride in their own community. Many mentioned the importance of a sense of humour as a survival tactic among so much misery, while here there seems to have been a defiant bravado added to the humour.

Though staff could move in and out in a way that patients could not, such movements were strictly regulated. Entry to Severalls was indeed an entry to another world, another community, but a community governed and guarded by its own laws of gender division, clothing regulations, temporality, hierarchy and secrecy. It was different and special, ultimately, because it was the place of madness, the place where people outside the gates feared to go, both literally and metaphorically. Partly, perhaps, as a result of that, it was in many ways a *protected* place, both for patients and for staff.

Paternalistic and patriarchal it certainly was, yet such paternalistic patriarchy also offered some staff – male nurses in particular, but also female nurses as long as they did not marry – job security almost unheard of in the first half of the century. While wages were low, they were regular, and there were perks: free uniforms, good wholesome meals, excellent sporting facilities (particularly for men), a pension, and a sense of belonging to a community. Many perks were illicit: there seems to have been quite frequent stealing by staff of patients' clothing, belongings, money and food. Estate workers would repair other staff members' bicycles, cars, houses, although these favours were part of a dense network of friendships as well as, quite frequently, kinship. A man who worked in administration from 1940, remembered how his father, who was the pharmacist at Severalls at the time, used to get odd jobs done by estate workers at their home:

> Before the war my father used to – you know, if he wanted a job doing, well you went to the carpenter – or one of the electricians – they all came up in the evening, 'Oh, can you let me have a bit of wood?' 'Yes, that'll be all right,' sort of thing. Or if they wanted, it could be a bit of cough mixture or something, he'd fix them up with a cough mixture. You know, everything was reciprocated. Black market – well, it wasn't black market, but – it was just a way of life, really. If the secretary's wife wanted a cake, her husband had to go down and see the baker or something – and receive verbal abuse from him! But he got his cake! It was all know-how, wasn't it? Well, my father used to like to poke his nose into a good number of things. He used to know the engineer, for example, they were good friends, and he'd get the engineer to come up and put the wallpaper up in the house and that sort of thing. My father was a very enthusiastic Freemason.

One male nurse remembered how an older, much-respected charge nurse used to smuggle coal from his ward in a bag on the back of his bike every evening when he left work, tossing his keys to the gatekeeper as he pedalled through the gate. Once, however, the cycle wheels got caught in the edge of the weighbridge and both charge nurse and coal spilled all over the front entry. Such transactions were mentioned most frequently by, and about, male staff and it is tempting to speculate if the bonds of Freemasonry, which certainly seem to have been strong at the top of the hierarchy, extended through the lower echelons as well.

For staff who grew up near, or on the periphery of, the estate, the sight of patients was familiar. A woman who was born in Mile End went to work at Severalls as a domestic, and then as the doctors' maid, in 1940. I asked her to what extent she was aware of the hospital as a child:

> Oh yes! Well, we existed round it! Everybody worked there, the people next door to me down the lane, the children I played with

– everybody, the children I went to school with. When we were children, you know, I'd say less than 8 years old – the early thirties – and Severalls' engine used to come by each day. It was a very large engine like a traction engine,[21] and I don't know, I can't remember whether it'd got one or two trailers on the back full of coal – or coke – I mean it could've been either – it was very high. And it used to make a terrific noise, you know, goin' along.

A man, a staff, used to drive it and there used to be – the patients used to ride, you know, one or two, and they were dressed in white cord velvets. They always had white cords – even dealin' with coal! The worker patients. Whether there was two or four I can't tell you, it's many years ago, but we used to run up the lane to see it going by. Well I can't tell you how frequently it used to go – it used to go down, load up with coal at the station, you see, and then come back later on in the day. I can't tell you whether that was two or three times a week.

Jackets and trousers the patients wore that all during the war, those that worked outside, you know, or doin' dirty manual work, you seen an' caps, tweed caps, and that used to make a terrific noise! Some of the people in the village was complainin' about it makin' the cracks in the ceilin's an' that. I mean it was as bad as that. Well then later on, later on, it was changed and Molly's used to do it by lorry, I think it was Molly's, because things got more cars about, more modern, you know, before the war.

Interestingly, however, when I asked her if she had been inside the grounds of the Severalls estate before she went to work there, she replied:

No. No. Fear might a' been the thing, you know. As I was sayin', I mean I was scared stiff when I went. I really – well, you don't know what you're goin' to find, do you? We wasn't frightened of it *this* side of it, if you know what I mean.

The gates and fences reassured the outside community that madness was contained, controlled and safe.

For children whose parents worked at Severalls, such fears do not seem to have existed in the way this woman described. Even if they grew up a few miles away, the sense of being part of a special community seems to have been strong. Julian Taylor, for instance, was born in 1941 and grew up in Great Horkesley.[22] His father, an active member of the Communist Party, worked from 1928 as the pathologist in the path lab and his mother had trained as a nurse at Severalls.

Mother was living in the house that Father and her had built about 1934 and which was Coach Road Corner in Great Horkesley. And what was fascinating, and at the time of Mum's funeral in 1996 we were able to identify, you go up the road and next door was Arthur, who was a male nurse, and his wife who was a nurse from Severalls, next door to us. The next house up, and I can't remember their names, but the two domestics who lived in the hospital all their lives, and – yes, most of their lives – and had retired and built their house, and lived together in the house. The next one up was Reggie, who was a male nurse at Severalls, and he retrained as a physiotherapist, and his wife was a nurse. The next house up was one of my father's temporary assistants, and later became assistant chief male nurse. The next house up was one of the carpenters and joiners, and was a very very fine cabinet-maker. Still alive. And both he and Arthur were Labour Party activists. The next person up was the hospital electrician, and he was very active in the church. And across the road, in the first of the Rampart Cottages, which was the local authority houses built in the thirties, was the – I think two of the sons became nurses in the hospital.

It was part of the change that happened in the village that the school in Horkesley was a voluntary controlled school, coming under the Church of England at that time, and both my parents, along with many other people, were not church members. My father was positively *anti*-church, and so we went [to school] out of the area. We went to the council school in Mile End. Most of the children from Severalls families, in fact, did not go to the village school, they chose to go to Mile End County Primary School. And coming home you just walked home. I mean, you went on the A134 – which it was then, which was the main road. You sort of took an hour to get home and wandered, two or three of you would wander home together. Very little traffic on the roads – in fact, we used to roller-skate on that road!

And then when I got a bit older, to about 8 or 9, I would walk to Severalls and go into the lab, and would get there at about four o'clock or so – and you'd walk into the grounds of Severalls and talk to people as you went in, stopping at the gate and the gate-man always knew you, and if you timed your arrival properly, you arrived at four o'clock and the gate-man would give you a piece of his bun or his tea to eat!

The gate marked status because most people had to hand their keys in and out at the gate, so it was actually, you were a signing-in position, you knew who was in and out of the hospital at that time, but if you were of sufficient status, you could take the keys home with you. So Father had the keys to the lab with him, but there were spare sets elsewhere, on the basis that he might have to come in in the middle of the night or do something urgent.

And there were parole areas, and there were certain posts marked around the perimeter track, about how far people were able to walk and go when they were on parole, and they were duty bound not to – not to wander beyond that. And you played with your friends who lived on site, you know, who were there all the time, and the people who you met within the hospital were – who were patients, you know, patients, you didn't think of them as patients, they were really rather kind to children and really very nice. And they certainly weren't frightening.

What the – bits that were, in retrospect, frightening, were the – were the people who were wandering aimlessly around, seen to be walking aimlessly around outside – the walking areas or courts, and there was a sort of – the hospital was designed so that the fences could never be seen, so you just looked and you just saw people walking around the courts, because the fences were in a ditch. They were all sunken. So you didn't actually see. But one of the things you were conscious of was noise, and of people shouting and being very very noisy. But I don't think one thought, as a child, you didn't seem to think of it as frightening. Just how it was. And it was OK – your dad worked there, and he was safe, and he was OK.

For those who came to work in Severalls without kinship connections or community proximity, their first entry to the hospital was often terrifying and traumatic. A man who worked in Severalls as a driver remembered:

That would be about '47 I went up there. And the job was a joint job. It was on the transport side and in the stores. That was their big stores, that department up there that supplied the whole hospital with everything. But when I arrived the first morning, I was cycling in those days, and I cycled into this yard and there was one of the patients – he was shovelling up a sort of anthracite/coal stuff for the kitchen boilers, because the kitchen, those days, it wasn't gas-fired. They had big boilers. And I don't know whether I want to say he was mad as a March hare – but! He was yelling and cursing while he was shovelling this – and I thought, 'Oh my God!' I was scared stiff of him! And he looked, he looked quite – well, I felt very apprehensive of him. Yes. He looked quite mad. But – and he used to strip off in the yard and wash himself afterwards – out in the cold! You know, in cold water. And I thought to myself, 'Whatever have I let myself in for?'

And of course, then when I started this delivery, you used to have to go into the kitchen to pick up all the cooked meals and that, and the kitchen employed a lot of patients. And there were patients making the tea and scrubbing the benches down and – and they all had their different personalities. And some of them were doing what I thought were crazy things then. Staring up at the ceiling and shouting and throwing their arms about and – it wasn't until you really worked there for a period of time and you got to know them that you took it as a matter of course. But it's a bit of a baptism of fire really, when you went up there first time, because they didn't, they didn't have the tranquillisers that they have at the present day. They must have had some kind of medicine, but they certainly were most queer.

I used to have my meals at the cafeteria up there and there were patients employed in there, in the kitchen area of the cafeteria – because you met them all in amongst the corridors. You used to have to walk round the corridors to do different jobs. And when I had to go through a ward for the first time, I was absolutely scared stiff. I was walking along, you know, and looking from side to side, and wondering who was behind me. And of course, some of them were yelling, and some of them were running about – and they were doing all sorts! I can't describe everything they were doing, but they were doing all sorts of peculiar things. And I thought, 'Oh my God!' I was ever so pleased to get out the other end of the ward! And of course, some of the patients used to lean out the upstairs windows and yell in such a loud voice, 'SEVERALLS MENTAL HOSPITAL!' and you could hear them all the way down Mill Road. Yeah. But it was quite a traumatic experience, really, going to work there.

An endemic labour shortage, most notably after the Second World War, and particularly among female nurses, but also later among male nurses and doctors, led to an increasing number of immigrants being recruited and employed. While boundaries between inside and outside, sanity and madness remained more or less in place, as did the gate and the fences and railings, local and national boundaries were changing in ways that eventually also challenged the more traditional barriers around, and within, the hospital, while at the same time new ones were being created.

Nursing staff had, prior to the war, been traditionally recruited in Ireland, Wales, Scotland and the North-East. After the war, these sources had to a large extent diminished, if not dried up, and recruitment was taken into first Italy, France, Spain, and then eventually the West Indies, Africa and China/Hong Kong. Though pay was poor and conditions still harsh, displaced persons and young people seeking the prestige of working and training in a British hospital gradually began to arrive, starting work as untrained nursing assistants, then later as student nurses. Yvonne Caron, a woman who was born in Neuilly, France, in 1938 came to work in Severalls when she 18:

It was quite complicated because even on the *boat* I had to have a medical! There was two of us – a girl who was coming to Nottingham to be an au pair, and I was coming to Severalls – so we sat on the boat and we talked and we both had to go to the doctor. And I said to the doctor, 'Why do we have to come here?' And he said, 'To make sure we're not pregnant'!

Then we got to London, but because she was being an au pair she had a lady waiting for her to put her on the train. Well, I didn't, but she was kind and said, 'you go to Victoria and to go to Colchester you have to go to Liverpool Street.' So we talked to someone at the station and the lady was very nice, she brought me back to Liverpool Street. And her French was sort of broken French, but – and she put me on the train and she actually asked people on the train where they got off, and she found someone was getting off after Colchester, and she said, 'Can you remind this young lady to get off?' And I was watching out for Colchester – because I was petrified as well!

And of course Colchester came, and a man told me and so I got out. Of course, come to Colchester – deserted! Wasn't it? There wasn't a soul anywhere. And I didn't know what to do, so I walked out of the station and there were two telephone boxes there – they were red in those days! And there was a young couple kissing in the telephone box. And I opened the door, and I gave him my purse and the letter from Severalls. And he didn't want to take my purse, he just phoned the number and he told me to wait, you know. Fine. I understood what he said. Then this big black car came. One guy. And I thought, 'Oh my God! Where is he taking me?' This big black car on the wrong side of the road – I was petrified at that time!

There was a lot of girls then. Yes. A lot of them. The Spanish. Italians. Not so many French, funnily enough, because a lot of them came here and a lot of them who came later went to Canada. When I was here I remember, must have been about ten or twelve of us, and we used to have separate corridors, you see, the French corridor, the Italian corridor, the coloured corridor. Well, yes, we stayed together. We used to speak our own language, we used to work all together. I mean, on the wards it was no different. It's just that we all had our little clique, if you know what I mean.

Perhaps it was inevitable that a hospital so demarcated already by boundaries, hierarchy and divisions, would instigate a system of differentiation based on ethnic origins in the nurses' dormitories. Racism as such had not been openly addressed in Britain in the mid-1950s, a point when immigration was at its peak and actively being encouraged as the only perceived solution to the chronic labour shortage. It was not just in Severalls that boundaries between ethnic groups arose, of course. By the 1960s these, along with other gates and fences, were also being challenged if not destroyed. A man who came to Severalls from Hong Kong at the age of 18 to work as a student nurse in 1963 remembered:

It took more than twenty-six hours to fly from Hong Kong to Heathrow, and in between, I think, there were ten stops. My first impression of England, actually, was rather grey and grimy. Sitting on the BOAC coach towards Victoria Station all I could see everywhere is grey. It's either black or grey, and people wearing grey suit, grey mac – and everything is grey. And I thought, 'Cor, this is a bit – sort of foul!' It was May. It should have been quite warm. But it was, I remember, it was quite cool. Yeah. And – but then, coming from a place like Hong Kong it would have been, it would be cool. So, Severalls was a big massive place to me. It was quite horrendous, quite frightening in a way, because to me there was acres and acres of space, and acres and acres of unknown to me.

The very next day I was given a day off because of my travel. I was being looked after by a chap who was quite well known in Severalls Hospital – he's dead now. His name was Tony. And he was a nice chap. He took me into Colchester, introduced me to the Colchester Castle and so on. He took me to Jacklin's restaurant in Colchester, where his aunt used to work. And then on the third day I started work.

We had to start work before our training started. I was placed, put on a ward – Firs Villa, the male admission ward. Now, Firs Villa is only just across the road from the entrance, the main entrance, but what we called the 'male mess', where people eat, is what is now the building of the Institute of Health Studies, about 150 yards away. But I was brand new, I didn't know the place, I couldn't get my bearings. And in those days an afternoon shift finished at quarter past nine in the evening. And by the time you get told to go it's about half past nine. And I happened to be the only resident nurse working that shift, so nobody else was coming off duty. And I came out from Firs Villa and I couldn't find my way to the dining room to eat! I walked round and round, and you couldn't see anybody in the corridors. Not that I would ask anyway, I was too scared to ask anybody. Eventually I found my way to where my room was. But I missed my supper the first night because I couldn't find the place and I was too scared to ask.

Having made the decision I wanted to leave Hong Kong, I didn't really want to go back and say I didn't like it. So I thought, 'Well, it's up to you to make something out of it'. So I did. I had some good friends, I made some good friends, which makes life more bearable. I wasn't always aware of any obvious overt prejudice, apart from being called names, which you just accept. Not by everybody. Some people called you names. Some did it, some people did it in a friendly manner, which is politically not correct these days. But those days, you know, you can accept that there was no malice in it, and the fact that they call you names is – wasn't – particular – because the fact that it is life. It's just their way of expressing. But at least that's how I took it anyway, because it was important I took it that way to survive. But when it comes to work I think there is, there has been a hierarchical role as to – first of all, via the seniority of your status. But secondly, I think your race did come into a little bit to it. You see, nobody wanted to feel that an outsider would come in and upset the – the family unit that is working here.

Those who worked at Severalls, especially those who had been born into Severalls of parents who worked there, regarded Severalls as not only their home, but their community, their special place with its own set of special ways and privileges, some official and some not. Of course many staff came from all sorts of different places and backgrounds and there does seem to have been a tolerance for a good amount of difference – as long as the space itself, its boundaries and rules were honoured. But from the 1950s, and especially in the 1960s, all these began to shift, change and be challenged, both from within and from without. Doors opened, railings and gates came down. Patients left – and frequently came back on a revolving door basis. The changing pace of life and work, both outside the hospital and inside it, new patterns of treatment and medication, changing philosophies and policies of mental health care, impacted on the place itself and all those who lived and worked in it in myriad ways. Ultimately such changes led to the closure of the hospital altogether. The gate to the hospital itself has gone, as has the hospital community it was set up to guard and protect, yet the less visible fears it served to calm – unclear boundaries between madness and sanity, safety and danger, them and us, inside and outside – continue to plague and perplex people and culture at the end of the era of asylums.

3

THE CORRIDOR OF POWER

The medical superintendent? Oh, he was *God*!
(Administrative worker)

The front gate to Severalls led to an imposing facade; from here the front doors opened into a long corridor along which were located the medical superintendent's offices, the committee meeting room, the clerk and steward's[1] offices, financial and administrative offices. It then divided into two branches which both bifurcated the male side from the female side and enclosed the kitchens, the stores, and the recreation hall. Matron's offices and flat ran along one side in the middle, the chief male nurse's (earlier, the inspector) on the other. At the far end was the pharmacy, the operating theatre and what was first the deputy medical superintendent's house, and later doctors' flats. Changes were made to these arrangements and the location of different offices from time to time, but throughout its life, this was the corridor where administrators and doctors met the outside world, both in person and in paper, a place where patients were rarely seen (at least during the first half of the century), but where decisions were made about their treatments, certification, rehabilitation, departures or, indeed, their deaths.

THE MEDICAL SUPERINTENDENT:
THE EARLY YEARS

To the right of the front entrance were the medical superintendent's offices. He[2] was the ultimate authority within the hospital to whom, like the father of a middle-class Victorian family, all were expected to defer. From 1948, however, the medical superintendent's power and authority were to become increasingly questioned, and eventually challenged, at a national level, but also at Severalls itself, until in 1971 the post was abolished at Severalls. It was not, however, abolished without a struggle, and much

59

Figure 3.1 Facade of the main building, *circa* 1930
Source: North East Essex Mental Health NHS Trust

of the 1960s, though a time when enormous and far-reaching changes were implemented, was also characterised by an increasingly bitter and divisive feud between the superintendent, one of his consultants, and the Regional Board. Before that, however, the superintendent was an awesome figure whom staff held in great respect. As one male nurse, who came to Severalls in the 1930s, remembered:

> The superintendent, of course he was a well qualified man. He was always the gaffer, you know, the head man, at the top! He – he did run this and rule the place with a rod of iron. He could rule it with a rod of iron! Dr Turnbull was superintendent when I came. Course he'd been there since it first opened. Dr Turnbull. Ever such a nice gentleman he was, very nice, and a real homely, fatherly type, you know. And his deputy, he used to take us for our exams. Course he took over, Dr Duncan, the deputy, took over in 1938, and *he* ruled with a rod of iron.
>
> You had to wear the right clothes, you couldn't come down that corridor like they do now in that time of day, some of the young lads like they are today. And one chap did go along – brainy chap too he was – he come along and he met him and he had a black shirt on – that was the time, you know, more or less Hitler – Mosley

was leading the Black Shirts – and he stopped him! Said, 'What department are you working in?' Course he said, 'On the nursing staff, Sir.' 'While you're in the hospital, never wear that shirt again!' He had to go, didn't like it, had to go. He changed his shirt. 'Don't ever wear that shirt in this hospital again!'

While he may have seemed god-like to those within the hospital, the medical superintendent was nonetheless subject to the dictates – and funding – of political and economic constraints outside the hospital. The Lunacy Act of 1890 stipulated that central government, the Lord Chancellor, was responsible for appointing Commissioners in Lunacy,[3] who had powers of visitation and inspection; visitors from the Board of Control made yearly inspections of the hospital and some of its wards and facilities; reports on deaths, illnesses, treatments were submitted to them, and they then produced an annual report on their visit. At a local level, however, the County or County Borough Council was responsible for building and maintaining asylums, as well as appointing visiting committees.

The medical superintendent, who combined both administrative and medical duties, was responsible legally and personally for the treatment of all certified patients he received in the hospital. He had to make sure they did not escape and were not subject to cruelty by hospital staff. If a patient escaped and harmed somebody or some property, the superintendent could be sued. By definition all certified patients 'were incapable of intelligent or reasonable behaviour, potentially violent, always on the lookout for escape'.[4]

Within months of Severalls' first medical superintendent, Dr Turnbull (1913–1940), taking up his post, the First World War began. He was immediately confronted with a number of serious problems: the most serious, and one which was to persist until very recently, was staff shortage. Even by January 1914 he noted 'I am now finding great difficulty in obtaining female staff and it will not be possible to open the new buildings unless some radical alteration is made in the conditions of service.' Low wages, harsh conditions, isolation did not attract many nurses, who, unlike their male counterparts, could only be entitled to security and a pension if they chose not to marry.

From 19 August 1914 the Suffolk Brigade of Territorials were quartered in the detached buildings and surrounding grounds of Severalls. There were four regiments with a total of 3,632 officers and men.[5] Very soon severe problems with water supply and drainage developed; largely as a result of these problems, at least initially, disease broke out, and many patients and nurses on the female side were stricken with scarlet fever. Two nurses died. Influenza then broke out and both flu and scarlet fever were problematic throughout the winter of 1915. In late winter of 1916 they broke out again, and so did typhoid, which continued until 1918, when the records ceased for over a year. The last few entries were written in such shaky handwriting that I presume Dr Turnbull was himself seriously ill by that time.

By October, 1914 Severalls had already lost twenty-one of its attendants who were Reservists and as a result, annual leave had to be cancelled. By November only ten experienced attendants were left on day duty on the male side. In March 1915 Dr Turnbull had to find accommodation for 175 patients being sent from Norwich. Meanwhile, more attendants had left to enlist and in the summer of 1915 Dr Turnbull decided to employ female nurses on the male side. Women nurses also worked as hall porters and clerks, for the first time. By 1916 the shortage of male attendants was dire, and Dr Turnbull tried to get an increase in pay for them; attendants at Brentwood, he pointed out, were paid 17s. 6d. per week plus 3s. war bonus and 1s. 6d. lodging allowance to married men. Severalls, however, paid only 15s. plus 3s. war bonus and a lodging allowance. Virtually no replies had come in to a recent advertisement for attendants, and later that year he complained that 'lately the class of men . . . have been of a very inferior stamp. I have lost several of the better class married men, who informed me that they cannot afford to stay at the wages offered them by the committee'. Inflation at this time, of course, was high.

Throughout the war, Turnbull struggled to manage the hospital and its estate so that patients could be kept warm and fed adequately. Nonetheless, rations dropped and mortality increased, not helped at the end of the war by the influenza epidemic. From October 1914 difficulties arose in obtaining coal. Delivery from North Station was impossible to arrange; eventually, he was able to enlist help from farmers and have it hauled by farm carts. But then supply of coal became increasingly difficult. These problems remained throughout the war. In 1919 the problem of haulage was solved by the purchase of a traction engine. The superintendent's tasks were overwhelmingly managerial and administrative, while shortage of doctors and nurses, and a general lack of viable treatments meant that patients were contained, controlled and managed rather than treated, listened to or cured.

On the whole, Turnbull's relations with the Board of Control and the Management Committee seem to have been cooperative and peaceful. Much of his work, of course, was delegated; the engineer effectively ran the estate and dealt with the artisanal staff, the clerk dealt with administrative and most financial matters; the matron ran the female side; the inspector (chief male nurse) ran the male side, the farm bailiff ran the farms. The medical superintendent oversaw the other doctors and discussed cases and treatments with them, as well as making regular visits to the wards. Much of his routine time went on liaising with the committee and various officials in the huge catchment area of Severalls, as well as with the Board of Control. He also gave lectures to the nursing staff, and the inter-war period was one in which a very high proportion of nurses gained qualifications. Many of the doctors at this time were also actively engaged in research. I could find no records of Turnbull's departure – minutes for the years 1938–45 are missing – although one respondent informed me that Turnbull committed suicide.

THE MIDDLE YEARS

The second medical superintendent, Dr Duncan, began working at Severalls in the 1920s, for years was deputy medical superintendent, and became medical superintendent in 1940. He, too, began his superintendency in a time of world war. Like his predecessor, his main concerns were with chronic understaffing and underfunding. Shortage of female nursing staff plagued all his years there, and showed signs of improvement only towards the very end. Nationally, half the mental health accommodation was taken over for emergency purposes. Work in outpatient clinics collapsed with severe understaffing. Shortages of food, clothing and heating plagued efficient care and management of the patient population. A Board of Control investigation found dramatic weight loss among patients during the war years.[6] All these developments 'meant the return of the locked door, of inactivity, of isolation; and again the tuberculosis rate soared'.[7]

Dr Duncan also had to contend with the increasing power of unions from the late 1940s. Before the war, union activity was highly disapproved of, as one male nurse, who began work in 1936, remembered:

> When I first went to Severalls, they asked me if I wanted to join the union. I said, 'Yes.' I thought that was the natural thing. I didn't realise there was only fifteen, twenty of us in, until one junior bloke said, 'Oh by the way, can I have your one and sixpence for your union due?' I said, 'Yes, that's OK,' and give it him. And this bloke in the next room to me, he said, 'Are you in the union?' I said, 'Yes, well aren't you?' 'No,' he said, 'don't let anybody else know,' he said, 'don't let the office know, otherwise you'll be out the gate!' I said, 'What?' He said, 'God, you mustn't let anybody know you're in the union!' Course then I bowed out. So then I never. I made sure every time it was due fees I used to take it over the ward he was on, cause he was a charge nurse.

After the war, however, unions increased their membership and influence, and Dr Duncan began negotiating with them openly. Whether it was union pressure or Masonic connections and allegiances (he was an officer of the Grand Lodge of England and the Provincial Grand Lodge of Essex), Duncan agreed to a closed-shop situation on appointment of male nurses in the 1950s, against Regional Board advice and directives; Russell Barton said that Duncan's relations with the Regional Board had not been good.

The medical superintendent had to negotiate both with groups inside the hospital and with groups and official bodies outside the hospital. He had regular meetings with the Management Committee, which was made up of a number of local worthies and medics and interested parties. Denis Hooton described the Management Committee, when he arrived as secretary in 1956, thus:

> Oh, they were country gentlemen – Colonel This and Colonel That, you know. There was one or two from the County Council. Oh yes, always one or two Labour members – and they were very good. I mean, those old school Labour members were conscientious. They were mainly from the sort of nonconformist school. I mean, the County Alderman I had up there was a brilliant member. She knew hospitals inside out. She – they – were very conscientious and experienced. We could do with some of them now.

Generally speaking, their concerns were financial and material; there were sub-committees that dealt with buildings and maintenance, the farm, clothing, stores. David Clark, appointed superintendent of Fulbourn Hospital in the early 1950s, said this about his Management Committee at the time:

> The committee seemed to me at that time to take little account of the treatment and welfare of the patients, which I saw as the only reason for any of us being there. They took the news of a number of deaths of patients and the inquest with equanimity, but when it was announced that swine fever had broken out in the pig herd, they were deeply concerned.[8]

Reading through committee minutes over the years at Severalls suggests that a similar agenda of concern prevailed here, too. Yet if the committee was not ostensibly that interested or powerful – for the finances were determined and distributed by central government and not at a local level – these people were a vital link to the local community and undoubtedly had considerable power and influence through political organisations, secret organisations such as the Freemasons, and various charitable organisations such as the Rotary Club, to either help or hinder the work of the medical superintendent. For example, every year, for many years,

Alderman Piper provided some fifty or sixty free tickets for patients to attend a Christmas show at the Colchester Theatre. A supportive committee could help a medical superintendent cut through red tape imposed by central government, providing, for instance, cheap or free supplies from local businesses for hospital projects.

By the second half of the 1950s the Severalls Management Committee was getting anxious to promote change in the hospital, to modernise it, to improve conditions for patients, at a time when Dr Duncan was nearing retirement age and less interested in such changes than he might have been when younger. Denis Hooton remembers this situation clearly when he was first appointed secretary:

> My first day at Severalls was amusing. The chairman was a well-known figure. And he came to see me in the morning and he said, 'Now, look . . .' He'd just been to some conferences, some Chairman/Management Committee, and he'd picked up all the bright ideas. And, 'Look,' he said, 'We've appointed you as secretary to *the Committee*. You're not secretary to Dr Duncan.' I said, 'Oh.' As I said, my predecessor was a dear old man who didn't – never opened his mouth, you know. 'And,' he said, 'you're responsible to us, and we want to see some changes. We'd like you – when you've settled down and looked around a bit, to bring forward a programme for the next few years of how you can upgrade the place and do things.'
>
> He'd just had the King's Fund in to look at their food, because he'd met one of the King's Fund people on this course and they'd upset the supplies officer and the cook by condemning half of the food that was being served. Any rate, they put a lot of new kitchens in for them. They did it very well. So he said, 'Now do be careful of Dr Duncan,' he said, 'and don't get under his influence – and don't just be his yes-man. We want you to be our independent officer.' So I said, 'Thank you. Thank you.'
>
> That afternoon, Dr Duncan came in. He said, 'Well, how are you getting on?' And he said, 'Can I give you a word of advice?' He says, 'I saw the chairman in this place. Don't trust him!' He said, 'He's a most untrustworthy man.' And that was my first day! I couldn't believe it. I thought, 'What have I come to? What have I come to?'

The secretary was in a position to make informal recommendations to the Board of Control on appropriate people to be appointed to the Management Committee. He was therefore in quite a powerful position. Where conflict arose with the medical superintendent, the secretary had the ability, if he chose to exercise it, to influence the Management Committee in ways that would make the superintendent's tasks if not impossible, at least more difficult. Denis Hooton remembered how such tactics had to be used in order to implement what he, and the committee, saw as crucial changes:

> This lady who was chairman of the Supplies Committee – and she was a very great friend – did me a lot of good with the supplies side of it, and we had a general practitioner on the committee, and I became friendly with him, and he helped me. If I wanted to steer something round the committee – Dr Duncan – one of these two would say, 'We'll support you,' you know.
>
> And in the end, Dr Duncan, against his advice, the committee decided they'd like a review done of all the wards that needed upgrading and improving. And this doctor and I did this. I could tell you how many toilets there were all over Severalls, where they were situated! I mean there was a ward with 104 patients in it, I think, with three lavatories. Patients were sleeping in corridors. The overcrowding was unbelievable.
>
> You see, at that time, we got that 'Mental Million' that Enoch Powell got, and that's how we upgraded that laundry and all the rest of it. We did a lot of upgrading. You see, I remembered the Regional Treasurer coming down and having lunch with Duncan and me, and Duncan said they'd always been short of money. And the Treasurer turned up his book and said, 'Look! Underspent so many thousands! Underspent so many thousands! What do you mean, we kept you short of money, doctor?' And I took the Regional Treasurer, I took him round the wards. He said, 'I've never been allowed outside the secretary's office before. I've never seen these wards.' And he was shocked, you see. Went back to the Board and told them. That was 1956.

Essentially, it was the Regional Hospital Board that controlled and oversaw the medical superintendent's work – and finances. Poor relations with the Regional Board meant acquisition of funds to implement changes, reforms and innovations generally could be seriously thwarted at every turning. The Regional Hospital Board was set up as part of the wide-ranging changes brought into effect with the National Health Service in 1948. At this time the role of the consultants in hospitals was strengthened at the expense of the medical superintendents; this was to have important repercussions at Severalls in the 1960s. It also had far-reaching effects on the status of psychiatry generally and its attraction to young doctors specifically: 'The strengthening of the consultant's autonomy encouraged the entry of a younger generation into hospital psychiatry, while before some of the best psychiatrists tended to work outside it.'[9]

The medical superintendent's authority was further challenged by the implementation of the 1959 Mental Health Act. This abolished the Board of Control; its function of inspection and review was taken over by local health authorities. Mental health review tribunals took over as 'watch-dogs' which had the power to discharge patients in cases of compulsory detention. Certification – but not compulsory detention – was abolished. This came at the peak of a wave of protest about cruelty and disgraceful conditions in mental hospitals specifically and institutions generally. The BBC's programme *The Hurt Mind* (1957) had already contributed to this and throughout the 1950s there had been a number of heated debates about reforming mental hospitals, both in the media and in professional journals such as *The Lancet*. Then, in 1959, Russell Barton argued in *Institutional Neurosis* that institutionalisation was so bad in mental hos-pitals that it actually caused a further form of mental illness. Bringing together innovative ideas and policies tried by earlier reformers, Barton argued that it was crucial for patients' environment to be enriched through activity and work. Then in 1961 Enoch Powell, then Minister of Health, announced a policy that would abolish mental hospitals altogether, cutting psychiatric beds by half, and promising to improve community services.

THE 1960S: RUSSELL BARTON

Dr Russell Barton was appointed as Severalls' third – and last – medical superintendent (now called physician superintendent) in 1960. He was a young, ambitious and outspoken man of 37, who had already made a name for himself with the publication of his book. His appointment in Severalls, however, was controversial, for it broke with the tradition that the existing assistant medical superintendent should be appointed as superintendent. Presumably the Regional Board wanted someone who had the vision, energy and drive to implement new policies and new reforms. This they cer-tainly got, and probably to a greater extent than they had bargained for.

By the end of his first year in power, Barton had built and established an industrial unit for male patients, found employment for over twenty-five men outside the hospital, set up and run postgraduate refresher courses for senior nursing staff, de-certified 800 patients, proposed dividing the hospital into five units as well as setting up a psychogeriatric unit.[10] He introduced an unrestricted visiting system for the first time, a move not initially popular with nursing staff, and one that caused a great furore in the local press, where it was seen as dangerous and 'absurd'. The iron railings that surrounded all the airing courts were taken down in 1960. The gate was rebuilt and made more open and accessible in 1962. Corridors and wards were repainted. Paintings were donated and purchased for display in wards and in the hall. Barton finally managed to pressurise the Ministry of Health to agree to change the catchment area – which was huge – by losing Dagenham and part of Hertfordshire. Even after this was accomplished, in 1964 Severalls still had a catchment area of most of Essex and part of East Hertfordshire, with a population at risk of 714,000.[11]

In 1964 Barton summarised his aims and changes implemented at Severalls over his first four years thus:

> The principal changes in Severalls between 1960 and 1964 are aimed at accomplishing the following objectives: to improve patients' contact with the outside world; the provision of useful occupation to every patient; the adoption of an attitude of encouragement and friendliness to each patient without foolish concessions; an emphasis on the quality of personal life of patients; a reduction of drugs; the provision of a friendly, permissive ward atmosphere with the provision of wardrobes, chests of drawers and individual territory for every patient; assistance with work, accommodation and friends outside hospital.[12]

Art therapy and music therapy were brought into widespread use, as were various jobs and rehabilitation programmes. When I asked Russell Barton what he saw as the major problem needing attention when he first came to Severalls, he replied:

> To change the attitude of the staff. Well, it was a Dotheboys Hall sort of, a rather grim institution. They had a social system that substituted for the sort of social hierarchy in the country. I think it was a hangover from the imperious Victorian mistress who usually could afford one or two maids and felt she was elevating herself by treating them abominably, because people in bigger houses usually treated their maids, their workers, with a certain amount of respect and kindness. But I think this was part of it.
>
> And second was that there were large numbers of people who reckoned controlling people was like controlling children. So you smacked them and you said, 'Ah – you dirty girl!' And all that sort of thing. So they found that they could lord it over 60 or 100 other human beings who had no chance of doing anything back. As I said to them, 'They're like animals in a cage, you don't poke them with a stick humiliating them.' And they didn't like that one, by the way.

Figure 3.2 Women patients on a ward, *circa* 1960
Source: Russell Barton archive

Certainly Severalls had a lot of catching up to do with most other hospitals when Russell Barton came. Comparison between Severalls, Netherne Hospital and Mapperley Hospital in 1960, for instance, showed that while only 6 per cent of all female patients remained during the day in their wards at Mapperley, 87 per cent did so at Severalls. On selected wards it was found that during a typical day there were 10 nurses and 20 patients at Netherne, 8 nurses and 81 patients at Mapperley, but 31 nurses and 488 patients at Severalls.[13] While all patients at Mapperley had some personal possessions, there were 33 patients at Severalls who had none whatsoever. Severalls patients spent 5 hours and 39 minutes of their waking time doing absolutely nothing, compared with 2 hours 48 minutes at Netherne.[14] By 1964, the research found a dramatic improvement at Severalls had taken place:

The amount of time spent doing nothing was still higher than at the other two hospitals in 1964, and the amount of contact with the outside was still less. However, the social environment provided by Severalls in 1964 was little different from that of Mapperley . . . Severalls nurses were much more inclined to think that patients should have their own clothes in 1964, compared with 1960 . . . There was an all round increase in the ownership of less obvious articles [than clothing], such as handbags and toothbrushes . . . fewer Mapperley patients owned make-up material or personal ornaments than in 1960, while many more Severalls patients did so . . . There is a striking increase in the amount of time engaged in work or occupational therapy at Severalls . . . and in leisure activities of various kinds . . . The changes account for the large decrease in the amount of time spent doing nothing by Severalls patients.[15]

Russell Barton brought into effect widesweeping, much-needed reforms to Severalls in a short period of time. Patients and younger nurses in particular admired him, and what he was doing, enormously, as one woman patient who has been living in institutions for over sixty-five years remembered:

> That was Dr Barton who got this hospital open! I can remember him. He used to *talk* to me! I liked Dr Barton. That was him that opened this hospital. Took the railings down. He used to come round the wards and speak to the patients. Reopened the hospital. We could wear our own clothes when Dr Barton took it over. I was pleased as punch. Used to get me hair done once a week. They were the good old days. We did used to get a laugh. Talking and that. We was happy in them days. Yes.

In other quarters, however, he was less popular, particularly with some senior staff and older doctors, as he himself realised:

> But in my first month I got nineteen working full-time outside and there was a queue outside my door, 'Can we go out and work and earn proper money?' 'Yes!' Most had been certified and become chronic. But money was a spur. I used to say to them, 'You're earning nearly as much as I am, you're getting seven quid a week, I'm getting thirty!' That was true.
> *What about the work the patients did in the hospital itself?*
> That was unpaid, but I kept them at it. There was one woman who used to scrub the stone flight of stairs – it went down here and there was a landing and then it went down there – it was

concrete with sort of non-slippery stuff. She used to scrub it from top to bottom every day. And one day my colleague said, 'She's got to stop that, it's servitude.' So I spoke to the woman, I said, 'Would you like to stop?' She said, 'No, Doctor, that's my work, that's what I'm here for!' It gave her identity. So I said, 'Let's let her keep on with it and you talk her into it if you can.' She kept doing the stairs for years. She was simple and couldn't do other things.

I set up the industrial units right away. I asked that the patients be allowed to make bricks and was told brickmaking was difficult and required firing in a kiln. I said 'Well, I meant cement,' because we used to do it at Shenley and we could put this up. Then there was the famous story of someone blocking the girders that were necessary. An old owner of a sort of shipbuilders in Wivenhoe, he said, 'I can get you those!' And he brought them in I think, or his trucks brought them in a few days, and the place went up in just over a month. They built the first bit on and then began using that and they began making dolls' houses. At a time when all the industries were working I think we were earning getting on for £200,000 a year the total income from the – the total cost of the hospital was only about £600,000. And if they would have let me do as I wanted to I could have more than paid the cost of the hospital.

What did they – how did they thwart it?

Well, it was interesting. They were mainly thwarting me. I heard Hooton once saying, 'He's too bloody clever by half.' And I corrected him. 'Too bloody clever by twice!' No, there was a – you know, it's awful when you've done something for twenty or thirty years and some bright young bastard comes in and starts changing things around, stopping the normal promotions, wanting this here, demanding that there. I could understand, but I felt there was an urgency to do it. You see, if you do something and you change something – unless you get a Nobel Prize – it looks, they look on it as a reflection on themselves for not having done it.

Most of everything I did had been done before – at Crichton Royal or – somewhere it had been done. And they realised it should have been done – if you look at the end of the reports before I came, you'll see many innovations have been made without much disruption or disturbance. You know, they were preparing, they knew what was coming when I was coming because I'd been over and told them what I was up to. In fact, I did say to the chairman, 'These are the things and I'm going to try and put them into action and if

you don't want me, tell me now, because there are plenty of other places that might be glad to have me – *at first!* They might change their mind later. So might you!'
Did you have support within the hospital?
Nobody at first. No – well, from some of the younger ones. But from the older ones there was sort of resentment, hatred. Not because I was, or they were, bad, but it's a normal response and reaction. And they thought that what they'd been doing was the right way.

Older nurses in particular – who Barton saw as needing re-education in their attitudes towards patients and patient care – were often upset by Barton's changes and the manner in which he dealt with staff:

Then Dr Barton came. Well – he went mad when he found we still got keys! They all come with *keys!* Well we had this meeting and I thought, 'Cor! We got a bright one here!' I thought, 'There's only one way to get on with *him* – you got to go with him, you mustn't go against him.' 'Cause some of them *did* – try and say, 'I don't think that'll work.' 'But it *will* work, Mr Kniveton! 'Cause we're going to *make* it work!'

And he had that way about him. I thought, 'Somebody from Whitehall sent *you* down, right.' So of course he said, 'The backs have got to be open, the wash-house' – 'cause we used to lock up the wash-house, make 'em look lovely – so the patients could go and wash their hands. But the trouble was, to keep the place nice and clean, some of them used to run the taps – gallons and gallons of water, so you wouldn't go down there.

And then he started. He came to do what he was sent to do. And he was to break the hospital up into six groups.[16] Now when he started off these six groups, we thought, 'Whatever's going to happen?' First thing he done he did for the patients. He broke up the habits of being in the same wards – now, see? He turfed them all over the place! He turned female wards into male and he turned male wards into female. Anyway, when they changed – that was a male ward, they made it into female. When the females went they'd got a big urinal – and only two seats! See?

I was in charge of the admissions ward then, over at Maplehurst. He closed that down. He had a row with the matron. She couldn't get on with him at all. She couldn't – as you know, the matron's been used to being God Lord Almighty. And when he turfed 'em all upside down – course there was a lot of patients then were allowed to go out, then they started to make 'em informal. Well of course everyone that time was certified. So to gradually get the numbers down, the doctors used to say to us as charge nurses, by the way, 'I've got to find two more now, for goodness sake find me two men I can make informal!' So I used to say to 'em, 'You'd better admit to so-and-so,' I said, 'because they'll never realise what being informal is!' I said, 'They've been here so long.' Yes! I did! He said, 'You're sure they won't do anything – er – dangerous?' 'No!' I said, 'if I asked 'em, they wouldn't go out the door!'

That was it. That was what Barton had been sent by the government to do and it was what he was doing. And I'll never forget – 'cause somebody said, 'I've been looking at your book. I see you've made so-and-so informal!' He said, 'they've been certified thirty, forty years.' 'If they want to go, they go,' I said, 'they've only got to say they'll discharge themselves. Let 'em go? They wouldn't know – they only know those courts out there!' Course we used to have courts then with all the railings round. Course Barton had that knocked down. 'Cause when the patients used to walk round they didn't see that. They used to see this side a nice little hedge, and the other side a nice little hedge. But there was a big ha-ha with about 12 foot drop. With these big iron railings going round, which they couldn't climb over. So of course they had to come down. And then the patients were allowed out. Go out on their own. Right. Open the doors and let them out!

But when they first opened 'em, old Freddy said to me, 'You got the doors open then?' I said, 'yes.' He said, 'Well we'll have to go and *push* 'em out!' 'Why?' He said, 'Them's lined up down there on the stairs down there, there must be thirty, packed like sardines!' 'But haven't they gone out?' 'No,' he said, 'we got the doors open, but they've never been out in forty years, have they?' But they wouldn't go. He said, 'Come on then! Come on then!' But they all went to the same old places. And they looked. And they got round. They went there. They went round here. 'Go on, you can go where you like! Don't worry about the staff!' They kept looking, where's the staff man? Anyway, Barton was very unpopular because he was beginning to get things *done*.

Male nurses in particular were upset by Barton's deliberate appointments of staff outside the hospital. As early as 1961 he appointed a charge nurse from Friern Hospital in London as assistant chief male nurse, fully knowing this would upset many: 'This appointment will give rise to some discontent among male staff since had one of the charge nurses already at Severalls been appointed, it would have made a vacancy for promotion through the bottle-neck which exists at the level of staff nurse.'[17] His policies of getting patients back to work, and, whenever possible, back into the outside community, caused problems with senior staff, whose pay was calculated according to the number of beds in the hospital:

The senior administrative medical officer from the Regional Board was coming down and saying, 'Oh, you've got 500 empty beds now!' And at one time the chief male nurse, the matron, the chief engineer and the hospital secretary had increments according to each fifty more patients they got. So they were paid to keep them in. The definition was the number of beds erected and in use.

I designed the wardrobe-bed – a bed was upended, a board was put at the top and the bottom, hangers were put in, and the patient's clothes were suspended. So that now you doubled the number of beds in the hospital! And according to the law, they were erected and in use. They were doubly erected! But I was called – he was furious! He said, 'We've been trying to do something about this!' So I said, 'Are you trying to help us, George?' And then – but you see, all our staff were being threatened now with cuts because we'd gone below 1,500. They'd been aiming to get it at 2,000 because then they would have the second or the third increment.

Constant debates and conflicts over beds were a feature of Barton's relationship with the Regional Board, but they also affected relationships with senior staff adversely. Denis Hooton, the secretary, remembered:

Well, he was a brilliant psychiatrist – who thought that everybody else had looked upon mental illness in the wrong way. Now, in a way, he – there was some sense in what he used to say, but he went the wrong way about it. He was obsessed with the idea that most of the patients had been in there too long, and had the idea that became current with the passing of the 1959 Act that if they weren't seriously mentally ill, they shouldn't be there.

The question of community care was non-existent. There was no provision for them, you know, and it was pathetic in some cases. But that was his motto: 'Get them out'. Well, now, of course, it reduced the population from what it had been when I went there in 1956, of nearly 2,000 – about 500 went in the space of six or seven years. I mean, nobody was opposed to de-certifying all these patients and – it was a very good thing – I mean, nobody was opposed to that in principle, but it was a bit ruthless. And I think he upset most of his medical colleagues.

Because, like many young psychiatrists at the time, Barton was keen to see psychiatry allied with general medicine, he was receptive to suggestions to use what the Board saw as Severalls' (new) surplus accommodation for general hospital purposes. Towards the end of 1962, visits and discussions with members of the management committee about having a surgical unit at Severalls took place. Barton very much favoured the idea. Soon after this was agreed, in 1963, after years of pleas, the Regional Board appointed a new consultant: Dr Richard Fox. It was just after this, in 1964 – whether as a result of concessions the Board made to his requests is not entirely clear – that Barton agreed to amalgamate with the Colchester Group of Hospitals to form the St Helena Group. It was a decision he – and almost everybody else at Severalls – would soon regret bitterly. Not only was his power within the hospital thereby curtailed, but it was soon to be further challenged by his new consultant, as well as by others, including the St Helena Management Committee and the Regional Board.

The amalgamation was viewed by almost all staff I spoke to as a major turning-point, a sea-change in Severalls which resulted in it no longer feeling 'like a family', where close community relationships began to dissolve, fragment, become embittered. One male nurse remembered:

> The hospital changed when we became amalgamated with the Essex County Hospital and became the St Helena Group. And then things changed, because, to be quite honest, to put it into the words of the old chief male nurse I worked with, the only thing that the Essex County Hospital was interested in was our money. Because we being a great big hospital, we got a lot more money than they did.
>
> I remember I was in the office with him one day, and we were talking about furniture and he said, 'We want a new three-piece suite for Ivy Villa.' I said, 'Yes. A three-seater and a two-seater would be nice.' So he wrote to Supplies and said he wanted a three-piece suite. And somebody phoned him up and said, 'What do you want a three-piece suite for?' He said, 'To bloody well sit on!' Because people at St Mary's who ran the Essex County and St Mary's and Mile End Hospital had never bought three-piece suites.

A man who worked in the Treasurer's Department of St Mary's remembered with sadness how bitter the staff at Severalls were about the amalgamation generally, and towards him particularly:

Then, of course, we were all moved up to Severalls. And to start with we were given offices within the building itself – quite nice offices, really. And we were a very efficient organisation because my boss made sure that we applied the book. And there were hand-books on each type of occupation, you see, and when it came to the manual workers and porters and all that sort of thing, the rules were very, very strict and, of course, when we got there, the rules hadn't been applied strictly.

They'd been applied in a friendly manner, you see, and if there was any doubt, you gave benefit of the doubt to the employee. So when we got there and we applied the book, really, everybody was up in arms. And this is the way we were trained to practise, and this is the way we did it. So things like shift work, you see, you had to make sure that the terms of the shift were properly carried out, whereas if, I suppose, in the old days, if the person, perhaps, missed the proper two-hour period or whatever it was by half an hour, well, they probably wouldn't take much notice, you see. But we – all worked very, very strictly.

As a consequence there was one particular workman, I don't know what – I can't remember what trade he was in, but he wouldn't speak to me. And when I retired – and I lived – in another part of Colchester – he lived in, this chap, lived along the same road, and we used to go and collect the pensions on the same day. And he would pass me in the street and would never speak to me. It's so absurd, because it wasn't my fault that we took them over. You see, I used this word 'take them over', because when we went there, there was this terrible fear that we were going to take them over, and as far as they could, they all got out of the – certain people got out of the jobs that they were in, so as not to come under our aegis.

And because so many of them slipped into different positions in the hospital, we did, in fact, take them over. Couldn't help ourselves, because we – we dominated, you see, in the administration. So – there were a number of people, even higher up ones, who found it difficult to deal with us for a time, but gradually it began to wear off. Some of the senior staff weren't friendly to us. Not at first. Oh no. You had to wheedle information out of them if you wanted it!

Administrative staff felt the amalgamation changed the nature of not only their own work, but the entire hospital, irrevocably. Three administrators who had worked there since the 1940s, said:

A: For me personally it all changed when we amalgamated with the other hospitals in the area. I physically remained here, but I was transferred to the new group and I wasn't part of Severalls any more. But it just so happened that the group officers moved here from Colchester, so I was still here, but I wasn't part of the Severalls staff. I didn't want to leave. I didn't want to change anything.

B: I didn't like that change at all. Didn't like it at all. It was much harder work administratively, because the medical superintendent in my early days, he was the boss here, he was in charge. We had committees: house committees, works committees, and it was all here. You see, we didn't have to consult anybody outside. So it became more difficult, there was much more work. You had to consult the group before – not always, but very often, you had to tell the group.

A: Because of course the group was dictating to Severalls. The idea was that it was an amalgamation, but we all knew it wasn't. And the group told Severalls what to do and what not to do, and all the rest of it.

C: Before, it felt like we were here for the patients, and I think I lost that feeling then, and it's gradually gone completely and I haven't got that feeling *at all* now. I feel the welfare of the patients has gone to the bottom of the list. Nobody here minded not having a carpet, not having pretty coloured walls. I mean, nobody minded that you had a coal fire, say, nobody minded that you had to stay perhaps a little later. You know, you didn't have any of those things, and you did your work *thinking of the patients*. Everything seemed to be orientated towards the patients. Nowadays you seem to have all these staff parties and staff things, and somehow the patients seem to have got pushed to the background. Perhaps because we thought it was the patients' home. You had a lot of dedicated people in those days that believed in the work they were doing. They *liked* the patients. I don't think you've got that dedication any more.

B: But don't you think a lot of this came when they did away with the matrons? I felt very strongly in favour of the matrons. They seemed to have more discipline and control over the nurses. They were respected.

A: Well, then they started organising it so the domestics would have a domestic manager and the domestic manager would have to have a series of assistants. Ordering all their stuff was being done in a separate office – and the whole grand thing would sort of grow and mushroom up into an organisation on its own! Whereas once upon a time, as I say, the matron dealt with everything.

If the medical superintendent had always been regarded as the most powerful person in the hospital – and he was – generally the matron was seen as the second most powerful. She had sole responsibility for the entire female side of the hospital, which was considerably larger than the male side. Ruth Clarke, who came as matron in 1957, describes her responsibilities, and some of her difficulties, below:

> My main responsibilities were nurses, and the nursing of the patients. So the patients were my responsibility – the nursing of them. And I used to disagree with one or two doctors over my suggestions. So – nursing, and the staff, and the staff welfare. Of course, I had people to help me, but dealing with their duties and off-duties, and of course there was night staff to consider, and hours changed from time to time, and then one had to get busy, wondering how we were going to cut down the hours and cover the hours that were wanted.
>
> Well, when I first went, I was responsible for the ward maids also, and for the sewing-room and the laundry. They all came into my ambit. But then, in due course, that was all removed to – I don't know, I suppose to Denis Hooton. Must have, because he was more or less responsible for the extraneous bits and pieces. Engaging staff, of course. And firing, if necessary. And student training, which, although we had a tutor, I was involved with.
>
> And one thing I almost fell out with Dr Barton over. Well, we had overseas students. I had a letter from this person who wanted some of his staff to come over. And I wrote back and said, 'If he would hand-pick them, so that I really got people who were suitable for training' – and we eventually had five. And one of them was an absolute – well – not very bright! She was *hopeless*. And her written work was so terrible that I wouldn't sign the form for her to take her exam. I said, 'No way would I do it.'
>
> And she saw Dr Barton and told him. So he sent for the papers of this girl. The tutor, Miss Robinson, rang me and I said, 'You don't send them! It's nothing to do with Dr Barton. You don't send them!' I used to stand up to him, which he didn't always like. Anyhow, I went to his office and I said, 'I have told Miss Robinson not to send the papers. It's *nothing* to do with you!' He said, '*I'm* the medical superintendent!' And I said, 'And *I'm* the head of nursing!' 'But,' he

Figure 3.3 Matron and senior nursing staff, *circa* 1965
Source: North East Essex Mental Health NHS Trust

said, 'the medical superintendent covers the nursing.' I said, 'But *I* sign the form for the GNC!'

And we really had a little ding-dong. I didn't give in. I think perhaps he admired me for it, I don't know – because he never said so! Oh, I had a few ding-dongs with him, a few rows. I used to give as good as I got. And – you see, he used to play one person off against the other. That was always his way of working. And he used to play the chief male nurse off against me. I knew this – and I didn't, I didn't let it bother me. But he was a very nice man, the chief male nurse at that time, it was the early days, but he felt everything Barton said was gospel, and he rather did everything that he was told to do, where I was a rebel and I wouldn't, you see. So I wasn't very favoured.

In October, 1964, the chief male nurse retired and Barton appointed a man who had previously worked as deputy chief male nurse at Highcroft Hospital. Once again, he appointed someone to a key position who had not worked in Severalls before.

A year later, Barton wrote to the chairman of the St Helena Group Hospital Management Committee concerning a proposal by the group to move the surgical ward from Fleming to St Michael's:

> Since our discussion I have given this matter full thought, and I regret to say that I do not think the surgical patients should be moved to St Michael's Ward, if they are to come under the care of the Matron of this Hospital. It would be a great blow for our hospital morale which has been suffering in many ways since the amalgamation ...
>
> Since the Committee insists in trying to effect this against my advice, I have written to Dr Ramsay[18] in the first place and will have to take it to the Group Medical Advisory Committee in the second before taking it up with various other professional bodies. The development of a willing, enthusiastic hospital staff is absolutely essential in a psychiatric service. I am afraid the approaches which are being made at the moment are having a serious effect and it will be necessary for me to protect the psychiatric service which is so essential to our catchment area. I regret that the Committee should be so short-sighted in these matters.

It seems clear that Barton by this time was feeling cornered and increasingly disempowered by the amalgamation, as he wrote (on the same day as the above letter) to the chairman of the Medical Advisory Committee at Essex County Hospital:

> I am concerned that the Management Committee may be over-riding my advice without having obtained any other medical opinion – but especially psychiatric advice ... In any case the wisdom of placing further responsibility on the Matron who has more patients and more admissions than the Chief Male Nurse is dubious.

On the one hand, Barton was apparently protecting the matron and her staff from too much work, yet on the other hand it seems possible he was also trying to curtail her from accessing further power, particularly at the expense of the chief male nurse, whom Barton regarded as an ally in a way that he did not regard the matron. He was probably also trying to recover some of the power which the Group had increasingly usurped. He did not get his way on this issue. In 1967, when the matron resigned, the post of matron was abolished at Severalls, as recommended nationally by the Salmon Report, and the chief male nurse became principal nursing officer at Severalls, responsible for both sides.

On another front, Barton was struggling to have personal control over the appointment of medical staff at a time when bureaucracy in the health service was increasingly defining ways and terms of promotion which Barton regarded as defined more in terms of existing rank rather than actual skills or expertise. In September 1964, he wrote to Dr Ramsay at the Regional Board to express concern over the 'impending machinery to be set up for the upgrading of Senior Hospital Medical Officers at present receiving consultant allowance, to consultant in post', expressing the view that among his senior medical officers, he was willing for only one to be so promoted, his reasons being 'It is not that I wish to deprive these doctors of extra pay. It is that I am very concerned that consultants may be forced on us without adequate supporting junior staff, social workers and secretaries, and without the necessary money to build an office each . . . If the doctors are informed that it is I who have opposed their being made into consultants at Severalls, it may have a serious effect on their morale and degree of co-operation.'

Then, in early 1965, what had begun as a friendly and cooperative relationship with his new consultant began to show signs of strain:

> I didn't dislike Ramsay. Fox used to call him 'Breadhead' – you see, Fox was quite fun in a way. I mean, he was outrageous! But he had no time for Ramsay, he would threaten Ramsay, 'Oh, Dr Barton will do this!' I *think*. This was in the early days, and then eventually, as I said, an assistant medical officer from the Board came down, and he said, 'I've got a file of letters this high from Fox and people complaining about you – staff at the hospital – and I think I've only got one letter from you about Fox, regarding a matter of leave.' But they did nothing about it. They never told me about them – which again, is very sneaky. I mean, it's dreadful. You know, it's like being accused anonymously, and I was never allowed to see the letters.

Barton felt Fox was jealous of him, as well as of others, and wanted his job. Increasingly he thought Fox was taking the law into his own hands and making decisions which should have been made by the physician superintendent, for instance, late in 1965:

> Richard Fox announced to the press 'Severalls to start Alcoholism Unit' and appeared on Anglia TV without consulting me. The chairman of the Management Committee was furious with me for not having informed him. I refused to delay or block the enterprise – I had just returned from four months in the USA. The seeds of dissension, already sown, escalated from here.

By this time, Russell Barton's reforms to Severalls Hospital, his educational programmes both with nursing staff and with the wider community, were increasingly well known as innovative, dynamic and imaginative. Doctors from overseas came in ever greater numbers to visit and attend seminars. Barton was publishing a great many articles on his work and his ideas of community care in both medical journals and more popular magazines.[19] He welcomed visits by the media and frequently appeared in the media himself. As always, he was outspoken, a trait which some found charming, but others found infuriating. In 1965, Barton became involved in a public furore over criticisms he made of Whittingham Hospital:

> What happened was, one of our assistant chief male nurses, who was very good, went to Whittingham for an interview, and he told them what we were doing here and how advanced Severalls was. And they took exception to this and ticked him off at the interview and didn't give him the job. Well, that was that. I sympathised with him and I said, 'there'll be plenty more' – and all my best nurses had gone by the time I'd left.
>
> But anyway, I then was asked by the National Association of Mental Health to give an annual lecture and – the Duchess of Kent, before she had her bad head – she was there, and I showed some pictures, including some that I'd taken at Whittingham. And I said, 'This is the result of this long-term neglect – sitting, drooling, looking straight ahead. Because they've been convinced there is no future for them and nothing they can do can make any difference' and so forth.

At the time, the duchess applauded Barton's comments, but the press took it up and Whittingham became the target of a moral panic about cruelty and neglect in mental hospitals.

The British Medical Association then held an inquest on Russell Barton, and an inquiry was made into Whittingham Hospital, in which virtually all Barton's allegations were eventually confirmed. But such incidents undoubtedly damaged his reputation, and were used to his disadvantage by those hostile to him within Severalls. Staff told me that from this time onwards Severalls became increasingly divided into what was repeatedly described as 'two hostile camps'. Generally, there was no apparent rift between Barton and Fox on matters of principle or policy, and even those who supported Fox saw Barton as an excellent psychiatrist who took good care of his junior doctors. Rather, it was seen as a personality conflict, 'the clash of two monumental egos'.

Throughout 1966, Barton was engaged with a fairly acrimonious correspondence with the Regional Board, in which he pleaded for them to reconsider, and revoke, the amalgamation. His requests were always refused.

Throughout his time at Severalls, Barton regretted the amalgamation deeply, particularly in the ways in which it made psychiatry, and decisions about psychiatric practice and psychiatric patients, subsidiary to those of consultants working in general medicine. He also held large bureaucracies and bureaucrats in great contempt, particularly those of the Regional Board who made decisions, he felt, solely with regard to numbers of beds, finances and budgets and never took into account patients' interests:

> They were constantly trying to get geriatric beds for the geriatrician to run in Severalls, which would have meant he would get rid of 200 geriatric patients which he shouldn't have accumulated in the first place. But he wanted 200 beds I think, and I refused. I said, 'We're here for *psycho*geriatric patients, geriatric is another matter. They're easy to deal with.' And you find if you read through those notes you'll find that Ramsay's bringing it up, or the Board has visited to see why these beds can't be used. And I used to have a little sign: 'Beds, Bricks and Buildings never Healed a Fracture, Helped a Haemorrhage, Let Alone Dealt with Anything Really Complicated like Depression or Schizophrenia'. As I used to say, they're uninformed bureaucrats masquerading as physicians and they've no right to make such decisions because if they did it in diagnosis they would be sued for malpractice, and if I were the boss I'd be suing them for malpractice myself. I used to say these things aloud at the Regional Board meetings.

In May that year it was decided by the Group Management Committee that all appointments in all hospitals would be made by the Group's Staff and Establishments Sub-Committee, thereby eroding still further the physician superintendent's power. The Group were also attempting to take over Severalls' pathology laboratory and X-ray facilities.

In 1967, Barton again hit the national headlines, and in so doing deeply annoyed the then Labour government. In that year Barbara Robb wrote a scathing critique of malpractice and cruelty towards geriatric patients in hospitals, *Sans Everything*. In this she argued for the desperate need to set up a Hospital Advisory Service and a Health Ombudsman. Russell Barton wrote a foreword to the book, and I quote below extracts from this:

> Institutions develop powerful instruments of defence for their protection and perpetuation. Sometimes their officers or governing bodies lose sight of the primary purpose for which they were planned and their energies become deployed in rituals or personality conflicts. The purpose becomes subordinated to the personnel . . .

The one thing administrators and other people fail to learn is that kindness, pleasantness, sympathy and forbearance cannot be commanded by giving orders or passing resolutions ... Commanding these qualities is even more complicated ... the nearest I can get to describing the background in which they flourish is 'morale' or 'team spirit' which arises from the way in which an institution is run; the way in which members of the staff are praised, promoted, recognised, considered, disciplined or dismissed. For no institutions of any size can run without rules and regulations.

Staff of institutions develop neurotic self-propagating traditions such as misplaced loyalty of one staff member to another. Only a deviant will shop a colleague. Officers and senior staff develop misplaced loyalty to committee and boards. To criticise forcibly rather than to cover up is to rock the boat. Victimisation of anyone who is critical, whether justifiably or not, may be automatic ... Yet doctors and nurses have two contracts: one with their board or committee which is written, and one with their patient which is unwritten. When conflict arises between the two it is the unwritten contract which should be observed.[20]

Barton's loyalty to, and honour of, his unwritten contract with his patients was almost universally acknowledged by staff and patients alike, but his written contract with the Group Management Committee, and, after his foreword to *Sans Everything*, the central government as well as the Regional Board, was increasingly shaky, as Barton remembered:

Kenneth Robinson was furious. He called me up and he said – I said, 'Well, I didn't realise it would have political repercussions.' And he said, 'Well, *of course* it will have political repercussions! You've probably done more harm now than – and da-da-da-da.' Because it was a criticism of the Labour Party – I think they were in office at the time – and it was a reflection on the competence of the Minister to ensure that human conditions – da-da-da-da – were present and available for everyone who could possibly vote.

And I know Kenneth Robinson, he was – I knew him and I met him several times – he was very upset about it, and he did say to me, 'You must have known it would cause this outrage!' And I said, 'Well, I didn't realise it would cause such an outrage, because one assumes that a large number of people know these things. It's common knowledge. And I certainly hadn't any wish to attack you.' But then we had a television – Barbara Robb was very dynamic and she got a television thing going – and we had a sort of set-to on that. Robinson had a spokesman with him and made a statement, and I just said, 'You can't deny the facts, and if you just go in and see how these people are expected to live.'

Within a year, however, Severalls again hit the national headlines with the publication of an article by Irma Kurtz in *Nova* magazine. Barton had allowed Kurtz to come into the Severalls admission ward in Myland Court pretending to be a patient, as he told me:

Irma Kurtz was a journalist and she wanted to see what went on in a mental hospital, and she asked me and I agreed. And she came and she spent three or four days in the admissions ward. The patients knew she wasn't a patient. 'How did you find out?' I said. 'Oh,' they said, 'she's the only one that's taking notes, isn't she?' And then of course years later a guy did it in America,[21] he sent patients in and they told lies, they said they were hearing voices and they were all admitted, all diagnosed as schizophrenia. I think that's very good, but of course it was used tremendously to discredit mental hospitals.

But – so she came in – but, oh! It caused such fury. Well, more people from the committee thought I wasn't a safe chap to be a friend with or to follow, because I could encourage such an attack. Mm. You see, Fox and another doctor were going for me. It's easy to do because you shouldn't admit a patient unless they're mentally ill. My defence was – show me a mentally ill patient who'd want to come into hospital! And surely if a doctor other than I, and not in the know, admitted that patient there was a flaw in the hospital that needed correction!

I mean, they did have a little inquiry. Let's see – it was the hospital – no it wasn't the main group, the St Helena Hospital Management Committee, but there was a Severalls Hospital Executive Sub-Committee. They set it up. They concluded that it showed bad judgement on my part. But they didn't censor me. They knew perfectly well if they sent me a letter, a censorious letter, that it would be appearing in the journal that had done the article! When accused again, I would have said, 'Well, I thought you would want your views known.'

In November 1968 Barton reported that he had just learned that one of his consultants had sent a strongly worded complaint to the Regional Board and the Ministry of Health about the Irma Kurtz affair. He also reported that earlier in the year a letter had been sent to Dr Ramsay 'by a consultant psychiatrist on the staff at Severalls' in which it was alleged Barton drove two junior doctors to suicidal depression and that he was intolerant of junior staff, who were afraid of him. Following this letter, he had been called to see the chairman of the Regional Board: 'these allegations throw doubt on my ability as Physician Superintendent and an administrator, and of course, must discredit me to some extent. Apart from personal distress caused, such allegations may influence the Board's decision concerning administrative control of the X-ray and Pathological departments at Severalls, and also the control of the Surgical unit and proposed medical unit.' In a letter to Ramsay at this time he stated:

> Most of the hospital has been happy and agreeable to work under my direction, and dare I say, inspiration. I have battled in order to change things – that is inevitable. I have had to put up with Dr Fox plotting for power and attempting to reduce the executive control of this hospital to a political arena almost as soon as he came here. Two other consultants for various reasons are alienated from me. I wish they would find occupations elsewhere and leave the rest of the hospital to get on with developing and improving the very high standards of the psychiatric service we run.

Wider changes in psychiatric services, however, were being discussed and put into action at this time, changes which signalled the start of a new managerialism in the health services and social services generally. The Seebohm Committee (1965–68) recommended setting up a new managerial framework for local authority social services, and the Cogwheel and Salmon Reports set up new staffing structures for all medical and nursing staff: 'the structures were primarily dictated by the needs and traditions of general medicine and general nursing . . . Community care proved difficult to organise as the professional empires grew apart . . . mental health was the biggest casualty.'[22] New government policies for staff structures recommended the phasing-out of physician superintendents and their replacement with committees. Barton was highly critical of the suggestions made:

> So I was saying, the foreword to *Sans Everything* wasn't good at all, and then there was – there were other problems – because I never thought that I should descend to baiting or criticising Ramsay, I never did anything against him at all or spoke against him, I just said, when they were talking about district hospitals, I said, the whole idea was so bloody silly, the uninformed bureaucrats playing doctor, I think, but that was because there were a lot of other doctors

on the panels, usually office boys, you know, guys that sit in labs and don't see the problems and just stick the needle in: 'Did it hurt? This is just a little needle, just a little prick.' Oh, Christ, they don't understand what goes on in people's homes and hearts. And they make the decisions.

Cogwheel[23] was coming in, yes. And I said, 'Look, because a lot of you idiots have made a terrible mistake and they've got these fellows in like Cogwheel – and you had Lord Brain, who said there's no problem with drugs in England, and I told him outright it's a *big* problem and it's going to grow – and now you've done this and now you've done that' – I added much more – 'it's just ridiculous. I'm the physician superintendent and I have tenure there, and as you know it's actionable if you decide to try and push me out against my will.' 'We're not trying to do that, doctor, but we thought in the interests of the service' – and all that. I just said, 'whose bloody interests?'

Early in 1969, the chairman of the St Helena Group asked Barton to submit a note on the organisation and administration of Severalls Hospital, with particular reference to 'democratic exercise in administration to permit corporate decision making'. Barton was in no doubt that such a policy, apart from his own personal demise, would have disastrous effects on the psychiatric care and treatment available to patients:

If the Physician Superintendent ... is to command backing from an electorate of doctors he will have to overlook and play down incompetence, idleness and other shortcomings on the one hand, and maybe, play up minor deficiencies and mild shortcomings on the other. This will reduce the medical administration to a political arena. Recommendations made and executive action taken will result from the uneasy equilibrium of committee strife, rather than the planned policies and actions resulting from a sense of commitment and responsibility of one capable person who looks into matters thoroughly and takes account of personalities, shortages and the prescriptions of the Ministry of Health and Regional Board.

It is not possible for a Committee to produce morale in a hospital – by which I mean a keenness and willing enthusiasm to get on with the job of treating patients. Committees are essential to act as checks and counterbalances to arbitrary or unjust actions of officers, to provide an impartial source of scrutiny for contracts to prevent peculation and corruption and to act as a court of appeal in the multitudinous affairs of institutional life. The suggested election of a physician superintendent ... would have drawbacks. It would rob the service of its leadership.

In my view it is not possible for a psychiatric service to flourish if the leadership depends on local election. Nor can an executive committee comprising one psychiatrist among seven or eight other specialists without psychiatric skill and training, be relied upon to make wise majority decisions about priorities for psychiatric medicine. The obvious physical need of the scalpel and resuscitation machine will always be awarded priorities over the apparently frivolous needs of the psychiatrically ill.

Support for Barton in his increasingly acrimonious battles with central government, the Group Committee, and some of his own doctors, was nevertheless forthcoming, at least from the nursing staff and some of the doctors. In March 1969 a letter was sent from the chairman of the St Helena Group to the principal nursing officer, acknowledging a petition sent to him, and stating:

I was not aware that Dr Barton's position was in jeopardy and that it required the written support of some of the staff of Severalls Hospital. I am not aware of any pending change. Personalities aside, I hope that you are familiar with the modern thinking about the medical control of psychiatric hospitals. If so, you will be aware that the post of Physician Superintendent is now regarded as an anachronism and there are only two remaining in our region. I would suggest that if we all reacted to everything we saw in the Press about what is or is not going to happen to Severalls Hospital we are all likely to end up as patients.

A prolonged row between Fox and Barton as to the placement of a doctor on Fox's unit by Barton continued and reached Regional Board level late in 1969. The Regional Board told Barton in November that Fox was afraid Barton wanted to murder him. Eventually Barton sued Fox for libel. Fox conceded he had told untruths about Barton. Barton gave Fox's fine to charity. Then an article was 'leaked' to the local press saying that all the medical staff at Severalls were in favour of implementing the Cogwheel Report, thereby ousting, or reducing to the rank of consultant, Barton. The Medical Staff Committee then met and passed a vote of confidence in Barton by a majority of fourteen. Barton made a clear statement that he was not agreeable to stay at Severalls other than as physician superintendent.

In December 1969 Barton was excluded from the Hospital Management Committee's discussion on the administration of Severalls, and felt deeply aggrieved by this. As part of the reorganisation of health services, he was told by the Board, and the eventual provision of district general hospitals, they intended to implement the Cogwheel recommendations, but offered him a post as consultant, retaining the same salary he earned as physician superintendent. Barton replied at length, giving his reasons for why he was convinced the proposed reorganisation would not work, and adding that despite their denial of its relevance, he was sure that what he saw as Fox's sabotage of his reputation had damaged his standing. He concluded by stating he was unwilling to relinquish his post as physician superintendent and would not accept an alternative appointment. In April 1970 he reported:

> The manner in which the Regional Hospital Board has attempted to implement the Cogwheel Report has undermined my position as Physician Superintendent, reducing my effective executive control of the hospital. Two issues have become somewhat confused: (I) whether the position of Physician Superintendent is safeguarded by contract. (Ii) if the administration of Severalls is headed by a Physician Superintendent, whether I personally am a fit person to hold office. Doubt has been thrown on my personal ability by defamatory allegations received by the Board. I have made a complaint to the Department of Health and Social Security, requesting that a statutory inquiry be held ... Inevitably there will be some delay and I feel it would in the interests of the psychiatric service if I were to have unpaid leave until the question as to who is to hold the conductor's baton is settled. I request unpaid study leave for 6 months from 4.5.70.

His request was granted, and he went on study leave to the United States. A hearing was held in September and the principal medical officer of the Ministry of Health decided he had no tenure as physician superintendent, although he could appeal the decision and return to Severalls as a consultant. Instead, he flew back to the US, having taken the civil service examinations for superintendent of a mental hospital there, where he had been offered the choice of three hospitals.

THE END OF AN ERA

After Barton's departure, almost no records survived, although it is possible, too, that few were actually recorded, given the abolition of the physician superintendent's post altogether, and the shift to an area health authority system and the abolition of hospital management committees. Consultants took turns in chairing a committee, combining their roles as psychiatrists with managers, although only on a temporary basis. A number of nurses began to rise into managerial roles at this time. One male nurse, who had begun work at Severalls in the 1930s, and was a charge nurse for many years, said this about the rise of managerialism in the 1970s:

> I worked in that office for months – and on the ward. And I come to wonder, I wonder what some of these chaps are doing in there? I often wondered what they were doing, to tell you the truth. I couldn't understand it, what are they doing? What was they doing with themself all day?
>
> Then I found out afterwards of course, they were all everlasting attending meetings! Which *I* used to have to go. Nine o'clock. Until about eleven. Talking about rubbish. Talking about this. Talking about that. By the time we finished it was time, 'Oh I'm going for an early lunch!' It was getting on quarter to twelve and some of 'em were going for an early lunch! There was me going back to the ward. Took all the money, money for all the – they've done it now over the years, cor. When you think, the jobs some of those men had to do.

During the 1970s an increasing amount of community care facilities were set up; voluntary organisations such as Phoenix Group Homes[24] provided shared housing for ex-patients in the wider community outside Severalls. Community psychiatric nursing also began at this time, as one male nurse, who rose to a managerial position after working as a community psychiatric nurse, remembered:

> By the seventies we were beginning to be more progressive in nursing. I think people were starting to be better trained in those days. The fact that we were successful in actually relocating chronic patients in the community, and I was able to integrate the two locked wards and eventually dismantle the locked ward by using therapeutic community therapy more. And all the institutional fear that people felt wasn't happening, didn't happen. People would start to be more adventurous, starting to take bit more a chance. In fact, they actually found now that if they listened to the patient and work *with* them, rather than work *for* them, they actually get a better result out of it.
>
> Don't forget, at that time nursing training saw some changes as well. And I think one or two appointments in the senior positions in the hospital changed which enabled, encouraged this kind of attitude. The old concept of the old matron, the old chief male nurse, was

gone. And we had people called 'director of nursing' and in terms of people looking at management looking at nursing practice, rather than a means of controlling patients, I think that is fundamental in developing a different kind of skill.

When I first got the job of the community nurse I was working for not only North-East Essex, but North-East and Mid-Essex as well. That was still a big district at the time. But, thankfully, at the same time we were getting more community nurses as well, so there were a lot more of us, covering still what was then a very big district. The work at the time mostly involved working with people who had already been in hospital and have a period of treatment as inpatient, and at that time we mostly followed up, post-discharge, and supporting the person and the family.

What we did not have in those days was the kind of supporting facility like housing and social service network and that kind of thing to help us. So if a patient deteriorated mentally, apart from being able to recognise it early enough and perhaps being able to find out the reason and adjust medication, get the person to see the psychiatrists earlier and so on, there was little else we could do. Nowadays you can use all sorts of other facilities in a community to prevent admission.

Although a Labour government was in power for much of the 1970s, the oil crisis of 1974 forced the government to seek loans from the IMF, which were premised on conditions that they make cuts. The first big NHS cuts began in these years. Cuts really began to bite, however, in the 1980s, when the combined effects of Thatcherite ideals of managerialism and economic policies of monetarism (the two not, in fact, necessarily compatible) resulted in major changes in mental health policy and the organisation of health services and hospitals. Between 1980 and 1990, the first decade of Conservative government, thirty-five of the older 'water tower' mental hospitals closed. In 1982 the Area Health Authorities were abolished and the first general managers were introduced in 1984/5. Christopher Bridge and John Walshe summarised changes at this period thus:

It was a steep sided pyramidical hierarchy – Region, District, Unit – with a substantial acceptance of the authority of the superior tier(s). But it was not yet a managed or directed service ... the authority was not personalised or personally articulated; general managers still acted through consensus mechanisms with decisions left to team endorsement/veto; and doctors were denying any change in accountability ... the key feature was that the NHS did not know what it should do. Thus there were variations in investment in services that were historically originated ... The management ethic could be summed up as 'we did what we could afford, not what was needed' and success was measured in avoiding complaint from superior tiers.[25]

Although a male patient who had been resident both in the 1950s and 1970s, told me how much better the 1970s were for him, both in terms of nursing care and in terms of material comfort, a senior nurse I spoke to felt strongly that from the 1970s Severalls had rested on the laurels of Russell Barton. It had, he argued, reverted to a situation of poor leadership with a medically dominated organisation of traditional psychiatrists who prioritised hospital treatment and drug therapy. Overcrowding had increased again and old problems such as lack of privacy and patients having to wear hospital clothes had become rife once more.

Then in 1980 a new director of nursing was appointed who had wide experience in implementing multi-agency work. He quickly began to challenge the existing power structure at Severalls in a bid to weaken the dominance of the traditional psychiatrists, the unions, and the medical model of patient care. Here is an account by a nurse who was working in Severalls at the time:

> He came in and challenged the authority of the medical group. He made some major changes in terms of personal clothing, privacy, and reduced the beds, he systematically reduced all the beds. Instead of closing wards, he reduced the beds on each ward. They wanted him to close the wards to save money, but he didn't do that, because it wouldn't reduce the overcrowding. I know he put a lot of money into psychology of nursing and nurse education. I think he managed to get a lot of money from the Authority.
>
> It seemed to us he walked through the medical group, although they fought tooth and nail. They were all – individually – great people, or most of them, but like any group, if you get them together they can be a bad bunch. The power of social class, isn't it? But they can be knocked off individually, and that's what he did. He tried to keep them apart as a group, I think, and then individually got their commitment, got them to try and do things very differently, like not getting together too often to talk! I think what he was heading for was really to *manage* them.

This time was also, however, a difficult time when a number of staff were dismissed by management. There was, for instance, a tremendous amount of drug theft going on in the late 1970s and early 1980s, as well as wide-spread theft of food and clothing. One member of staff was fired for stealing a loaf of bread. Graffiti were painted on the walls protesting against such measures, targeting the director of nursing in particular. Trying to prioritise patient care, as well as increase his own authority, the director of nursing invested increasingly in community nurses, psychology, and bringing in psychological tests to measure patients' potential for rehabilitation in the community. During this time there was a General Management Board in the District with a chairman who many felt was disastrous for mental health. As a senior nurse commented:

> The man was an arrogant pig, you know, and he had no values but self, really. He ran the organisation how he wanted to, and did so with total arrogance. He and the District General Manager came up and visited some of the wards and they'd both been drinking very heavily. They had to be thrown out, you know. And then it was said that the chief medical officer eventually got the push because he wrote on application forms, medical forms and that sort of thing, 'not another wog'. And, you know, at that time there was a much more multi-cultural workforce than now.

In the second half of the 1980s, when general management came in, community mental health teams (CMHTs) became prioritised, thus enabling management and nursing practice to get away from the medical model. The old hierarchy with the medical superintendent at the top had kept the matron and chief male nurse in inferior positions to the superintendent, but the system of management that prevailed·during the 1980s meant it was possible for an energetic and forceful director of nursing to effectively seize control of hospital management to put into operation a particular vision of community care. An enlightened programme of nurse education in the 1980s, the professionalization of nursing generally, and the shift away from a medical model of psychiatric care to one geared more to empowering psychiatric nurses in the community, with nurses as therapists rather than as minions of doctors, shifted power relations in the mental health service generally, and in Severalls specifically.

One of the groups worst hit by such changes, however, was the unions. One man who was a union secretary for many years, said:

> I feel absolutely awful about Severalls closing. It's just politics that's done it. Because if fifteen or seventeen years ago it had been a Labour government, those hospitals would have still been there, they would still be housing and caring for patients. When I first started work, I joined the Transport and General Workers' Union,

and then I always went to the union meetings, which were held in the back room of the Dog and Pheasant. And everybody knew what went on at the union meeting, because everybody could hear through the side! And so I started off doing this collecting, and then as time went by, all of a sudden, the secretary of the union got promotion on to the management side, and he couldn't wear two hats, so he had to pack up his union job. So they said, 'Will you take over as secretary?' And so I thought, 'Well, I'll try' – I'd not had a very good education, I knew nothing about it at all.

And I did it for about twenty-five years, and when I finished, I had 700 members – because things changed, one of the things the Labour government brought in was that you could pay your subscriptions off your pay roll. Well, that absolutely let me free, that meant we could recruit people from other hospitals. I finished up negotiating about thirty or forty bonus schemes. A lot of them were very wary about these bonus schemes, because quite a lot of the ancillary staffs were doing overtime. And the overtime was at a premium rate, and they were doing well on the overtime and they thought replacing it with a bonus was going to lose them money.

The first bonus scheme we tried to put in, in Severalls, was for the biggest section, the laundry. And when it started off they first studied them, and of course they went like the clappers to prove what they could do, which was the thing they shouldn't be doing, because it was a study, and of course, they've got to work like the clappers all the time once it came into operation. And then when it got into its heyday, oh! They weren't half earning some money. They were working hard and they were getting what they earned. But all that went by the board, didn't it, because they privatised the laundries and shut them down. All the laundry transport was privatised.

So, you know, all the things, all these bonuses that we got for domestics, of course that all went up the wall, because they all lost their jobs and the firm that took it over wouldn't pay that kind of thing. What we gradually built up – a decent wage from a poor wage for what they were doing – has gone back to a poor wage again, because there's no wage restriction limit now, is there? The government's knocked that off, so they can pay as low as they like. And of course, when they got to private companies, they lost holiday entitlement and sickness pay and all sorts of things. Things just went up the wall.

Curtailing the power of the unions was one of the main targets of management policy in the 1980s. A nurse who rose into management said:

> The unions in the early 1980s – it was terrible. Terrible, because you couldn't satisfy them. It wouldn't matter what you did, they'd come back. There'd be ten letters a day, and letters sometimes three pages long, and each one of those had twenty or thirty points on them, you know. Extremely militant. What you have to do is to make sure that you get your staff on board with you. By getting them to come along with you and convincing them about – that you were honest, upright, that you weren't out to do them, that they could trust you, that they had a say in what they were doing. And that you had their interest at heart and you weren't down to screw every penny. If there was injustice, they could come and talk to you. People knew here that everybody had an open-door policy. It was really influenced by a change of government as well.

In 1988 there were a number of changes at Severalls: CMHTs became operational in Colchester and Clacton, John Walshe became chairman of the psychiatric division, and Christopher Bridge took up the position of chief executive. Within two months of Bridge's appointment, a commitment to general management philosophy was made. Soon there was a shift away from a centralised management structure which operated mainly from a large centralised location at Severalls, to working towards a policy of decentralisation: 'Our central core objective was to have a community based service ... that was not stigmatising.'[26] It was agreed that the central site should be closed, as it was too expensive to run with a rapidly declining patient population, which stood at about 1,000 in 1980 but had decreased to 500 by the end of the decade. This decision involved many other decisions regarding the authority structure of peripheral agencies and organisations, and meant a radical change in patient care and treatment.

In 1989 the government published 'Working for the Patient', which stipulated that services should be locally responsible as far as possible. The idea was that this could give patients more power over their treatment. 'Trusts' could also be set up and compete with each other: 'These changes were enormous and sensitive to political pressures, which made them even more difficult to ... achieve.' Eventually the decision was made to become a Trust, and the Trust became operational in 1992. By then two acute clinics had opened in Clacton and Colchester, each having space for about twenty-four patients at any one time. A nurse who moved into education, however, felt that these changes had impeded the development of a more enlightened nursing practice and patient care:

I think that change was *about* to thoroughly happen when they became a Trust. I think that the potential for it to thoroughly happen still exists, because I think the nurses are trained well enough for it to happen, but what appears to be happening since they became a Trust is that turnover – or 'through-put' as it is now described – and extra-contractual beds and *money* – have become more important than patients' needs. So what we get is people who come in in crisis, and their crisis is dealt with and they go out again, which means that the revolving door is getting faster. Not slower. Whereas I think that what we had got to just before we became a Trust was real investment in terms of *time* with people. And that's gone.

Well, it's difficult, because it leaves a frustration in the nurses, because it's what they want to do, and they do try, a lot of them do try. But they'll say, 'What's the point of me getting involved with this person, really, because in six weeks they'll have gone?' And you know, what we're talking about is someone who needs a *real* investment in terms of time. So if we were to invest, just as a hypothetical situation, if you were to invest two hours a week, say, two separate hours a week with an individual for two years, possibly in the community, possibly in a day hospital or something like that, they might never come back. But that won't happen, so what will happen is that you're going to invest six weeks at a time, every time they have a crisis and they don't deal with it. But – it's very frustrating for nurses, I think. Very frustrating.

People I interviewed perceived the Trust as having an overtly Conservative bias. A man who worked in Severalls for many years, for instance, felt deeply sceptical about current changes in mental health care:

I think it's a big political thing. You see, they're obeying – we've been under seventeen years of Conservative government now, and their object has been to close these type of places. And the people who are in charge are people who are answering to the government. I mean, someone asked the question when we went over to a Trust, someone asked the chairman and the chief executive a political question, 'Are all these non-executive directors and chairmen going to be Conservatives?' And the answer was, 'yes' because the Labour Party did not believe in the Trust, so how could they appoint Labour people to work in Trusts? And that was the point-blank answer, you see. That is the type of attitude, because whatever they say about it, these people have got to obey their political masters. I mean, you hear these people making their grandiose statements – well, they tell you point-blank lies as if it's the truth.

Severalls ended its eighty-four years with one individual still having considerable power and operating from the same office where the medical superintendent had first come in 1913. It was the same, but it was not the same at all. The chief executive was not a medical man, but a full-time director. The power of the medical profession was still important in patient care, but it had been curtailed and weakened by the rising importance of the nursing profession, and to a certain extent, social work. The care patients receive now comes as much from nurses and nurses as therapists as it does from psychiatrists who, some might argue, have become peripheralised in their role as dispensers of medicine. Central government is still dictating general policies on mental health care, and, though more decisions are taking place at a local level than before, mental health care undoubtedly remains a thoroughly political arena.

4

THE GREAT DIVIDE

Rule 233. The male and female patients shall be kept in separate wards, and no male attendant, servant or patient, except workmen in discharge of their necessary duties, and under proper supervision, shall be allowed to enter the female wards, nor any female to enter the male wards except where the Medical Superintendent shall deem it advisable to appoint nurses or female servants to attend for that purpose. Any attendant or servant transgressing this rule, unless a satisfactory explanation be given to the Medical Superintendent, shall be immediately suspended. No male persons, excepting the Medical Officers, Engineer, and the Chaplain, shall at any time have keys admitting them to any of the female wards. In visiting the female wards during the night the Medical Officers shall always be accompanied by a Head Day or Night Nurse.

(County of Essex Manual of Duties for the Asylums: County of Essex and the Borough of Colchester, 1914)

The spatial division of asylums by gender affected the daily lives and routines of all who worked and lived within them. The few who designed and administered asylums – all of whom were men – constructed ideals of masculinity and femininity, male and female behaviour, that reflected their own ideals of gender, class and family. These often both defined and reflected ideas, and definitions, of mental illness itself. Definitions of mental illness have varied and changed over time; in the nineteenth century both 'moral insanity' and 'masturbatory insanity' became newly defined as pathological. Neither category now exists. Categories of mental illness, in other words, are socially and historically constructed, and such categories include ideals of gender: 'gender is embedded in the concept of mental disorder itself'.[1] In the twentieth century women have been more frequently defined and treated as mentally ill than men. The female patient population of Severalls was consistently greater than the male, but this did not necessarily mean mental illness was, or is, more common in women than in men. Rather, it suggests women are treated more often *as if* they were mentally ill. Busfield points out that 'much psychiatric theory regarding women is revealed as more ideological than scientific' and that clinicians' concepts of adult mental health varied considerably between women and men.[2]

Severalls' division into a male side and a female side meant there were for many years effectively two hospitals. Each side, although ultimately governed by the medical superintendent and a shared set of rules, had its own regime, routine and ethos. On the one hand, the female side seems to have been run on the model of a Victorian family, with matron the supreme power within the 'house' – yet always second-in-command to the patriarch, the medical superintendent, who many regarded more as God than as father. The male side, on the other hand, was run much more along the lines of a military model. This was reinforced in the first half of the century by military-style uniforms for the male attendants, many of whom had been recruited from the army in the first place, and many of whom found promotion and social mobility by entering the police force. The inspector, later renamed the chief male nurse, who was in charge of the male side, played more of the role of a military commander than one having any familial associations. Discipline was firm and the regimes strict on both sides. Although violence often erupted between patients, especially on the male side, staff could be dismissed instantly, and sometimes were, for inflicting any violence on patients. The actual practice and implementation of rules against violence almost certainly varied considerably from ward to ward.

Fear of contact between male and female patients was great and reflected definitions of mental illness that emphasised heredity and 'faulty genes'. In the early twentieth century in particular, the influence of eugenics was widespread, and there was a strong belief in the urgency of forbidding any reproduction between 'unfit' and 'diseased' people who might perpetuate the wrong sort of people, the wrong sort of race. Perhaps equally important was the idea that the asylum acted as a custodian of its patients and as such was responsible for protecting them on behalf of their relatives. In effect, this related more directly to women patients and reflected the widespread belief that women belonged to men; male relatives did not want their wives, daughters and sisters 'interfered with' by other men, especially lunatic men.

Strict segregation by gender meant that each side of the hospital had its own routines, methods and, to some extent, culture, although obviously each was ultimately directed by hospital administrators, and the medical superintendent in particular. Work activities, when available, reflected narrow definitions of gender roles. Interestingly, however, the strict gender divisions meant that no female domestics worked on the male side, and both male attendants and male patients had to perform cleaning tasks normally associated with women's work. There were no female artisanal staff, except for a 'lady gardener' working on the female side. This meant that electricians, plumbers, glaziers, carpenters and painters had to work on both sides. Hospital rules stipulated that they should always be escorted by a female member of staff when on the female side. Where a building for a specific purpose was located on either the male or the female side, but needed to be used by both sexes, it would be divided. The isolation villa for infectious diseases was divided in this way, as was the villa for private patients (Myland Court). Even the mortuary had a female side and a male side with a room for post-mortems dividing the two.

There were times and places, however, even in the earliest days, when female and male patients met within the hospital itself. The first 'cine-matographic entertainment' at Severalls took place on Boxing Day 1914. From 1919 films were shown fortnightly, then weekly from the 1930s. These took place in the main hall, with women and men patients sitting on separate sides. The nurses sat at the doors and at intervals along the aisles: guardians of correct gender division. A similar arrangement applied for concerts, which were put on once or twice a month from the 1920s. There were also weekly dances, which one man who began work as an attendant in 1934, remembered:

> That used to be comic. They used to have a dance every week in the big hall, because Severalls they had their own band, and all that sort of thing. And there was a dance every week, but the females sat one side the males the other. And then when the band struck up it was just a wild dash – to run across. I mean they had quite a lot of them. They had their own fancy – you know – partners. They used to hug each other and kiss each other going round. Somewhat, you know. Yes. Well, that was the only time during the week when they were able to mix.

Services in the hospital church took place weekly – there was a hospital chaplain – and male and female patients sat separately there, too. A woman who worked as a nurse in the 1930s remembered the church services:

> The patients seemed to enjoy the services and used to sing very loudly – and more often than not sing out of tune. In fact, it was awful. But they enjoyed it. As I said before, the men were sat separate from the women, and we manned the aisles.

Gender divisions for staff were almost as rigorous as for patients. If a male attendant was found on the female side, instant dismissal followed.

The same applied to nurses. A male attendant who worked from the early 1930s to the 1970s at Severalls remembered the importance of temporal and spatial rules and divisions in their regime:

> Course, you had to be in certain times. You always – everybody had to be in by half past ten. In your rooms by quarter to eleven. If you were goin' with a girl and you come up – you had to be in before that, on the drive up there. You used to stand along there, all of you, kiss and a cuddle before you went in.
>
> But we used to, you know, sing our way home. An' the matron used to come down an' with her dog an' put it amongst the bushes an' say, 'Come on nurse! Out of there! Nearly half past ten!' An' I used to say, 'Don't move! Let the others move,' I said, 'when I move that dog'll follow me and then you go with the other girls up the end and she won't see you, she won't see us.' But we had to be quick once we start runnin', 'cause once we was out of the bushes – by what they call Firs now, it used to be called Farm Villa – an' then we used to nip through there.
>
> We – male – were never allowed to pass the centre. You know where the clock is? Well, the female side was that side. They could walk right round, but we weren't. We were allowed to walk from the centre, round the boundary to as far as Ashley. We couldn't go past that. If you were seen over there, especially in the evenin' time, if you were caught there after half past ten – you were out the next mornin'.
>
> And we used to call it 'ten minutes notice', 'cause next thing you'd be up before the inspector and he'd probably say, 'Well, of course you know you'll see the superintendent. I advise you to go and pack your bags ready. He wants to see you at eleven o'clock'. And then you went down, and the old saying was, you went in, and course he said, 'I understand you were so and so. Well, you won't become an efficient nurse. You must abide . . .' Very nice. Put it over nicely. And then he used to say, 'When you go out, call in the pay office'. He had your pay all made out, your papers and everything. Your kit packed and you were escorted from your room, which used to be over the cafeteria. Course we used to sleep on the wards an' all, about four of us. And then they used to see you right out the gate. One nursing officer would take you down with your bag right to the gate. But the trouble is, the trouble is, you daren't take that chance! There was so much unemployment in the country that you got a job an' you – you hung on to it.

Anomalies in the hospital's division by gender, however, existed, and gender divisions could change abruptly in times of labour shortages or economic crisis. During the First World War, when the shortage of male staff was acute, female nurses worked in male wards and on the farms. As early as November 1914, female patients began working with a tailoress to do 'some of the tailor's work'. From 1915 female nurses began to nurse in male wards. In June 1918 a party of five women patients and two nurses began working regularly on the farm. Dr Turnbull noted that 'they have been provided with suitable costumes and are now engaged in hoeing mangold'. The farm bailiff apparently found their work very satisfactory.

After the war ended, however, previous gender divisions reverted to their original state. In 1922, a time when some hospitals were experimenting with bringing in female nurses permanently to male wards, Dr Turnbull noted that 'the employment of female nurses in male wards had been tried, but the experiment did not prove successful.' No reasons were given, but usually there was opposition from the unions and male attendants who were afraid of women being used as cheap labour. Given the chronic underfunding of mental hospitals, this fear was undoubtedly correct.

When Severalls opened, the entire kitchen and bakehouse were staffed and run by women, including women patients. The early years were hard ones. The First World War created severe shortages in food supplies. Patients' food rations were cut. Sugar and potatoes were scarce. Wages were low, work was hard and hours were long. After the war ended, a new cook was appointed at an annual salary of £70, plus a war bonus of six shillings a week. There is little mention of kitchen technology in the records until 1922, except for a meat mincer; work depended primarily on labour by staff and patients. Washing, peeling and cutting hundreds of pounds of vegetables each day would have been done by hand. Bread was cut by hand, dough kneaded by hand.

In May 1922, a kitchen-maid accidentally put her hand through the meat mincer. Her hand had to be amputated. The hospital first offered her a small award during the length of her incapacity, then offered to re-employ her at some other occupation. Then they bought her an artificial hand. In September 1923 her husband requested compensation of £250, but the committee turned this down as excessive and only agreed to pay £150. Earlier in 1923 another kitchen-maid brought action against the committee, which she lost. She was apparently 'absolutely penniless and permanently incapacitated as a result of her illness' (it does not say what that was; presumably she argued it was contracted while working at Severalls). Her father was a labourer who earned little and now had the expense of her maintenance. The hospital, who won the case, agreed not to press for expenses.

In that same year, 1923, the hospital committee decided to staff the kitchen with a male cook and male assistants. Dr Turnbull's reason was that this was 'owing to the difficulty in obtaining an efficient kitchen staff', but I wonder whether the previous two court cases by kitchen-maids were connected to this sudden change. The entire kitchen staff were given one month's notice in November 1923, and a male cook and three assistant male cooks from Brentwood mental hospital were engaged. Two months later orders were placed for a whole range of mechanical aids for the kitchen: a vegetable attachment for the mincing machine, a half-sack dough kneader, a two-sack dough kneader for the bakery, and a wheeled trolley for transporting pudding from the bakery to the kitchen. Soon after these were installed, the old earthenware sinks were replaced with teak ones. The male staff were paid higher wages than the female and the new equipment was costly. It is tempting to wonder whether anyone considered mechanising the kitchen as a way of making the female labour-force more efficient. The result was better conditions and higher wages for the men who worked there.

Gender divisions were made explicit by wage and salary differentials as well as by formal rules. Interestingly, the matron received a higher salary than the inspector. His maximum wage was £5 17s. in 1920, while hers was £7 12s. She had a higher status than the inspector and seems to have been in many ways a far more powerful and respected figure, acting as a kind of 'supreme mother' throughout the hospital. She was the head of the whole female side, and in that position commanded considerable power and authority, the pinnacle of a female hierarchical pyramid within, but in many ways quite separate from, the hospital overall. The female side was invariably larger, and matron was also responsible for the Laundry and needle-room, two enormous enterprises servicing the whole hospital. The inspector was for years bandmaster, a task which, although important to the hospital's dances and sense of pride, did not carry quite the same burden of work or responsibility.

In 1967, however, this system ended. When Severalls' last matron resigned, Russell Barton appointed a – male – nursing officer who was responsible for both sides of the hospital. The position of nursing officer had been recommended by the Salmon Report of 1966; this made it possible for nurses to enter into management – and many did. Many who did so, however, were men, and where this happened, as it did at Severalls, there was a marked loss of a woman's power base. A male nurse who worked there at the time remarked:

> When this was all changed and the matron fell out with Barton, Barton said, 'Well, I've got to have a male or a female' – it was a male – who he could control. The old chief male nurse hadn't got

a clue what he was talking about. But the matron knew her job. So of course matron got out and went down to Southampton. Heads – things – started to roll then. He had the whole lot done then, didn't he? Of course the matron – the God – he'd got her out of the way, 'cause she went against him on everything.

In the 1960s male management also took over the laundry, and the laundry itself expanded at this time. Instead of two separate hierarchies divided by gender there was increasingly just one hierarchy, with men over-whelmingly at the top of the pyramid.

The 1960s, of course, was the era of the 'sexual revolution'; the intro-duction of the contraceptive pill made sexual relations between women and men much freer without the age-old fear of pregnancy. From the 1960s changes in spatial gender divisions at Severalls also occurred. With most wards unlocked, patients could now meet and mix in most social situations, although the division of labour in patient work remained strictly along traditional gendered lines: women patients worked in sewing and laundry, men worked in new industrial units as machinists, carpenters, painters. Rehabilitation for men emphasised getting a job outside the hospital, for women, the stress was on household management. Women and men patients could meet in the grounds or in town without recrim-ination, although sexual encounters were forbidden. This was not unreasonable, considering the following account by a woman who was a patient in the early 1970s:

It was then I got raped. Somebody'd been to prison and was put in a psychiatric ward and he systematically made love to somebody who was married – made love to me – he was generally very sexu-ally over the top.
Made love or raped?
Well – I don't – I mean – you see, you're not well – you see things differently, do you know what I mean? If anybody's interested in you or takes notice of you – you – you're, you know, you feel as though you're *somebody*. He took me and made love to me and I didn't sort of stop him. He took me out into the grounds into some ward that was being redone up. It *was* rape. Because I was not – I mean I never would have – normally – would never have done it. But I was high, this is the problem. ECT makes you peculiar. I was on ECT then. It was a very spaced-out time.

Heterosexual relations between patients were seen as problematic partly because of the fear of pregnancy, and partly because administrators saw themselves as acting *in loco parentis* for female patients. A blind eye was turned to homosexual relations between patients, however, as one man who came to work in the late 1950s remembered:

> I caught one patient in a compromising position with another male patient on the bed, you know, under the bedclothes. And I didn't, I couldn't say they were having a sexual relation, because there was a cover on top. But he shot out of bed and sort of came at me, and then he decided to back off. And I reported it. Of course they said, 'Well, forget it.' You know, I suppose this happens all the time. I didn't realise it. I think I was on the first ward, and I couldn't believe it.

Wards remained strictly segregated throughout the 1960s, except occasionally for meals, as Russell Barton recalled:

> I did bring in mixed Christmas dinners. I never brought in mixed wards, because people farting and so forth embarrasses some of the older ladies, and some of the older ladies will hold their water or won't go to the toilet because the thought of a man being the other side and hearing the water running is terrible 'They wouldn't know if it was the cistern or me.' So I didn't do that.
>
> And then of course there was sex between patients. And the big problem there is – was – if you see a couple of patients *in flagrante delicto* in the bushes and a journalist has also been tipped off – usually by one of the evangelistic nursing types – and he comes and witnesses it, you're likely to get some remarks such as, 'SEX BETWEEN PATIENTS ENCOURAGED AT SEVERALLS HOSPITAL'. I don't think we ever went as far as that, but I remember once being called, 'Do you let patients have sex with each other?' And I said, 'No'. 'Well, what would your view be about it?' I said, 'Well, if it's someone who hadn't thought about sex for many years, it would be a sign they were improving, because they were behaving like normal men.' 'So you think it's justified?' So I said, 'No! Of course not – *all* sex should be stamped out! You know it's filthy as well as stupid!' But you have to be silly like that – and then of course they try and get you some other way.

Most wards remained segregated by gender until the 1970s, and some remained single-sex into the 1990s. A male nurse who was involved in the first attempts to bring in mixed-sex wards said:

We were very brave at that time, that we actually made a decision that some of the patients we'd had in the hospital for years and years and years don't actually need to be in hospital. They can actually live somewhere else with somebody else looking after them, and can be just as happy, if not happier. And then through that kind of thinking we would then say, 'Well, the reality is that if you say they are going to live outside hospital you have to give them some fairly realistic living situation.' Like you don't live in a segregated world to begin with, and if you walk round the street then you have women who walk round, men who walk around. You might even have people in the same sitting room, and you might even eat together! That kind of thing. So then we actually started our first mixed-sex ward in 1972/3.

The integration between male and female patients took place almost entirely during mealtimes, in the dining room. Breakfast, lunch and supper. And afterwards, they went back to the respective wing of Myland Court, where they were strictly segregated. Now, that's not to say they don't see each other, make plans to see each other in the grounds. Having said that, it was very much frowned upon, and the notion that they were coming here for treatment – your normal heterosexual social activities should be the last thing on your mind. And I remember that it wasn't uncommon, particularly for a husband, to complain that their wife were allowed to visit and talk to the male patients. It was quite common at that time for that kind of complaint to be made. Although we did try our best to point out to the relatives about normality, about life, and the fact that it could be part of the recovery.

Single-sex wards began to be run by both male and female nurses from the 1970s. Here a woman who was in Myland Court during the time mixed-sex meals were being introduced, remembers how she and her friends and fellow patients felt about the changes:

I was always in a single-sex ward. Mixed sex, really, has only started – apart from the chronic wards – the mixed-sex wards really only started with The Lakes being built. In Myland Court quite often there would be visiting between the two wards, and I always hated it when the men came down. Didn't, didn't want them round me. I'd got enough to cope with without them. They tended to be noisier. They tended to try and take over the sitting room. In fact, everything women's libbers don't like about men was there to a marked degree.

106

And looking back, actually, it's quite funny, because, you know, the paternalism would be there, and the – seeking attention, and 'Oh, you've got to look after me, I'm a poor sick man!' 'I know better than you' – it was all there. It was a relief when they weren't there. They weren't there all that much, and if they caused a lot of problems they would be asked to leave. Most of them felt like that. And some of them were, 'Oh, thank heavens! A man!' But most of them resented the men coming down. Having male nurses didn't cause any problems. I think they were – given some form of training or guidance, because they came over very much as people.

This woman also played a pivotal role in a challenge to existing gender divisions within the occupational-therapy programme that operated in the 1960s and 1970s. Occupational-therapy programmes gave many patients a sense of dignity, worth and a renewed interest in life, but they also reflected a rigid and Victorian stereotype of gender perhaps more than any other aspect of hospital life. Women needed to be trained to be good housewives and mothers, whether they wanted to or not, as made clear in the Annual Report of 1960:

A Department of Household Management has been started in eight rooms which had been deserted since the War owing to bomb damage. A group of regressed patients is gradually redecorating these rooms, and as soon as they are ready, they will be used to help women patients recover their skill in housewifery, cooking, washing and household chores generally.

Of course much good work was being done in a genuine attempt to rehabilitate patients long abandoned, idle and institutionalised. Many activities were organised and virtually all patients were encouraged to work; undoubtedly much of this work gave many patients a new sense of hope and self-worth. Nevertheless, the messages conveyed were highly traditional and stereotypical ones in relation to gender, as this woman makes clear in her memories of the occupational programmes she experienced in the 1960s and 1970s:

The jobs we had were, literally, counting screws, ten to a packet. Or tying – you know the little bows on lingerie? They had a contract with Marks & Spencer's for those. So the neater-fingered ones of us would sit and tie these little pink and blue and white bows! We did get paid a certain amount. It went by results. I was quicker-fingered than anyone else. I got more money. And some of the staff got shirty. Not the patients – the staff! Why should I have £2 10s.,

Figure 4.1 Household management unit, 1960s
Source: North East Essex Mental Health NHS Trust

when the others would only have £1? There was quite a row about it. At that time it was decided I should be switched to the house-keeping unit, which is where we would be taught to cook and wash and iron and do all the housewifely chores – *again*.

I was furious! 'I'm not going there – I know how to do all that. I just don't *want* to.' 'Oh well, you've got to go.' And Kay[3] couldn't do anything about it, so I ran away. And I was waiting for the bus outside the hospital and Kay turned up to go home. And she looked at me and she said, 'What are you doing?' I said, 'I'm running away.' And she went to the other end of the bus. Well, I came home and my husband found me sitting in the garden when he got home from work. He phoned the hospital and took me back the next morning. And I was gated for a week! I wasn't allowed off the ward.

Then I was forced back into the housekeeping unit. We came to an agreement that I would go for a week, and if I proved I could do all the tasks they set me, I could go back to the industrial unit. I proved it, and the end of the week came. 'Oh, we'll see you on Monday.' 'No!' 'Yes.' 'No.' In the end I said, 'OK. I'll have to prove it's not a flash in the pan. I'll come back for another week.' I mean,

Figure 4.2 Women patients sewing bows on lingerie, early 1960s
Source: North East Essex Mental Health NHS Trust

this is me, I was as mad as a kite! I was *reasoning* with these stupid – ! And I went back for another week and even the head of occupational therapy came down to assess me. And she said, 'Yes, you're right. You don't need to be on this unit. Well, we'll see about sending you elsewhere on Monday.'

Came Monday, I was sent to this dolls' house factory, which was where long-stay male patients made doll houses to sell to the general public. The charge nurse there and I both agreed that it wasn't a good idea for me to go on a circular saw, because it was bigger than me. So I was set to finishing, doing the finishing off, as I was good with my fingers. I was too fast for the men. Within two days I was playing chess against myself to occupy myself. A battle started up between some of the men and me as to whether the radio was going to be on all day or part of the day. I couldn't stand it – it was on a pop station all day, so I kept switching it off, and they would stop their circular saw or hammer or whatever and realise it had been switched off and come and put it back on! I was the only woman there, you see, there had never been a woman in that unit.

And then they put another woman on who – I don't know if she was overdosed or overdrugged or what, but she was very slow and thick and couldn't understand the instructions, and things got even worse. But she could play chess! So the pair of us would be sitting playing chess. But then, I can't remember how long I was there, but one day I had a fit and the charge nurse said, 'That's it! I'm not having epileptics – *any* epileptics on this unit!'

Then I ended up going to Iris House, which was occupational therapy – making macramé pot-holders and banging drums and reading to each other and doing a bit of pottery. I got very fed up there. For the majority of people there it was fine. But I found it very unstimulating, and it wasn't until David and another chap joined as day patients and, thank heavens, I had some brains to work with, you know. Otherwise I think I would have gone mad! David and I had met before, we always talked philosophy and religion and psychology and sociology and – you know – the very first day we met we were introduced about half past nine at night and we were still talking at three in the morning. And this was on the ward, you know, this is how we always were. The other chap didn't talk very much, but he was very much into classical literature, so we did talk a bit. Finally in Iris house, the head of Iris House, bless her cotton socks, she said, 'Well . . .' I'd sort of been round the hospital, seen it all, done it all, got the T-shirt. What was the point?

Well, there was this small woodwork unit in Iris House and I always fancied doing woodwork, so I said, 'Can I go in there?' 'Oh! There's never been a woman in the woodwork!' So, eventually she overrode the therapist in there and I was in. Most of the men in there were very resentful of me, but one – my Mauritian friend who committed murder – he proved to be very supportive. If I was stuck, if I didn't know what to do, he'd leave what he was doing and come and help me. And he'd make sure I got a cup of coffee or tea at break time. The therapist wasn't really a carpenter or a woodworker. He didn't know much more than any of the patients. In the occupational therapy department they weren't trained, they certainly weren't trained for the severely disturbed people. And there were people working there who'd sort of come in off the Job Centre with no knowledge of – perhaps – how to do a craft, let alone how to handle people. Because the occupational therapy is actually where most of the treatment went on. It was where we were being forced into situations where we had to relate, to some degree, not only with staff, but with each other. We couldn't go and hide in our beds. We were having to handle some sort of work situation, receive a wage packet – and that was stressful.

Figure 4.3 Male patients doing carpentry, 1960s
Source: North East Essex Mental Health NHS Trust

MALE AND FEMALE NURSES

Since the proliferation of large state-run asylums from the mid-nineteenth century onwards, asylum attendants had been recruited overwhelmingly from the working classes. This contrasted with general nurses, who were traditionally middle-class women in the mode of Florence Nightingale. John Conolly regarded asylum attendants as on a par with household servants; their pay at the turn of the century was comparable, for women, to that of a domestic servant, while for men it was similar to that of an agricultural labourer. Their working-class origins, low rates of pay and large proportion of men contributed, in contrast with general nursing, to a high rate of unionisation.[4]

In 1910 the National Asylum Workers' Union was established and after the First World War a number of strikes broke out in asylums, one of which, at St Andrews in Bodmin, was by female nurses. Although records are missing for 1919 at Severalls, it is clear that there was substantial industrial unrest from 1918, when the National Asylum Workers' Union took up attendants' grievances about low wages. Dr Turnbull noted 'considerable unrest' existed both among women and men staff 'and great efforts[5] are being made to enrol the whole staff in the workers' union. The cause of this disturbance is largely the result of successful agitations in the Lancashire and London Asylums.' In 1920 the committee resolved to pay artisan staff recognised trade union rates of pay and to increase the wages of non-union employees by the same percentage as the unionised. A new wage scale was adopted, but differentials between women and men in equivalent jobs remained. A probationer attendant, for example, received £3 9s. weekly, while a probationer nurse received only £2 18s., a difference of some 30 per cent.

Low wages, residency requirements – attendants and nurses had to be residential, unless the medical superintendent gave a male attendant permission to marry – and a high degree of stigmatisation, not just of patients, but also of those who worked with them, would not seem to make it a particularly attractive job. Yet for many working-class men it was a godsend and a most unusual chance to gain security. Free clothing, cheap board and lodging, and a pension,[6] were attractive incentives to many, particularly during times of recession and high unemployment. One man told me how he was the youngest of seven children, his father died when he was young, and his mother worked as a caretaker to support her children as best she could. He began work as an attendant in 1934:

> And to me it was a good sound job. I mean, if you thought about it, it was a job for life. You had your holidays, you had a fortnight every six months, you had two suits of clothing – winter and summer

– so. And also it was a pensionable job, which was a big thing in those days. I mean, you were sort of on a par with the police and firemen, you know, that sort of thing. It was a good job, providing you looked after yourself and kept your nose clean, and I mean, there were people, I mean, they were very severe. You could get ten minutes' notice, no problem. But I liked the job. I liked the work.

The job, however, was far less attractive to women than it was to men, and recruitment of female nursing staff was an ongoing problem from the very beginning. Women who did come and stay could rise rapidly to quite well-paid and prestigious positions of responsibility, providing they did not want to marry. One young woman who joined as a probationer nurse in May 1913, for instance, had been promoted to head nurse by October of that same year and retired on a pension in 1930. Yet very few women who came to nurse at Severalls followed this path. The majority left after a short period of work, as Table 4.1 shows. Whereas in 1913 32 per cent of nursing had left in under a year, by 1924 this figure had *doubled*. The 1920s was a period during which many new job opportunities for women developed, notably in the clerical sector, but also in light industry. It was also a period generally seen as liberating for women; to what extent this applied to working-class women in Essex is hard to assess. Mental nursing, however, must have been one of the least attractive jobs to a young woman. Extremely long hours, poor pay and enforced residence under a

Table 4.1 Length of employment of (male) attendants and (female) nurses at Severalls, by groups of 50 recruited in 1913, 1919, 1924 and 1929

| Year joined | Length of service | | | Number |
	< 1 year	1–10 years	11–40+ years	
1913				
Males	30%	42%	28%	50
Females	32%	60%	8%	50
1919				
Males	26%	42%	32%	50
Females	62%	36%	2%	50
1924				
Males	32%	28%	40%	50
Females	64%	36%	0	50
1929				
Males	24%	44%	36%	50
Females	58%	42%	4%	50

Source: Matron's and inspector's employment records, Severalls

strict regime offered nurses little scope for leisure, freedom or fun. In times of unemployment, notably the 1930s, nurses left less quickly and readily. Almost none stayed long enough to receive a pension, and very few took advantage of career prospects. Of a sample of nurses and attendants appointed between 1913 and 1939, for instance, 24 per cent of the male attendants retired, while only 4 per cent of the female nurses did so. Of those dismissed – 25 per cent of the nurses, and 22 per cent of the attendants – the reasons for being so dismissed varied: the most common ones for men were drunkenness, violence and disobedience, while for women they were disobedience, theft, violence, sleeping with other (women) nurses, and pregnancy. Attendants left more frequently to take up other jobs elsewhere (21 per cent of attendants, 13 per cent of nurses).

Nurses often left to marry or care for relatives (28 per cent), while attendants never did so. The marriage bar was in force for women until 1946, which meant nurses had to resign if they wanted to marry. No such restriction applied to men; although they had to seek permission to marry from the medical superintendent, which was a mere formality, married attendants then became eligible for hospital houses in Mill Road and Defoe Crescent. Unlike men, women were also expected to give up their work if their (unpaid) labour was needed caring for relatives at home. Undoubtedly some gave this as a reason for leaving when it may not have been, in fact, true, but the fact remains that women's work was seen as secondary to men's. This was reflected both in their lower wages and in their lower rate of unionisation. At a meeting of the local branch of the National Asylum Workers' Union in 1929, for example, at a time when the union was pressing Severalls for better conditions and higher wages, the general secretary was reported as saying:

> Mr Gibson . . . touched upon the anomaly of fully-qualified nurses being rated as second-class nurses, as the majority were, and the promotion outlook – waiting for dead men's shoes. The wages scale at Severalls was outlined and compared with that of the Mental Hospitals' Association and Joint Conciliation Committees' recommendations, and those obtaining in Yorkshire and Lancashire. The Essex County Mental Hospital scale did not stand the comparison very favourably, Mr Gibson said. What was the reason, he asked, that the female nurses would not stay any length of time? He submitted that the wages paid did not offer a sufficient inducement to carry on work of a most uncongenial and discouraging nature.[7]

The way male attendants perceived female nurses, however, revealed a somewhat different story. A male nurse gave this account of unionisation among women and men at Severalls, when he was demobbed after the Second World War:

114

Then I came back here, but when I went back we were still on the old system of going to work at seven in the morning, finish at quarter to eight at night. But that time of day a Mr Wright, old Ben Wright, he had just taken over as the union representative, you know. They were working out a shift system. And they didn't want it, but anyway, it was worked out. A lot of men who wasn't in the union, as one would say, before the war, because that time of day before the war, if anybody knew you were in the union – you were out. So if you wanted to pay your subs you had to do it quietly, without anybody knowing. But, like, unknown to a lot of people, who later on become nursing officers, they were *all* in the union – so of course things broke down after a while.

Anyway, when they went to see old Duncan about this shift system, he said, 'Well, what does the union think of it?' And of course, he said, 'Well, we have 90–97 per cent of the males, but the females are not for it.' The trouble is, with the female staff – I don't like to say this, but the females who were sisters then didn't want to share the ward with another sister. Where the men were more adaptable – they said, 'Right. We'll share. We'll get – we'll have two charge nurses' you see. But the sisters weren't.

And years later this lady said, 'Do you know, you're very lucky to have this system.' And I said, 'Well, going back about ten years ago, you know,' I said, 'You were the ones that opposed this, because you were a sister in charge of a ward and you wasn't prepared to share it. And now you say we're better off than you are. Of course we're better off than you are!' I said, 'but it was people like you, along with three or four other women, who were against it. But you could have had the same system as we've got!' And that was the best thing in the world, the shift system we had there. 'Cause men seem to – get together better than perhaps the female does, you know.

Undoubtedly there were attitudinal differences between women and men about the unions, but what he fails to acknowledge is the deep structural differences between men and women nurses that made unionisation and commitment to union affairs far more difficult for women.

Turnover rates of female nursing staff were always high, but particularly so during the Second World War and for some ten years afterwards. Lifting the marriage bar in 1946 resulted in a new source of labour: part-time work by married women. The average age of female nurses joining rose markedly:

Table 4.2 Average age of nurses joining Severalls, 1939–1949

Year	Average age	Total number joining
1939	23	47
1940	25	49
1941	23	47
1942	25	26
1943	22	31
1944	26	17
1945	24	18
1946	34	26
1947	34	48
1948	35	44
1949	32	70

Source: Matron's records, Severalls

The first part-time female nurse at Severalls was appointed in 1943. The following year, out of a total of seventeen hired, four were part-time. In 1946, sixteen out of twenty-seven were part-time (59 per cent). In 1947 55 per cent of those hired were part-time (thirty-two out of fifty-eight) and in 1948 twenty-six out of forty-four (59 per cent) were part-time. A very small number of male nurses worked part-time; the vast majority worked full-time. Women who work part-time almost invariably do so because they also have family commitments and responsibilities. This means in effect that they have two jobs. Such a situation leaves little opportunity to participate regularly in union activities.

Interestingly, an interview with a woman who came to work at Severalls from France in 1956, reveals that part-time nurses were actually better off than full-time nurses, suggesting that management may well have encouraged this in order to save on superannuation and national insurance payments:

> I found I could get £1 10s. more a week – that was a lot of money then – if I became part-time. I was married by then and Mike was in his third year. So I gave up the training. I became part-time with quite a lot of hours. And I got £1 10s. more a week, so Mike could finish his training. I felt – wrongly or rightly – now I could be totally wrong – but in those days I found more importance for Mike to finish training. 'Cause we found we had difficulty – I mean, we had the rent to pay. We had difficulties and I just thought I had to – you know, for Mike – and £1 10s. in England in those days it was a lot of money, so we did it.

The post-war years were ones when the unions were gaining considerable benefits for their members. The main beneficiaries of these, as the
previous account by the male nurse suggests, were the men, although pay
awards were also given to non-union members. Throughout the 1950s Dr
Duncan and the committee complied with what was effectively a closed-
shop situation in the appointment of male nursing staff, thereby actually
going against central government policies. In January 1952 Dr Duncan
noted:

> There will shortly be two vacancies for charge male nurses. It
> seems to be a principle with the regional nursing authorities that
> such positions should be publicly advertised. I recommend,
> however, that instead of public advertising, applications be invited
> from the male nursing staff at this Hospital ... Regional Board
> regard it as very desirable that all vacancies of grade of Sister (or
> charge nurse) and above should be publicly advertised ... as far
> as the male staff is concerned ... we have a large number of
> qualified and experienced staff eligible for promotion ... and
> consider the cost of publicly advertising such posts would not be
> justified.

No advertisements outside the hospital were made for male nursing until
Dr Barton came as physician superintendent in 1960; he changed this
policy and brought in male nursing staff from outside Severalls. This did
not please many of the older generation of male nurses.

The Regional Hospital Board made it difficult for management at
Severalls to increase nurses' wages. Desperate for female staff, whom the
hospital was unable to attract, Severalls began to recruit untrained women
from abroad after 1948. These recruits, many of whom could speak little
English,[8] were cheaper than trained nurses. Interestingly, there had been
a policy before the war to recruit nursing staff from areas *outside Essex*
whenever possible. This was apparently part of the general policy to maintain silence and secrecy of both patients' identities and hospital affairs. It
undoubtedly contributed both to stigmatisation and fear in the wider
community. A woman illustrated this policy in the following account of
her appointment to Severalls in 1936:

> An ex-Severalls nurse was telling me all about Severalls: wonderful
> pay, wonderful opportunity, and all the rest of it. 'The patients do
> all the work. You don't do any work,' she said, 'they do it all.' So
> I applied. I had no idea what I was going into at all. I suppose we
> thought we were doing a very dangerous job. Well, I had the appli-
> cation form and it said you'd got to be – this was, I think, one of

the first big lies of my life – you'd got to be 19 years old. I was 18. 'Oh,' she said, 'put down 19.' Then there was another question, 'Are you musical?' I said, 'No. I'm not.' 'Oh – put "yes",' she said! So I – I sent off the application form, then I was given an appointment.

And – oh! This matron was a great big – a great big lady. Oh, she was frightening! So she said, 'Well, you were 16 when you left school, so you've had a good education.' Oh dear! I felt so guilty! So then 'Oh', she said that they didn't take on local nurses as a rule, because they would know, they may know patients and may talk about them. So I was more or less told that whatever happened, I *never* spoke about patients outside. Well, my mother knew somebody who was here, and my mother used to ask me, 'Have you seen – seen her?' I think she was something to do with The Grapes pub. I told my mother I'd never met her. I had. As I tell you, there's lies after lies!

During the severe labour shortage in female nurses at Severalls between 1938 and the early 1950s such a policy was simply untenable. The introduction of part-time nurses and the removal of the marriage bar meant that a high proportion of the female nursing staff were local women. Many were women who had trained at Severalls earlier, married a member of staff and lived in hospital housing. In 1939, for instance, 17 per cent of all nurses recruited had worked previously at Severalls. In 1946, 82 per cent of all new nurses recruited had worked previously as nurses (or sometimes as maids or laundry maids) at Severalls. This must have meant that networks of Severalls workers in and around the local community became more cohesive and tight-knit. This high influx of local, married, older women on the nursing staff, many of whom later became full-time and often stayed for twenty or thirty years, may have resulted in nursing patterns modelled on the parent–child relationship which was later disparaged and discouraged by reformers like Russell Barton:

It was the method of management: 'Come here, Mrs So-and-so! Do as I tell you!' They were treated as naughty, wilful children, which was the way these middle-aged women who'd gone back to nursing after having their families used to treat people who weren't immediately obedient. And so one got all these awful phrases: 'How dare you!' And, 'I didn't say you could do that!'

One woman – she was the mother of a policeman, he was a nice guy, the ward sister screamed at her and called her an Irish lout and said, 'Hey, you bag, get out of my sight, get out of my ward as soon as you can!' And this copper came up – very upset, because his mother *was* depressed – and she kept asking questions, you know, as they do – usually an obsessive touch, 'If I keep taking these, Sister, will I be all right?' 'Yes.' 'Can you be sure I'll be all right?' 'Sister, I don't want to bother you, I know I'm coming back again, but if I take it, how often should I?' And it can be very maddening, but that is a dreadful thing to do, say you're not wanted, get out of my sight. A lot of the male nurses did that: 'Get out of my sight!'

Problems with nursing staff were by no means unique to Severalls, but were experienced nationally. Throughout the 1950s there was ongoing debate in journals such as *The Lancet* – indeed, in Parliament itself – about the nursing crisis in mental hospitals. It was part of a much wider debate about mental health and hospitals generally and led to the Percy Commission 1954, which was set up in 1954, and eventually the Mental Health Act of 1959. In 1952, for example, *The Lancet* reported that Harry Crookshank, Minister of Health, regarded the recruitment of nurses for mental hospitals as 'one of the most difficult and intractable of our problems'.[9] While between 1948 and 1951 there was a 25 per cent increase in full-time nurses and a 38 per cent increase in part-time nurses in general hospitals in England and Wales, there was a mere 2.6 per cent increase in full-time nurses and 29 per cent increase in part-time nurses in mental hospitals. In these three years the number of student nurses in general hospitals rose from 30,603 to 38,284, but in mental hospitals there was a decline from 4,955 to 4,519. A 1954 Royal College of Nursing conference on staffing problems found that 80 per cent of entrants to mental nursing left before they completed training.[10]

From 1950 new recruits tended to come increasingly, albeit slowly, from abroad; they were younger, often untrained nursing assistants, but there was also a rise in the numbers of student nurses at this time. By this time the problem had begun to affect both female and male nurses; the older generation of male nurses – attendants – who began work in the inter-war period were beginning to retire. It was not until the end of the 1950s and the early 1960s that the chronic shortage of nursing staff began to show improvement. Pay increased for nurses during this period, largely as a result of union pressure. In 1951 mental nursing was subsumed under the responsibility of the GNC, and during the 1950s the GNC pressed for better formal nursing education. Nursing tutors' pay rose. The syllabus for mental nursing was revised. As the profile of mental nursing improved, so part-time nursing began a slow decline.

Russell Barton made nurse education and re-education a high priority on his agenda of reforms from 1960. Refresher courses, seminars and symposiums were organised both for Severalls staff and for those from further afield. Because nurses were the people who dealt most directly with patients, they were the ones whom he believed had to be targeted for the most important reforms if psychiatric care was to become therapeutic rather than custodial. Such a policy was often unpopular with the 'old guard' of nurses, but often very popular with younger nurses. The school of nursing at Severalls became well known and much respected in the outside world during, and after, the 1960s.

FEMALE AND MALE PSYCHIATRISTS

Problems with staffing were not unique to nurses. From the beginning Severalls had difficulties hiring, and keeping, medical staff, and this had repercussions on gender divisions among psychiatrists. Severalls was isolated and had no previous reputation to attract doctors. It was not a teaching hospital. It was large and overcrowded within a few years of its opening. Accommodation offered doctors in the hospital was by no means special or luxurious; in the 1930s the deputy medical superintendent's house was divided into doctors' flats, but some doctors were just given single rooms in patients' villas. Not until 1960, when Dr Barton opted to live outside the hospital estate, was the original medical superintendent's house converted into doctors' flats. At the end of the 1960s new accommodation was provided for doctors in the Severalls grounds, but it included provision for doctors from other hospitals, a move bitterly contested by Dr Barton.

Most of the patients were paupers from a largely agricultural catchment area; any doctors aspiring to practise the new Freudian approach or, indeed, to find facilities for research into bio-medical psychiatry could find relatively few opportunities at Severalls. Psychiatry had been, and continued to be, the last choice of the vast majority of young doctors. Consequently, psychiatry, especially in asylums, tended to attract doctors who, for various reasons, were unable to practise in any other field. Although this endemic problem improved somewhat after 1948, Russell Barton still found it a major obstacle:

> Well, the mental hospital became the sort of refuge for doctors who were alcoholic, substance abusing, epileptic, had been thrown out of other places for stealing or couldn't keep their hands off the ladies, and so forth, so that anyone who wanted to get rid of someone they would ring up the superintendent – a superintendent of one of the London hospitals did this to me once – I think I told you about the lady who was – I – I didn't mind her being a lesbian, that's up

to her, but what I did object to was that she was a psychopath. And, you know, she would blame the ward sister if – she was a les – and this superintendent wanted to get rid of her, so he did that on me. And another one who was – I liked him very much, he was a friend, too, he was at St George's – he tried to give me a guy with an MD MRCP who was a drunk and also a gay lothario.

There was another problem when you have a closed institution, we started having medical students – one or two of them chucked condoms, used, in the waste-paper baskets, which a waste-paper basket is for, of course. However, the maids would then tittle-tattle to the matron and the matron would go and talk to the telephone operators, who were the source of all gossip. We had a very amusing Irish girl in, she was great fun, but she began bringing Americans in for – I don't think she was charging them, but then the deputation came from some of the nurses who were offended: doctors' quarters were a cat-house!

Then there were people who just were lazy and didn't do their work, and there are people like that, that just don't get on with it, don't write up the notes. And they would be pushed from one mental hospital to another. So that virtually we had the dregs and everyone accepted this. There are no institutionalised patients, only institutionalised staff! Especially institutionalised doctors. You see, people settle down to do the least possible they can get away with – not all people – some have a sort of zealous personality problem – like one of the women doctors we had was always doing religious stuff on some of these people. It was all right until you got an Orthodox Jew – and then the shit hit the fan! The mental hospital doctor was the lowest on the totem pole, and mental hospitals often had a succession of doctors, locums, new people coming to the country. They were uninspired. They felt they were failures. And they really knew nothing about psychiatry.

Male doctors who came to Severalls during the 1920s did not fare well on the whole; one doctor, for example, was appointed as second assistant medical officer in September 1922. He was quickly promoted and became first assistant medical officer and deputy superintendent. On 22 June 1927, however, he was asked to resign, given three months' leave of absence, and ordered to leave on that day. What his transgression was is not recorded. In August the BMA sent a letter suggesting an inquiry, and in September a writ was issued for charges of slander against Dr Turnbull. The next month he was sent £210, his salary owing, but there are no records of the outcome of the case. That same year another doctor was convicted in August by Witham justices for being drunk while in charge of a motor car. He resigned. Not all, of course, caused such problems. Dr Duncan came in the 1920s and went on to become medical superintendent in 1939.

In Severalls' first few years there was hardly any medical staff at all; by 1917, all of them had been called up for military service. From the early 1920s, however, a number of women doctors began to be appointed. The generally low status in which psychiatry was held at this time offered women doctors, who had only recently achieved the right to practise in the medical profession, opportunities they would not have found in other fields. Not surprisingly, they tended to be appointed as locums or temporary doctors rather than given permanent positions. Of forty-one locums appointed between 1921 and 1959, for example, eighteen were women, or 44 per cent. Of thirty-nine permanent appointments, however, only 12 per cent were women.

The 1920s in particular was a period when a large number of women gained appointments as doctors at Severalls. Some came as locums for three or four weeks and then left. Others, however, gained their DPM[11] while at Severalls and either were promoted or found better jobs elsewhere. One woman, for instance, was appointed as a locum in 1922. She was given three months' study leave and passed her DPM. She then became a junior assistant medical officer and was awarded a pay increase of an extra £50 per annum Another woman doctor also came as a locum in 1922, then went on as a temporary assistant medical officer in Edinburgh. She returned in 1925 as senior assistant medical officer and stayed until 1929, when she was appointed to the London Hospital. A woman doctor who came as a temporary medical officer in 1927 was made permanent in 1928. She was successful in her DPM that year and, indeed, attended the International Mental Hygiene Congress in New York in 1931, when she became second assistant medical officer. A woman who joined as a locum in 1929, got her DPM in 1931 and became a permanent member of staff that year. In 1935 she was given permission to marry and remain on the staff and worked there for many years. Six other women came to work as locums at Severalls in the 1920s, but only stayed for short periods.

Medical staffing remained a problem generally, and became most acute during wartime. Retired doctors then came to work as locums, and a woman who worked as the doctors' maid during the war period, remembers women doctors, retired doctors and doctors who were displaced persons from the war working at Severalls.

The assistant medical officers' centre, up the top, I didn't stay there every day, but I was there most of the time – and from then on I was on the doctors permanently till '50. There was also another place where the lady doctors used to live – which was over by what was then the deputy medical superintendent's house, and that was round by the dispensary. It was a long way away – you used to go right down the corridor and turn left at the dispensary, and there was a house on the end of it – and he had the bottom, and up the top there was accommodation for three lady doctors – sittin' room an' all that – but it was shut up because of the war – except for just an odd bed for fire-watchin' for the medical officers.

The number of doctors varied, as the young ones were in the forces – and most were on short locums, the doctors we had. There was usually a lady doctor – Doctor Dorkins was there when I went. There was various ones, cause she left in '45 and went over to the British Legion Hospital at Nayland, but there was other ones that came in between, you know, but none stayed a long time. Dr Dorkins, well – she was – another battle-axe! She really was, you know. You took her tray of tea at half past seven – give her a knock at quarter to eight when she slept in – at ten to eight you put her wireless on for her! You know, precise in every way, but a bit of a taskmaster really, she was very difficult to please. I got on with her all right, but everything had to be on the ball all the time with her, you know. I don't think she liked the male doctors very much! An' you know, there was always a bit of a battle between them, really, but it didn't concern me directly.

But she was a very good doctor, oh yes, she was very good to the patients, I believe, in every way. She was very small, very dainty – dressed, well, she looked you know – one of the old-fashioned doctors, do you know what I mean? She dressed smartly, very smartly, but very austere. No, she wasn't married, never was, no. She rubbed everybody up the wrong way somehow. She couldn't bear – I had a male patient come with me, 'cause that was the male side – well, we used to come and clean the brasses and that sort of thing – an' she used to come out of her room, you see – he used to come up and he'd be in the billiard room cleanin' the brasses on the door – and she'd open the door in her dressin' gown and come through the bathroom, and that annoyed her, so SLAM! 'd go the door! Anything like that irritated her – well, I got on all right with her, she was better than a lot of others anyway!

Sometimes we'd have resident doctors you see, if they come as locums they came from away. One doctor came in 1941 and he was resident all the time I was there. He was a refugee, I think, from the Jews, you see, I think he suffered quite a bit, you know, that was the tale – he never spoke about it, but I think he had to do so many years more or less labourin' an' that sort of thing before he was allowed to come to the doctor. And in 1941, just after I came there, he came there. Another doctor, he went in the forces. And he was there all the time until he married, I think, but I got on very well with him, he was very nice. Then Dr Heffner was always permanent, but he lived on the male side for some unknown reason, but he had his meals at our place. And then there was the doctor who was there all the time, he eventually ended up as medical superintendent at Turner Village. Dr Heller came towards the end of the war, again, he was another refugee from the Germans – and he was a real character! He was a professor from Prague University, and he wrote to me and communicated with us till he died in the late 1960s. We had some displaced persons there.

We used to have the padres come in as well, you know, and the locum doctors, 'cause we had – the Red Cross had a villa for the wounded soldiers – we called it St Michael's, but there again it was on the male side. The nurses from there ate in our place – most of them were volunteers. We also had a doctor there, he was in his eighties I should think. He was the doctor for the St Michael's. He was a painter, he used to have pictures that got shown in the Royal Academy in 1898, and I don't know why, but during the war – you know, they had these big gold wooden frames, gilt – he used to come and put pictures in them, hung them all round the walls. I suppose he thought they were safer there! He took them away afterwards. Then we had a colonel from Jersey, you know when the Germans – they picked up and run sort of thing, and he done a locum, he was about 80, his wife lodged at the Wagon and Horses, used to come up there for tea with him and that sort of thing. Dozens of 'em!

The young ones had to go to the war, you see. We had another one there, he was a Yank – and he kept chickens or ducks somewhere, he lived near Walton, and he came one day and he said, 'Here, will you go ask the men if they'll get this ready for me.' Well I knew I didn't like feathers – I can't stand 'em! And that was in one of his briefcases, and I took it down and I put it to the men in the kitchen, and said, 'Well, doctor said –'. 'Cause he used to give 'em a drink for doin' it, you know. Well, when they took it out it'd still got the lasso on it! It was great times, it really was.

After the NHS Act in 1948 psychiatry became a somewhat more attractive option for young doctors. Psychiatry during the war had also made substantial improvements and generally had a higher profile than previously. From the early 1940s some progressive medical superintendents were initiating programmes of reform, rehabilitation and, as far as possible, de-institutionalisation. Pay scales and career opportunities, both in mental hospitals and in private practice, were improving. From the 1950s, more doctors came to Severalls with qualifications – the DPM – than had been the case before, yet recruitment remained a serious problem. In 1950, for instance, there was only one applicant for the post of senior registrar at Severalls – and she changed her mind at the last moment and went to Runwell instead.

Demoralisation of doctors, particularly the male doctors, seems to have been an ongoing problem. Dr Duncan, for example, reported to the Committee in 1958 that on 12 August:

> There was only one doctor doing ward duties for the whole male side. Dr Rosenthal was taking a normal day off duty. Dr Jefferson[12] also absented himself, spending the morning in bed. He admitted that he had decided to do this the previous evening, without any consultations. This was the culmination of a long series of negligence and incompetence and I gave him notice to terminate his appointment.

The problem with firing a doctor was that it often took months to find a replacement; such action presumably only took place when absolutely essential – or desperate. In the 1950s Commonwealth doctors began to work at Severalls. Several European doctors were also appointed. Adequate staffing levels and adequate staff remained a problem throughout the 1960s, although as Severalls' reputation improved, more doctors chose to come. Those who remained – and who were judged to be good at their job – had excellent chances of promotion, given the rapid rate of turnover. One such doctor, who had been educated and brought up in Pakistan, was appointed as a registrar in September 1968:

> I remember my mother saying to me, 'But psychiatry is for the riff-raff type of doctor!' You know, 'You were so brilliant in your studies, what are you doing specialising in psychiatry? You should be an obstetrician.' The interesting thing is, they were so short of doctors in those days that I – I was working as a house officer in obstetrics before I joined Severalls, and the hierarchical system of doctors' training is such that after house officer you have to be a senior house officer and then a registrar. In fact, these days, you have to be a senior house officer for at least a couple of years, if not more. Well, I was given the post of a registrar straight away. I never became a senior house officer.

I don't think they'd had an Asian lady as a senior registrar. I think I was the first one in that post, and I was appointed at the age of 29 as consultant, which was probably the youngest ever. The job came up – I was encouraged to apply. I applied on the first occasion and didn't get the job on the first interview, because I was told that I was too young and too inexperienced. But nobody else was appointed. And the job was readvertised. I was once again strongly encouraged to apply again – in three months I had neither grown up nor become that much more experienced – but I got the job. And it was in competition with other local graduates – white, male and female – and I still got the job. And I think it was only because of the local support I got from my other colleagues in Severalls that I was appointed. So I had tremendous support here.

Psychiatry offered good opportunities for women to advance in their profession, although even now there is only one woman consultant for the Mental Health Trust, and by far the majority of managers are men. Nursing has become a profession in its own right, although the new structure of the nursing profession means that male nurses tend to rise to higher managerial positions than women. What has been lost is an area unique to the hospital in terms of space in which women are only with other women, men with other men. From the 1960s it was generally assumed that integration, mixed-sex wards and so forth were a desirable goal and a sign of progress. Patients' accounts, however, suggest another interpretation. Not having to interact constantly with members of the other sex was seen by many women as a positive advantage to being in Severalls.

5

ON THE FEMALE SIDE

Much Madness is divinest Sense –
To a discerning Eye –
Much Sense – the starkest Madness –
'Tis the Majority
In this, as All, prevail –
Assent – and you are sane –
Demur – you're straightway dangerous –
And handled with a Chain –
                    Emily Dickinson (1830–1886)

The spatial division of Severalls by gender meant the men and women who lived and worked there led very separate lives. For the women this arguably meant the creation and reinforcement of patriarchal, Victorian ideals of femininity. The laundry and needle-room were located on this side, and many women patients worked in them. There were few opportunities for women patients to work outdoors in 'public' areas, as male patients did on the farms and gardens. There were far fewer opportunities for women to play games and sports outdoors; until latter years the provision for exercise for women patients was generally performed indoors in gymnastics classes, or movement to music. Male patients, on the other hand, had opportunities to play football, cricket, bowls, and many were members of teams and inter-hospital leagues. As in the outside world, women's activities were more confined to the 'private' realm of indoor space. Yet, paradoxically, this confined space meant that women patients and staff inhabited a place that was almost entirely and exclusively female, and for many women this provided shelter, protection and 'asylum' from an outside world in which violence and abuse by men could be, and often had been, terrifying. Moreover, this uniquely female space offered the chance to establish, maintain and reinforce friendships between women, both among patients and among staff.

ADMISSIONS AND REASONS FOR COMING
TO SEVERALLS

Women came to Severalls as patients for many reasons. Whatever the original causes of their anxieties, sorrows, manias and griefs, once they entered they became by definition pathological, ill, and not to be credited with powers of reason or judgement. To be seen as 'cured' or 'relieved' and gain the possibility of freedom meant being 'good' and 'normal' – as defined by ideals of womanhood laid down by psychiatrists and administrators, and as observed and noted by nurses. A woman patient who wanted to work in carpentry or on one of the farms would have been seen, by definition, as transgressive, more pathological than she already was by virtue of being certified as mad.

Many women came only for short periods, needing simply a chance to recover from extreme stress, often exhaustion, in their domestic lives. Many came because they simply could not cope in difficult circumstances any longer and, once rested, fed and relaxed, would be discharged from the hospital. One woman I spoke to, for example, was admitted to Severalls in the 1930s after her second set of twins was born, eleven months apart, when she already had ten children. Her husband was a fisherman who could often only get one or two days' work a week; they eked out a living on sprats. 'I just couldn't go on any longer,' she told me, but she was discharged after a few weeks and returned to her family. Others, however, had nowhere or nobody to return to or, by the time they were admitted, were in such a bad state that rehabilitation became unlikely; it was these women who made up Severalls' long-stay population.

Case notes suggest these were common reasons for women's entry to Severalls. One woman, for example, was admitted in the 1940s covered in bruises; she was an army wife 'with marital difficulties'. Her diagnosis was 'depression' and she received ECT, with little improvement. To be a battered wife rendered you liable to certification as mad. Another young woman was certified for nearly fifty years; the certificate read: 'She lies in bed gazing vacantly before her. She would not answer simple questions or carry out simple commands. On occasions she volunteers the information: "The Mother of God has put her in a trance".' Year after year a medical report reiterates 'she is in a state of catatonic stupor. She is mute.' She was diagnosed as catatonic schizophrenic. The father told the social worker his daughter was normal, a splendid scholar, but left school at 14 to care for her father and three brothers after their mother died. She was religious and in good health. One summer evening after supper she suddenly 'turned funny' and did not know anyone. She went stiff and mute and the father could not think of anything in particular that precipitated the attack. In the 1950s she was given a bilateral frontal leucotomy. Later she was given Largactil. Little change occurred. After she died in

128

the 1980s, a brother came and explained that she had been raped prior to admission, although the notes did not indicate by whom. After she was certified, the family pretended she had never existed.

Others were certified for bearing illegitimate children, undoubtedly some as a result of rape: the shame of both rape and illegitimacy for families was huge until the 1960s; psychiatrists were still admitting teenage girls who bore illegitimate children into the 1950s. A woman who worked in the laundry in the 1920s remembered:

> And we had one patient, she come from Hackney Wick and she – she was the favourite. When she was mental, she was terrible, when she really went off. But – otherwise – she was full of Cockney wit. She gave us all a name. And my name was Brown – she said I was a boy. And my friend, she called her Charles. And her history, we found out, was that she was jilted and had an illegitimate child, and it turned her brain. It did a lot, in those days. We used to take her out. They even brought her to my wedding – and several of the others, several of the others that were able, they brought to my wedding.

But married women who suffered post-natal depression or puerperal psychosis were also liable to lose their children. One woman who came into Severalls in the early 1960s said:

> I got married at 17 and had me daughter at 24. I had a breakdown after I had her because I found out he was carrying on with some-body else, and he wouldn't turn back. And through that I became very ill and depressed, and through that I wasn't capable of looking after me daughter. They thought at first it was just depression after having the daughter, but I'm not – I'm a manic-depressive. When they took her, they said I could have her back. But then they said, no, I wasn't really well enough – I was all right to live in the outside world, but not to have her.
>
> Severalls was a different world. When I was depressed and ill I didn't wanna go far, and I was quite happy there in my own way. I didn't have to do anything I didn't wanna do, did I? Or go anywhere I didn't wanna go. I could go out in the grounds, walk round, sit in the sun, go in what you call the tea bar, have a cup of tea or do the work that I did there. I spent ten years in hospital. Then after that I couldn't take her back because he'd remarried, and she'd got two sisters and I couldn't take her away from them. But in my own mind, I never forgot her. She's over 30 now. Last time I saw her was when she was 12.

In 1967 a mother and baby unit was finally set up at Myland Court, the acute unit. Women suffering puerperal psychosis or post-natal depression could come in with their babies. Babies would be cared for by the nurses, but given regular contact with the mothers until such time as they were again able to bond with and care for their infants. Valerie Moody described the mother and baby unit to me:

> I was the sister on Myland Court East when the mother and baby unit opened. Well, officially there were four beds in the mother and baby area. It was a sort of – a separate little wing, really. And there were four beds, and ideally we were meant to have four cots with a small kitchen – for preparing the foods and a little steriliser, you know, this sort of thing at the end. And of course their own bathroom and so on they had. And – but quite often we had to have an extra cot. We have had as many as six babies, but really that was too many. Their stay was fairly short – I would say about five or six weeks. Well, of course it would depend how long the consultant thought it was likely to be, you know, because obviously it wouldn't really have been suitable to have toddlers, for instance, tearing around where there are disturbed patients. I mean, you just couldn't allow that.

One woman told me how she suffered from post-natal depression after each occasion of her three children's births; she felt she had a much closer bonding with the third child, who was in the mother and baby unit with her:

> When I had my first baby I was quite young and quite naïve really, but everyone took it quite on the chin, had their babies did this that and the other, and I went inward, and started to have post-natal depression. I was in the hospital about ten days and I started to have problems so they shipped me out to Severalls. When they sent me away I didn't have my baby with me, they took my baby away from me, I mean my baby was only two weeks old, I mean it was dreadful. I was in Severalls for about three months without my baby. I was only 19.
>
> We were all in a long corridor with a fire in the middle and our beds were on the side, we didn't have separate bedrooms or anything. There were quite a lot of frightening people there – a lot of people that were elderly, screaming at night and, you know, people with large heads, all the sort of freaky type of people that

were always locked away from human sight. I was always very frightened I think, because at night there was always quite a lot of foreign staff and it was a power struggle, they had a lot of power over you. It wasn't a friendly place. I was just another patient. They didn't talk to you, they just sort of gave you medicine. There was quite a lot of stealing. 'All right,' the doctor said, 'you've got to do this that and the other', but it's usually the people that weren't really qualified that had the say, and you were subjected to their whims and feelings, you know.

They said to my husband, 'Well, don't give her another baby for another three years!' Baby-machines! My husband had a terrible temper, he lost his temper quite a lot. My husband was hitting me on and off, you know, it was quite horrible. Then he left me. He made me pregnant again two years to the day, almost, and left me. And I stayed in a holiday home with no toilet, no running water – and I was pregnant and, you know, I had a toddler and then my husband came back again and he found me another – awful – place to live in. He was away a lot of the time – God knows what he was doing.

When my second child was born, blow me if I didn't have another post-natal depression! This time I was put in Myland Court – that was a set-up – oh God! A very frightening place. It was a big Victorian sort of building, lots of corridors, dark corners. You just didn't know what was going to happen, who you'd meet, you know, who you were going to see next or if somebody was going to commit suicide – or what.

When I had my third child the whole attitude sort of changed. There was a mother and baby unit then, although the rest of it in Myland Court was exactly the same. We still sat round in circles with the smell of urine and everything else. The night nurses, the hate they had for you, was still there. And I remember somebody watched me breastfeed, and I said, 'What do you think I'm going to do, throw him at you or something?' They'd never seen this before, someone breastfeeding their baby, because everyone had bottles and let the nurses feed their babies, and you know, it was a funny situation.

Many women were admitted because they were confused as part of a physical illness, or simply could not cope with the problems of old age and poverty. There was, for instance, a convalescent ward for many years where female patients lived who had very little wrong with them

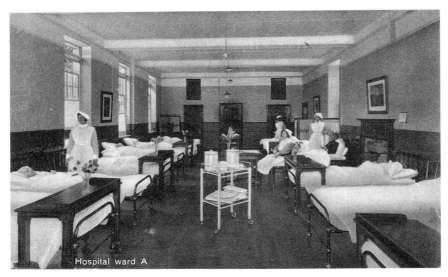

Figure 5.1 Ward A, female side, *circa* 1930
Source: North East Essex Mental Health NHS Trust

in psychiatric terms. Chronic patients who were physically ill or infirm were put in the infirmary ward, where they were confined to their beds both day and night.

Childhood sexual abuse was quite probably a frequent cause of women's depressions, anxieties and illnesses. Freudian theory and psychiatric practice, however, defined all women's claims of sexual abuse as 'fantasy', and such memories and claims were totally dismissed by psychiatrists until very recently; indeed, many psychiatrists still dismiss them as a case of 'false memory syndrome'. One of the women I interviewed had memories of being abused as a child, but the psychiatrists dismissed these as irrelevant. A nurse who trained at Severalls in the late 1970s described some of the women on a long-stay ward in which she worked during the early 1980s:

> Some of them had been in thirty years or more. Two of them, two very different ladies, had actually come in after childbirth. When you read back in the notes, it looks like it could have been a post-natal problem which was never recognised, you know, maybe in the fifties or early sixties, they were post-natally depressed or something like that. They were quite a mixed bunch really. I mean, there were some that were completely mad in a very lay sense of the word. There was no real contact.

132

I'll give you an example of one lady who I think has probably died now. She and I actually got on extremely well. She was very paranoid. She wasn't paranoid all the time, she was paranoid some-times, and she wouldn't eat if she was paranoid. We had to assume that was because she felt we might be poisoning her, because she didn't verbalise any of it.

When she was paranoid what we used to do was to make her jam sandwiches and leave them behind the curtain. So that then she would find it and eat it. So if she'd found it, it was all right. But other times her paranoia became rather manic and she'd march up and down, and then she wouldn't eat either, and you'd just hold her out a jam sandwich to take as she passed, and she'd march up and down eating her jam sandwich. And while she was marching up and down she'd be singing. Singing like, 'She loves a lady' and all sorts of little songs all mingled up together. And other times she'd be mumbling under her breath things like, 'We don't take other's children, do we? Do you like matches, nurse? What about your shoes then?' A load of absolute rubbish. But if you listened to her long enough, there was something there.

And there was another lady who, when you first met her, I mean she'd say, she'd ask you all about yourself, 'Got any brothers? Where's your mum live?' She wanted to know all this, and you'd think, 'Oh, there's nothing wrong with her! She sounds all right – what's wrong with her? What's she doing up here?' And then she'd start on about, 'Of course, when I worked for Mr Sainsbury, he told me I could eat the buns because I'm not diabetic, you know', but she was diabetic as hell! And so there was – not until you touched on the bit that was paranoid did you get it. She was blind, or almost blind, and she'd got like huge elephantine legs. And she was lovely, too.

There was a huge assumption that it was all too late. I think quite a lot of them, if they'd had intervention early enough, need never have become as mad as I experienced them. I think the probability is that a large number of them were abused. You know, with all the stuff that's coming out now about abuse, and the frequency of abuse in the population, I would guess that what we were seeing were other ways of being in the world for very painful experienced people. I have no doubt. I think they had retreated into total madness. They'd found somewhere else to be.

CLOTHING AND IDENTITY

It is axiomatic that the clothes we choose to wear form part of our sense of self and identity; clothes provide clues and signs to others as to how we wish to be seen and regarded, and are an integral part of our subjectivity and identity. For women, presentation of self by means of clothing and make-up has long been considered a vital way in which femininity and identity are constructed. In Severalls, however, all women (and men) wore uniform clothing until 1960; personal clothing and belongings were removed on admission. This was one of the principal ways in which an individual sense of identity was removed upon admission, and an institutional identity of 'patient' imposed; Goffman (1961) and Barton (1959) both drew attention to the deleterious effects of uniform clothing on patients. When Russell Barton became physician superintendent of Severalls in 1960, allowing patients their own clothing was one of his first priorities in reforming the hospital.

Until then, however, regulation hospital clothing was ordered in bulk or made by patients in the needle-room. In 1923, for instance, 600 women's calico bed-gowns were ordered and twelve dozen woven knickers. In the

Figure 5.2 Women patients arranging flowers, *circa* 1950
Source: North East Essex Mental Health NHS Trust

1950s more effort was made to provide varied clothing, but women patients still wore the same basic dresses and coats, albeit in different colours and patterns. Bras and corsets were not issued, and patients had to wear 'open drawers' until the late 1950s. A woman who was a patient from the 1940s remembered:

> Used to have to wear hospital clothes. Wasn't no choice. Used to have workin' dresses. They were all right – striped and short sleeves. They'd go right over you. You'd take your clothes off an' just put it right on. All the same they were. Like plus-fours, the dresses were! I didn't like the drawers we had to wear. I used to save up and get me own. Never used to have a bra! You had to buy your own. If you was in a locked ward you used to go without. We had to stick our clothes under our pillow when I first came. Under our pillows. An' we never used to have wash-bags. Used to have to wash with Severalls soap. Carbolic soap. It wasn't very nice.

'Strong clothing', used for patients who were prone to tear their clothes, was worn until 1953. The following is an account by a woman who worked as a nurse in the 1930s:

> Many patients used to tear their clothes to ribbons, so there were special thick twill dresses for them to wear – also bedding made in the same material. 'Strong clothing' it was called. For ladies who stripped off all their clothes we had special all-in-one suits tied at the back. We called them 'bunny suits' because they had feet in and trousers. One time I got into trouble. There were some visitors, and this patient was outside in one of the huts. I showed the visitor out, and the patient, was still in her strong clothes, and, of course, the visitors were never allowed to see the patients in strong clothes! We dressed them up for visitors!

The dresses patients wore were all made to the same pattern, although not always of the same material. Underclothes were made of strong calico, and all their shoes were identical, black with one bar, and were made in the hospital. The uniformity and harshness of hospital clothing constantly reminded patients of their loss of status, freedom and identity. Even sanitary towels were part of hospital regulation clothing, as a woman who worked in the laundry in the 1920s recalled:

> Sanitary towels of course, we used to make our own with towelling. And the patients, they wore – made in the sewing-room with old

sheets. And of course they all come down to be washed. And they had big – in the foul laundry – they had big tanks, and they used the – 'diapers' as they called them, were all put in there, tipped in there from bags, and they were covered up and they would be soaking in cold water. And then they were taken out and put in the machines and boiled, and they all had to go through the colander. All of them. There was nothing easy. Nothing disposable at all.

When the new matron came in 1957, she was shocked to discover some of the practices still extant on the female side:

Oh, the clothing was backward! And that was partly to do with a lady on the committee who rather felt that they must have open nightdresses and open-back dresses and all the rest of it. She thought all the old people would be incontinent all the time.

And when I first came all had chamber-pots, and I got rid of those pretty quickly! And, you know, the staff were a bit horrified then. I had to do it very carefully, because they said, 'Oh, what are we going to do?' I said, 'Well, take them to the lavatory when they want to go!' But once it got going nobody ever complained. I mean, we still kept the stalls for those who really were disabled and couldn't walk. We had to do that. But all of the chamber-pots went.

When I first went I was responsible for the ward maids also, and for the sewing-room and the laundry. I used to visit the sewing-room, the laundry – and I was horrified one day in the laundry! Something that had absolutely – well, I'd not thought about it – and this was 1957! But I found that the patients still had home-made sanitary towels. And when I was shown these in the laundry, I just couldn't believe it.

In the 1960s Russell Barton arranged for local shops to bring selections of clothing to the main hall from which patients could choose and buy their own clothes. Relatives sometimes brought clothing, although this could lead to problems, as Russell Barton remembered:

When I came the ladies were all forced to wear aprons in case they got their clothes dirty. At one time or other a woman was wearing a dress with a cigarette burn in it. A relative came in, 'That's not her dress! I gave that dress to so-and-so!' Now, I remember that, and she made a huge fracas about it. The result was the nursing staff tended to keep the possessions of the individuals out of the wards and never to issue the clothes in case they issued the wrong one and there'd be all this fuss. I changed that. In fact, a woman who was a member of the management committee – active on the Coop, got in a lot of beautiful cases that they had in tailors' shops, with drawers and stuff. The tradesmen who did it refused to have the patients into the place to see the clothes.

Not just patients wore uniforms, of course. The entire staff had some form of uniform that identified their particular role in the hospital; domestic maids, laundry maids and nurses were carefully distinguished by colour of uniform, attendants first wore military-style uniforms, then dark serge suits and, later, white coats. Doctors also wore white coats. Estate staff and kitchen staff also had their own uniform. Domestics and nurses wore starched caps, starched aprons, black cotton stockings, flat-heeled black shoes, and long fully lined dresses. Nurses wore bleached aprons, but laundry maids' and domestics' aprons were unbleached. Different uniforms give messages of hierarchy and order as well as role and occupation. One of the major changes in staff–patient relations was the phasing out of nurses' uniforms in the 1980s. This blurred the boundary between 'them' and 'us', 'mad' and 'sane', patient and nurse, and arguably facilitated more humanitarian relationships between patients and nursing staff.

WARD ROUTINES AND EXPERIENCES

Wards were by no means identical. Long-stay patients with few, if any, symptoms, usually lived in one or two villas from where they went out to work in the needle-room or laundry or, in later years, industrial units or kitchen. For a while these villas had an open-door policy in the 1930s. Yet even in later years, wards varied significantly according to whether they were designated short-stay, long-stay, geriatric or secure, as this woman, a patient off and on from the 1960s, remembered:

A lot depended which ward you were on. One ward I was on which was – I would call it semi-locked – and it was mainly old incontinent women. So there was one bath night a week and there were three baths. And everyone sort of queued up and had a bath and got a towel sort of dabbed at them, and off they went again. On one of these occasions they tried to get me to go in someone else's bath water. And I might have been mad, but I was still rather particular! And I threw a wobbly and it got quite, quite heated. This was years ago, back in the seventies I think. And I just refused point blank to get in this water. And on that ward as well the toilets only had half doors, so they could see people's feet and heads. It didn't upset me greatly, because I was too ill.

Those suffering from TB and other infectious diseases were kept separate. Acute patients were separated from long-stay and refractory patients. Epileptics lived together in huge wards, as a woman who began work as a nurse in 1936, remembered:

> The first ward I worked on was horrific: an epileptic ward with at least a hundred patients milling around. The noise was unbelievable – women shouting, fighting and cursing each other. There were some wandering around with draw sheets tied round their necks because they dribbled so much – their mouths wide open – not a pretty sight. The dormitory was huge with four rows of beds and side-rooms along three sides of the room. The beds were only about a foot high for safety reasons, as all these people were prone to have fits at any time. The most difficult patients slept in the side-rooms – what a fight it was to push some of them in and get out quickly enough to get the door locked on them!
>
> I was taken to the charge nurse who told me to go and clean the baths. I asked where were they? She just yelled at me and said she had better things to do than show new nurses around. Somebody took pity on me and showed me the bathroom and produced all the cleaning materials. Later a patient fell down and had an epileptic fit, and one of the nurses went to the cupboard and when the patient came round, she said, 'Here you are. Down the backs!'[1] A clean pair of pants to go and change herself! I was called to help with the teas. What a shock! Two thick slices of bread and margarine and an enamel mug of tea poured from a very large urn. I helped to feed some patients and then assisted another nurse hold down patients who refused to eat. These were force-fed with a sop made up of the bread and tea all mixed up.
>
> We then had to clean up, wash the tables and clean up all the mess on the floor and count all the spoons. By the time this was all done, medication given and all taken to the toilets, it was time to start getting them ready for bed. Most of them had to be undressed by us. What a struggle that was! I was undressing this patient to put her to bed and she was going, 'Oh my head! My head!' And I called another nurse, and I said, 'She's got a bad head'. 'Oh, don't take any notice,' she said, 'she's always like that.'

From the early 1960s epileptics ceased to be thought of as 'mentally ill' in the way they once had. New drugs on the market from this time meant many epileptics were able to live and work in the outside world. Until that time, however, they were one of the main groups confined to mental hospitals.

There were often outbreaks of typhoid in Severalls, even in the 1960s. Diphtheria, dysentery, scarlet fever and severe influenza were also endemic problems, and patients suffering these were kept isolated from others. Refractory patients were also kept separate, usually in 'back' wards never, or rarely, visited by commissioners or local worthies, as this nurse, who worked at Severalls in the 1930s, remembered:

> Here it could be rough and tough most of the time. Most patients were really violent, and one had to remember never to let anyone creep up on you from the back. Many a time you could be attacked for no reason at all, and end up on the floor with legs and arms flailing in all directions. Windows were smashed almost every day. We spent a lot of time sweeping up glass.
>
> Most of the patients here were up and dressed all day. We kept them fairly quiet with paraldehyde, which was a most foul smelling medicine, but most patients came to love it and became addicted to it. Quite a few had to be cared for in the side-rooms and padded rooms. I will never forget the first time I saw the patient in one of the pads. She just had a sheet over her shoulders – no other clothes, and when she was wet or soiled we just changed the sheet. She never moved and was fixed in a crouched position.
>
> At times we had outbursts of violence and had to call in the help of several staff. We often had our clothes torn from us, and it could be a hard time to get the patient in a side-room or the pads. Then there was the afternoon for the giving of enemas. We spread a sheet on the floor and on it put all these rubber chamber-pots, gave the enemas, and had the patient on the pot. Often these were emptied all over us. I did get used to this ward, but was not at all sorry to leave it.

When patients became violent, the main solution for nursing was to seclude them in padded rooms. Here a woman who worked in the laundry in the 1920s describes her impressions of seeing women in padded rooms:

> I used to have to go round for different things to the wards and I used to take great notice of what the nurses were doing. There would be sometimes up to ten or twelve nurses on duty on some

of the wards. When the patients got very violent, and they'd tear everything and do a lot of damage, and they had no option but to put them in these padded cells.

They'd got padded walls, but everything was padded like – like you'd get a settee or a chair, and they padded with in those days, oilcloth stuff with buttons in, holding it down. Otherwise they'd tear it. And the door had a peep-hole in it like a prison door, because if they were very bad you couldn't open the door, not anybody, unless there was three or four nurses open the door, because they'd spring at the door.

And the patients were dressed in strong clothes, or naked, because if you put them in the strong clothes – they were the strait-jackets – with the arms tied up. They were using those because otherwise if they could use their arms they ripped everything. And they even ripped these strong things. We had them come down the laundry in ribbons. The mental illness – the strength they had!

Befriending patients was not considered essential, or even desirable, until well after the Second World War. Cruelty, of course, was always taboo, and if reported would result in instant dismissal, yet it is worth remembering that definitions of cruelty can change and vary, and what may seem cruel by our standards now would have been regarded as appropriate fifty or sixty years ago, as the following extract from a nurse who worked both in the 1930s and the 1960s suggests:

I can't remember any cruelty going on at all. As I said, we had to be so careful we didn't bruise or do any injury to them. But I'm afraid, to tell the truth, we rather looked down on patients. Because when I went back to nursing in 1962, as I said, we were friends with patients. We loved them. We called them by their Christian names and we took them in presents, and they were people.

But in the days of Severalls in the 1930s, they were just patients. They weren't part of the human race somehow. I cannot remember a nurse making a fuss or putting her arm round a patient. When we used to hand-feed them I can't remember saying, 'Come on, love, this is nice. Try it. Have a mouthful,' or anything like that. It was, 'Eat it!' I suppose we treated them almost as if they were inferior.

We used to get the old people up and just sit them in chairs where they'd be all day, except when you carted them off to have a meal. It never occurred to me to think, 'Oh, you poor love, sitting there doing nothing all day.' We just took it for granted – or at least, I did. But I think it was a general thing.

Ward routine followed a set pattern for years. Patients rose at 7 a.m. Their breakfast – during the inter-war years – consisted of a pint of coffee, cocoa or tea, porridge and bread and margarine. On Wednesdays and Saturdays they had tinned fish or sausages instead of porridge. Women always received less than the men. The privileged few who had jobs to go to in the Laundry and needle-room would be taken there at 8:25. Some would work in the ward, scrubbing and waxing and polishing (known as bumping). The others, those who had no work, would sit around the ward until at 10:15, rain or shine, the doors were unlocked to the airing court, in which they could circle in a small area surrounded by ditches and railings, for exactly one hour and fifteen minutes. Dinner was always at 12:45. Mutton, corned beef, Irish stew, fish, boiled rabbit, and pea soup were standard fare. These were served with potatoes and a vegetable – unless it was a stew day. A hot pudding followed: rice pudding with jam, rice and rhubarb, date, fig or raisin pudding, plain boiled pudding, bread pudding, fruit or rhubarb pudding or tart. At 2:30 another hour and a quarter in the airing courts took place. Tea was at 5:30 seven days of the week. For this they received one pint of tea, bread and margarine and three times a week, 3 oz of cake. They were also allocated 2 oz of jam each a week. For supper they had oatmeal biscuits or bread and either Oxo or coffee to drink.

For years, because of staff shortages on the female side, patients were dosed up with paraldehyde and put to bed at 7:30 p.m. In the summer, this meant some three hours spent in bed while it was still light. In winter the rigid routine was broken by Christmas. In summer, there was Sports Day and, for some, trips to Clacton. Film night was special, and so were dances. Occupational therapy was available from the late 1920s, but a shortage of staff, swelling patient numbers and chronic underfunding meant only a few benefited from this. The space patients inhabited was incredibly small. Body rhythms were controlled by outside routine and medication. A woman who worked in the Severalls laundry in the 1920s and 1930s, and returned again in the 1950s, remembered how patients were bathed and what she perceived as cruelty by the nurses:

Each ward had a day when they bathed the patients. And they had big bathrooms, and the patients used to have to go down with their nurses to the bathroom, and they all carried a bath sheet. And I went in and had a look one day, when I was supposed to be getting back to the laundry! I knew the nurses well and they said, 'Well, come and have a look.'

So I went in there. And as they went in, all they'd got was a dress on, a dress on, and they sort of – that was taken off and they were put under showers, poor souls, and there they were with all the water running down over their hair and everything else. And the nurses had big sponges and they did sponge them down after a fashion, but they weren't all that fussy about going in certain places, because sometimes they weren't all that clean, you know. And then they wrapped themselves in these bath sheets and dried themselves as best they could, or the nurses helped them best they could – a bit on the rough side, some of them.

It wasn't all, you know, as it should be. I saw rough handling in patients. 'Oh, we've got this lot to do,' you know. I mean, there was about I don't know how many on a ward – fifty, something like that. They've got a job to do, I know. But they didn't handle them gently. I've seen them pull them by their hair and all that sort of thing. And with their – if they can't get their arms, pull their arms. I've seen them slap them and all that. Seen all that. And you didn't say anything about it, that was all taken for granted.

Undoubtedly from 1960 onward enormous changes took effect in the whole hospital. Working conditions for staff by this time were better than in the past; the unions had achieved substantial gains in shortening hours, improving wages and conditions. Russell Barton sought to instil, above all, new attitudes to patients and patient care. Conditions in the wards and daily life of patients improved in many ways, although undoubtedly this varied from ward to ward, and certainly conditions seem to have deteriorated again in the 1970s. The next extract is from a woman who spent many years in and out of Severalls from the 1960s:

The first year I was in about eleven months. The next two years I was doing the revolving-door bit – in/out, in/out. In the seventies I was on a long-stay ward and very withdrawn. And I used to go down to the library and hang around the library every time they were open. And eventually the librarian found out that I didn't go anywhere, I was just on the ward. And she was very annoyed about this, because she felt I needed some stimulus. So she put her tuppence in – her twelvepence in – or whatever was necessary! And I was allocated to the industrial unit.

Work in the industrial units made a great difference to patients, giving them a sense of usefulness and self-respect. Untrained care assistants often worked with small groups of patients and in many cases were able to stimulate conversation, trust and interest both between patients and between patients and staff, as the woman patient quoted above explained:

You were divided into tables, and each table had a nurse or a care assistant. My care assistant was Kay, she was Scottish. She was an absolute poppet. Swore like a trooper, probably drank like one as well! And smoked like a chimney. She was everything a good carer – in apostrophes – shouldn't be ! But she was so strong that she made our table into quite a good group, a healing group, and she got us communicating with each other. I thought she was terrific. She's now dead, but I think she was in her sixties then.

She found out from me that I wasn't taking my medication, and she said, 'What are you going to do with that?' I said, 'What do you think?' you know, 'Don't be such a bloody fool!' she said, 'You let me have it.' And she talked me into handing over a big plastic bag, like a sandwich bag, full of tablets that I'd saved up. There was enough to kill the whole table, let alone just me! She talked me into giving them over to her. But I made a condition that she wasn't to tell on me. So she was in a very invidious sort of posi-tion. But she took a chance on that. And then she said, 'are you going to start taking your tablets?' I said, 'No.' She said, 'Well, bring them down to me every morning. I'll remove them a day at a time instead of a month at a time.' And that's what we did for the rest of the time I was on that unit.

Increasingly, after 1960, previously abrupt and dismissive treatment of patients by nursing staff gave way to a more enlightened and humani-tarian pattern of care; as a result, nurses came to play an increasingly therapeutic, rather than custodial, role:

On the whole the nursing staff were extremely supportive. In some cases, very loving, would go to terrific lengths to support or stimulate me or whatever. And there was one in particular, gave up her, her day off, and took me to Felixstowe for the day. There was one nurse, a male nurse, who took great delight in twisting my arm up behind my back when I was trying to do a runner. And he was a vicious piece of goods. I wasn't the only one who complained about him. There was another male nurse who could divert me from running by making me laugh. There were some nurses who took the time to cuddle me, to sit with me. One day I was trying to rip my face apart and they just got me, somehow, into a chair, and they just sat and stroked my arms until I calmed down. I can remember that so clearly, it was so calm. And – and they were very forgiving. I think I was probably at my worst at the changeover of shifts, the disturbance with changing the shifts, which is three times in twenty-four hours. I was frightened at those times.

I know one evening I started to blow and tried to break a window. And there were a couple of nurses on who knew me fairly well, and the nurse in charge said, 'Oh, I'll ring the doctor.' And they said, 'No, give her half an hour.' And they got me away from the window and they sat me in a chair, and I was trying to tear my face out. And they got hold of my hand. They sat on my feet. They held my hand and talked. I can remember them sitting close to me, holding me. I can remember the – the wanting to tear myself apart and them holding me so I couldn't. They were protecting me. They were caring for me. And I never did need an injection that time, because they had the time to just hold me, with their own body contact. I can only remember hearing their voices and feeling them close to me and holding hands – just gradually easing me.

Few patients I interviewed felt that doctors played a central role in their healing process. Doctors were seen rarely and for very short periods of time, usually just to adjust or change medication. Increasingly from the 1960s there was a division between psychiatrists who embraced a bio-medical model of hospital care-cum-medication, and others who, although reliant on drug therapy in many cases, sought to introduce and implement other therapies that would hopefully lead to rehabilitation in the wider world. Here the patient quoted above discusses her feelings about doctors:

Doctors were very frightening, some of them. They were remote. There was one I liked immensely. If I asked him a question, he would answer it. And there was one episode where in review he had his registrar with him, and in review he suggested I went and had my hair cut and washed. I must have looked a bit witch-like, I think. Well, at that time, I was absolutely phobic for having my hair or neck touched, and I threw a wobbly and smashed a window.

And the registrar slapped me to try and calm me down. And my doctor said, 'You don't do that to my patients!' And then he turned to me and said, 'It's all right. If you don't want it, you don't have to have it. Perhaps you could tell me why later.' End of episode. He was very calm. He was an ex-Auschwitz man, I believe. He certainly had a number on – on his arm. And that registrar became a consultant. And time after time they tried to put me under that consultant, and I said, 'No!'

There were two doctors I hated. There was the one who slapped my face, and I didn't trust that one, and I never have trusted that one. And the other one I've seen a couple of times since doesn't listen. I wouldn't take any medicine they prescribed. I wouldn't do any therapy they prescribed. So they gave up trying in the end, more or less gave me my pick of doctor.

There was one doctor, oh, he was terrible! He was African. Black as your skirt. And when I came back from the general ward after the overdose, my ears still buzzing with aspirin, he called me in to see him. And in this very very thick accent told me how sinful I'd been, and if I'd have died I'd have gone to hell, and what right have I to destroy the life God had given me? And he went on and on and on. And I saw him several times after that and he still took the same attitude. But then he – then he disappeared. That was in '86.

The trouble is, you see, the nurses would be with me for twenty-four hours a day, they'd get to know me, they'd accept when I was absolutely fighting mad if they could tickle my sense of humour, they'd somehow get me to cooperate, or if they gave me a cuddle or gave me some little sign that they considered me a person – they would get through to me. But the doctors would see me for ten minutes a week at the outside. Dr Jacobs got nearer to understanding me simply because he saw so much of me over the years. And he's sort of a rather slow grandfatherly type, and he's very laid-back.

WORK

Work by patients had always been seen as beneficial both to patients' well-being and to the economy of the hospital itself. Overcrowding and understaffing, however, meant that many women patients had nothing to do at all. Long-stay patients with no, or few, obvious disorders worked in the laundry and needle-room. Those more prone to outbursts of violence or disruption might work in the ward or scrubbing corridors. The following extract is from interviews with a woman who was a patient in Severalls from 1947 until the 1990s. She has never lived outside an institution since she was 5 years old:

I used to break a lot of windows at Essex Hall, so they sent me up here. I was certified. Didn't much like it, but you had to bear it. Wouldn't let you go out on your own. You had to have a nurse.

That was all railings when I first come. That was when the railings were up. I used to scrub-wax the floors. With a scrubber. That was hard work! Yes, on your hands an' knees. There weren't no buckets an' mops then, you had to do it on your hands an' knees. I scrubbed all the bathroom. Dust. We used to clean the floors every day, put some wax on 'em an' polish 'em. Heavy old deckers! Oh my goodness! We used to enjoy that. I like housework, long as nobody don't get in my way. Me and my friend used to do that. She was my mate. We was in Orchard and Ward C. She went to another hospital, near her parents. Her parents got her out. Probably she's not there now, probably she's passed away or somethin'. Don't know why she came here. We didn't want to talk about the past.

Finding ways for patients to spend time was an ongoing problem. Those who were ill and infirm spent most – often all – their time in bed. But those who were physically fit, and often full of manic energy that could easily slide into violence with frustration, inactivity and confinement, were more problematic. Many were both well and fit and had little to do; these were generally the women who worked in the laundry and needle-room. Patients who worked in the laundry or needle-room only worked there part of the day, and were designated as 'good' to be able to be there in the first place. Here a woman who began working in the laundry in the 1920s recalled her first day and some of the main aspects of laundry work at the time:

I had a shock on the first day. It was freezing cold in January. The laundry looked enormous to me. There were twenty-four girl staff, with a head laundress and sixty women patients. It was the duty of the 'last maid' as we were called, to fetch the patients from their various wards and villas at nine o'clock in the morning, and return them at dinner at twelve, and fetch them again at two o'clock and bring them back the laundry until four o'clock, and then we had to take them home.

I had to go out across the grounds to Chestnut Villa – it was mostly where the workers for the needle-room and the laundry were. It was a problem to keep them together in line. They were all counted in and out of the villa, so I would weave around them like a sheepdog, scared stiff I'd lost one or two. Some would slip in amongst the trees or lag behind. Though they were all big strong women, it wasn't often that they would harm any of the staff.

It was the duty of the laundry maid to go round the wards on Mondays to collect the weekly general soiled linen. And to do this we had to take four patients – strong ones – and a long heavy truck. And we had to go through the ward – day rooms, dormitories – to the soiled linen store at the 'backs', as they were called, which were the toilets. And this is where all the dirty linen was bundled up, in bundle-sheets, and tied up. The clothes were all wet and the stink was terrible in these wards, in the dirty wards. I couldn't stand the smell. I'd cover my mouth with my hanky to stop myself from retching.

We had a large bunch of keys round our waist because every door in the corridors and the wards was locked, and had to be unlocked. Even in the corridors there were intervening doors – all had to be unlocked as we progressed with this trolley and the four patients, which were so good and so helpful. And we had to lock it afterwards. If we defaulted it was then instant dismissal. No one wanted that, with two million unemployed waiting for every vacancy.

And there was the big, what we called the 'hydros' which was like a massive spin-drier, and they were huge. We used to have big wooden trolleys and they would have those come from the washing-machines all full of wet stuff, that was pulled out by patients, the strong patients. We didn't have to do that. And then the patients used to push the trolleys up to us on the hydros. We had to pack those. They were huge, 3 or 4 foot diameter, and used to get nearly a huge trolley full of wet stuff in, but they had to be packed evenly, so we had to do it. The patients didn't do it right.

That was my first job, filling them. And that was winter. And in the morning they'd been left overnight, full. In the morning they were frozen, and I, sometimes, my hands used to bleed trying to get them out, get the stuff out. There was no heat, only what comes from the machine. I went from there to the top of the laundry where there was a big room, and that was called the 'blanket room' and that was all bars – and that was heated. We liked that because you could go in there and have a warm. And that was to put things like from the – what they wore in the padded cells, the strong things.

And everything had to be shook out and put – several garments, all on to a frame, and that was wheeled to the colander. So the colander girls, there was four of us feeding in, four rollers, and two patients at the bottom taking the stuff out. And we used to feed in. And we stood on a platform, and behind we had this big rail with all the stuff ready, to get – so the sheets were laid so that we could just get a corner each. The other girl got a corner and I got a corner, and there was four of us feeding in sheets on that. So, and

147

you had to be careful because otherwise it tangled up. Patients used to take them off but patients weren't allowed anywhere where they could get fingers in or anything.

Women who worked on the female side worked hard and long hours for low wages. Yet for many, particularly during the inter-war years and the depression, the relatively secure work at Severalls was a godsend. This woman, for instance, was born locally and started work as a domestic at Severalls in 1932:

I slept in up there then. We all slept in, yes we all slept in. We had two days off a week, but we worked from — we were knocked up at half past five in the morning an' we were on duty at six. The first job I had we did the nurses' breakfasts — we used to go down in the big messroom an' lay all their breakfasts up. We used to serve their breakfast an' all that and after that was all done then all the chairs went up on the tables an' we had to clean the mess-room out — an' that was hard work then.

When I finished I was working for a Miss Lennox, she was assistant matron at Myland Court. And she had a flat over Myland Court — she had her bedroom upstairs and a sitting room and a spare bedroom. I used to sleep in that spare bedroom. And I used to cook — well there was three breakfasts, there was three of them to breakfast an' I used to cook their breakfasts. Midday meal used to come over in the van with the patients' dinners, their dinner used to come over — put that in the heat until they come in — and it got to half past one, well then I was relieved by the girl that was in the kitchen and she would finish it for me.

And five o'clock I had to get Miss Lennox's tea — tea on a tray — an' the evening meal I had to get a patient an' take her over from Myland Court right over to the centre an' right through to the big main kitchen an' with this big old basket an' a patient on one side of me — ever so creepy! We always had a patient come — well, to help me carry the basket. They used to send quite a — you know — decent one with me. I used to hate goin' — it was so creepy goin' over there that hour — well, it was *dark*.

And then of course in the morning when I come down I had to clear all that lot away — supper things — lay the breakfast up, cook the breakfast — an' after breakfast Miss Lennox went across from Myland Court into the matron's office, then I had to do her bedroom and sitting room an' bathroom and toilet an' all that — an' fires, yes

I had fires, I had two fires, one up and one down. Yes, I had the
fires to do. It was hard work!

If work was hard for women there – which it was – it is hard to imagine
what life must have been like for the thousands who were patients. For
many, of course, simply receiving three good meals a day and living in a
warm and dry place meant far better material conditions than they would
have experienced before or elsewhere. Poverty and mental illness were –
and arguably remain – close partners. To be incarcerated, however, with
dozens of other women, to have no privacy whatsoever, not even your
own clothes or belongings, undoubtedly reduced the majority of the patient
population to the worst sort of institutionalised behaviour. Subservient,
passive, deferential, often mute, in the late 1950s Russell Barton would
describe such behaviour as in itself an illness caused by mental hospital
regimentation.

Early on, however, attempts to provide occupational therapy were made;
in 1922 Dr Turnbull set up a special department to 'encourage work and
handicrafts of various kinds among the female patients'. Miss Smith was
engaged for six months. In 1923 a weaving-room was set up, and over
the years goods were sold from there. Only a small number of women,
however, could benefit from this facility. In 1926 Dr Turnbull put up a
notice on the female side

> The Medical Superintendent wishes to draw the attention of
> the Female Staff to the Instruction in Handicraft Work which
> has been started in connection with the Weaving Room. The
> Medical Superintendent is of the opinion that the teaching of
> Handicraft Instruction is likely to take a large part in the future,
> in the treatment of mental cases ... and that there will be good
> openings in the future for Nurses who have knowledge of
> handicrafts. Should any members of the Nursing Staff wish
> to take advantage of the opportunities offered, they should give
> their names to the Matron. The number of Nurses who can be
> so trained is necessarily limited, so that early application should
> be made.

Another woman was employed to help in 1927, and one of the nurses
had her wages increased that year to acknowledge her services in training
staff and patients in gymnastic exercises. In 1928 female patients gave a
display of gymnastics with the assistance of the hospital band. From
this time onwards, and throughout the 1930s, however, numbers of new
female admissions rose dramatically. Staffing on the female side became
problematic once more. The weaving-room was converted back into a
dormitory. In the early 1930s staff helped produce plays with patients as

149

Figure 5.3 The weaving room in Chestnut Villa, *circa* 1930
Source: North East Essex Mental Health NHS Trust

actors, and gymnastics continued to be taught by one woman, though again, probably only a very small number of patients had such facilities.

From 1939 both financial and staffing problems were severe. All that was not essential was cut. Sports stopped altogether (this occurred nationally, too, of course), although one handicraft mistress remained. After the war, facilities were reintroduced when and where possible, but a combination of overcrowding, understaffing and underfunding, which hit the female side hardest, meant substantial changes were hard to implement. In 1948 four handicraft huts were built. In 1949 a male occupational therapist was appointed on the male side, and Mrs Doreen Hamze was appointed as head occupational therapist on the female side. In 1953 the first television sets for patients' viewing were set up in the hall, and over the next few years further sets were installed in wards. Television undoubtedly had a huge impact on ward life and routine; although a passive activity, at least it offered idle and bored patients a chance of both entertainment and information.

A woman who came to work as an occupational therapist at Severalls in 1957 gave this account:

> Mrs Hamze was a very kind sort of person really, but talked the hind leg off a donkey – and walked at a rate of knots! There was just Mrs Hamze and two other women who had started before me, so there were just the four of us. After that we gradually got more staff.

150

Weaving – that was about the state of occupational therapy when I arrived. There were rug looms, looms of every shape and size, and there used to be one patient there who was absolutely superb at it. She was a paranoid-schizophrenic, and would blast off at us every so often, but she was really in her element weaving. We had to collect patients from the wards. Patients who came to weaving were mostly from the admission ward, which was then Ivy Villa. Of course, all that's gone.

When we got a few more of us there we started work on some of what they called the refractory wards, where there were very disturbed patients – if you weren't careful you got things thrown at you. Nobody would tackle them, so we had to try and get something going on there.

OT was basically craft work in those days – simple things, like sewing, painting, or toy-making. You had one pair of scissors attached to a macramé cord, and you wouldn't let them out of your sight, you know – this had been drummed into us at college. You had to be careful with knitting needles – otherwise they'd be used for the wrong purposes!

We talked with the patients, oh yes, although you'd try and not collaborate with their delusions. We'd try to interest them in the normality of things – take them out in the gardens – there were still railings up, of course. We'd go out in the garden and perhaps play ball games, you know, have exercise sessions and things like that.

From the 1940s there was increasing concern nationally about the condition of mental hospitals in Britain generally and reformers like Duncan Macmillan and David Clark sought to implement humanitarian reforms in mental hospitals. Ward doors were opened, leisure and work facilities improved for patients where possible, some experimented with therapy, group therapy and therapeutic communities. In Severalls, however, few such reforms occurred at this time. Not until the mid-1950s did staff come who wanted to – and were in a powerful enough position to – begin to implement reforms. Ruth Clark was one such person. She began work as Severalls' new matron in 1957. Trained as a general nurse, mental nurse and midwife, she had worked both as a sister tutor and an assistant matron in other hospitals. This was her account of her first impression of Severalls:

Oh dear! I thought, well, there's an awful lot to do! Because it was backward. The medical superintendent was a very nice gentleman, very charming, but he was getting towards retiring age, and of course I presume that was why he had not kept up with the times. And mental hospitals were changing then.

You know Myland Court? Well, half the ward were patients who really need not have been there at all, but, I suppose, had nowhere to go, or their relatives didn't want them. Because this is what happened so much in the old days. They went in – and there they stayed. And I said, 'Couldn't they have an open door?' And he readily agreed that we try it. And then later, on one of the geriatric wards, I thought, well, they'll never run away! And so I suggested it again. And after a bit, he said, 'Yes, we'll try that.' So, had he stayed, I think, in time, we would have gone ahead a bit more. I know Dr Barton takes the credit for all the open wards, but we had just started before he came. Mr Hooton had been there about eighteen months when I went, and had had some of the wards upgraded a bit in that short time.

The patients who could have worked, were not working. They were just sitting around all day doing nothing. And apart from the nurses looking after them, they were not helping them to do anything. You know, it was just a question of, 'Just sit where I put you!' and that was that.

The occupational therapist was there, but she – considering the number of patients, there were over 600 women when I went, and she didn't have very many out of that number. And the wards were so large. It was impossible for the staff to really do a lot on some of the wards.

Occupational therapy changed radically from 1960 when Russell Barton built the industrial units, set up the household management unit and brought in policies to get all patients working, whenever possible. The aim of occupational therapy then became rehabilitation and enhancement of existing skills rather than a means of just passing time or enjoying a leisure pursuit. The woman quoted previously, for instance, left in the early 1960s and then came back in 1966, when she noticed a marked difference:

Occupational Therapy by then had changed its face, and it wasn't just craft work. Staff were trying to encourage people to get back into the community really. Some went to household management, where they learned how to cook and look after themselves and shop and things like that. Then they developed a payment system to give patients some incentive to go to work.

Upstairs, opposite the laundry, we had all that area as an OT place. It was quite a big area with a veranda – it was the building that was bombed during the war. And there was a lot more going on then – we had a kitchen and we did cookery and art and all sorts of different crafts. We took them swimming. And then we went on the wards where people actually couldn't come to you.

FRIENDSHIPS AND RELATIONSHIPS

So much is written about 'the community' with regards to mental health, yet almost nothing is said about friendship. Friendship is not a topic that has interested researchers, politicians, psychiatrists or social workers. There was a veil of silence around the existence – and importance – of friendships at Severalls, despite the fact that one side of the hospital was exclusively inhabited by women. Here hundreds of women lived together – at very close quarters – day in, day out, often for years on end. Under the certification system, a member of a patient's family might petition for her to be removed from the hospital. A friend, however, could not do so. The woman cited earlier who had spent sixty-five years in institutions still expressed great sadness that her friend had left the hospital many years ago. When she left, nobody thought to tell her friend where she had gone to, what her address was, or suggest that they might be able to meet at some later date.

Even in later years, however, friendship was not considered important between patients. If they had no families, then they could be rehabilitated alone or in some nursing home or half-way house. When such decisions were taken, the patients were rarely, if ever, consulted. A nurse remembered how in the early 1980s management carried out a large assessment exercise of all patients:

In all of the wards that were old long-stay wards, all the patients were assessed for their rehabilitative potential. And what happened was that as a result of that massive exercise, a lot of the patients were moved around, which meant that people who'd been together for a very, very long time were often split up. And a lot of people died. They just died, because their friends were gone.

There were nurses that made you know very clear that this was about the changes that had occurred, that you know these were two friends. I can think of two ladies in particular who'd been on my ward, on this rehab ward together, and they'd been together in various wards, but always – for donkey's years. Like twenty years

153

or something. And all of a sudden because one of them has more potential than the other, they're split up. And there were something like half a dozen deaths. If not more. I think that was about 1984.

Some more psychologists had been employed who specialised in rehab work, one of whom had done prison work or something like that beforehand. I don't think they'd really thought it through, you see. I think they'd done it as an exercise thinking to sort people out with a view to moving out the people with potential, and they hadn't really thought about the repercussions of long-term relationships. They never thought about people as having really good friends.

Goffman's work in the early 1960s drew attention to the importance of networks of friendship among asylum patients. Friendship seems to have been crucial for many patients at Severalls, especially long-stay patients. A woman patient, for example, said:

There were two sitting rooms – one for smokers, one for non-smokers, but everyone sort of made up their own little friendships. And also their own little enmities. And I know, on one occasion, I was very edgy, and two patients I didn't like very much were squabbling. And these two women squabbled and squabbled – they were always doing it. And I shouted at them to shut up, and then they started again a minute later. I just jumped up and thumped the table, and really shouted at them. And then I ran out the room, because I knew if I stayed in the room I'd – I'd really start hitting them.

And I did a trick my therapist has given me, which is holding my wrists under cold water. And I raced off upstairs and was doing this, and two of the other patients came looking for me to make sure I was all right. And then they took me to the kitchen and made me a cup of tea and gave me a cigarette and sat with me. And one of the squabblers came in to apologise. But I was still het up, and I went for her, and these other patients just caught hold of me and sat me down. One sort of cuddled me, and the other got the squabbler out of the room.

And that sort of thing was happening all the time. 'So and so's upset.' 'Do you want a cigarette?' 'Do you want a cup of tea?' 'Come on, let's have a little walk.' I was friends with one woman from Severalls for years and years and years, and exchanged visits with and without our respective kids. There are others. And some I sort of see around and still talk to. There was one nurse in particular, but then we were friends before I was in there.

Figure 5.4 The nurses' recreation room, 1950s
Source: North East Essex Mental Health NHS Trust

Friendships among nurses and other staff also flourished at Severalls. Women who worked there spent so much of their time within the hospital estate that previous networks and friendships often dissolved, and new ones were made within the hospital. In the early 1920s many women came from outside the area in groups of two or three friends to start work together. Frequently if one was dismissed or decided to resign, the others also resigned and they all left together. At this time a number of nurses were dismissed for sleeping with another nurse. One was dismissed for sleeping with a patient. Severalls may have been a haven for many women who preferred relationships with other women, particularly in earlier years when such relationships were heavily stigmatised. A nurse who trained at Severalls and moved into education remarked:

> Oh, there were a lot of same-sex relationships, or quite a few. It just seemed to be accepted. It felt like it. I mean – I guess one of the things that it feels like is that it didn't bring the same kind of closure that having a gay relationship can bring about in other circumstances. So, for example, I know of two women who have

155

been married and then gone on and had quite long lesbian relationships, you know, over a number of years. And then gone back and got married again. So there was no closure. And people – there were two sisters, two ward sisters who were obviously having a relationship and had been for years, and still live together, although they've both retired. That was just accepted. I think it was tolerant. I think it was tolerant of gay people, drug addicts, alcoholics, whatever. Where better to hide the stigma than in a stigmatised population?

6

ON THE MALE SIDE

''Tis 7:15! Arise! Arise!
Show a leg! Show a leg!' The Attendant cries.
Whether it's fine or whether it's wet
Up the patients have to get.
Some would fain stay in bed
But all they get is a clout on the head!
Down to the wash-house do they stream
Some half asleep, some in a dream.
Some wash their faces, some brush their hair
But others look on with a vacant stare.
'Buck up there, and don't be silly!
What ho! For the bread, marge and skilly!
Stand for Grace!' The Attendants yell.
'Move from your place, 'tis your death knell!'
After breakfast they disperse
Some to cry and some to curse.
Some rub the windows, some wax the floors
But others look out through the glazèd doors ...
A voice is heard: ''Tis close on four!'
'Boots off! Boots off! And hold your jaw!'
See how they come with madden'd run
To drink their tea and munch a bun
To count the hours from now till seven
To end the day in so-called heaven!
To doff, remove, throw off their kit
To see Jack Smith have one more fit
To enter 'gain the rubber'd pad
To play the fool, to act the mad.
                    (Jerry O'Toole, 'Asylum Life in Verse')[1]

Beyond its imposing facade, Severalls looked like a large barracks. True
to its appearance, the wards on the male side ran very much along military
lines. Paradoxically, however, the fact that the turnover rate of male

157

nursing staff was very low compared with the female side meant male patients had greater stability and were more apt to feel their ward was 'home'. For staff on the male side there flowed a network of invisible and sometimes secret, yet interrelated, allegiances – trade unions, Freemasonry, kinship – which almost certainly had far-reaching effects on jobs, promotion possibilities and the daily lives of the men who worked there. Combined with greater job security than existed for female nurses (because of the marriage bar), it meant male nurses, unlike their female counterparts, stayed longer, could build careers, could establish and maintain quite powerful positions within wards, and could act collectively to press management for material advantages and improvements.

Originally designed to take the same number of patients as the female side, the male side of Severalls was generally more spacious owing to the consistently lower number of male patients. There were fewer villas and more single rooms than on the female side. The ratio of staff to patients in 1947, for instance, was 160 full-time male nurses for 715 male patients, or one for every 4 or 5 patients. On the female side, however, there were 68 full-time and 47 part-time nurses for 1,060 patients, or one for every 11 or 12 patients.[2] Male patients may therefore have received proportionally more attention than female patients.

THE ENGINEER'S YARD AND THE FARMS

Just as the laundry took up much of the space on the female side, so the engineer's yard occupied a great deal of space here. It contained a range of workshops for glaziers, electricians, plumbers, carpenters, upholsterers, tailors, cobblers and, in the earlier days, a blacksmith and tinsmith. The engineer had overall control and responsibility for all work that took place here. Severalls' huge generator was here, with the engine-room measuring 50 feet by 36 feet. It produced DC electricity until the 1960s. One man, who worked as an electrician at Severalls for many years, explained:

> When I came they were just in the process of changing over from DC to AC, because we generated our own electricity here. We had big reciprocating steam engines that drove the generators. All the wards were being upgraded, because it was all – I don't know if you've ever heard of 'capital casing'? This was what the hospital was wired in: beautiful, elaborate, wooden casing with the wires running parallel. You had to be a carpenter in those days to be an electrician! And, you see, the engineers were nearly always ex-naval people, people who had worked in ships as engineers. They're used to steam and things like that, you see. We had big steam

Figure 6.1 Severalls' generator
Source: North East Essex Mental Health NHS Trust

> boilers then. And ships are all DC, or were in those days, you see,
> so we were generating direct current, and the steam boiler-houses
> – so engineers nearly always appeared from – either from the Navy
> or from the deep-sea ships, cargo ships.

Male patients worked as coal stokers, coal dressers, bootmakers, tailors,
upholsterers as well as on the farms and gardens.[3]

The farms played an essential part in the hospital economy; Whitehouse
Farm was acquired in 1931 to increase food production for the ever-
growing patient population at the time. Severalls was virtually self-sufficient
in meat, milk, eggs and vegetables until 1956. A man who worked on
the farm in the 1940s and 1950s remembered the importance of the potato
crop for the hospital:

> We used to grow all the potatoes, and they used to put them in
> the old potato cones, where you put all the bales of straw around,
> and then you put the potatoes in that, then you put straw and stuff
> on top, and soil on top. Then you'd dig them out in the winter. And

159

that protected them from the frost. Then they used to riddle them out, they had a riddle which sorted the potatoes out, and they'd bag them and then we'd take them in to the hospital for the winter.

In 1920, 32 cows in the dairy herd were producing on average 82½ gallons of milk for the hospital. Barley, clover, lucerne, mangel, swede and furze seed was purchased that year, as were 81 pigs. In 1921 it was reported that a pig was killed each week to be consumed at the hospital. In 1923 Dr Turnbull bought some chickens and had hen-houses constructed at the north end of the orchard; Cuckoo Farm had its own slaughterhouse built in the 1930s, and new piggeries were built in 1934. By 1945, 63 cows were producing some 200 gallons of milk daily, in 1948, 398 hens were laying on average 230 eggs daily, new blackcurrant bushes were planted, but 4 hives of the apiary had to be destroyed because of foul brood disease. In the late 1940s, new farming techniques were introduced: battery-hen farming,[4] spraying the orchards with pesticides, artificial fertiliser. New tractors were bought. In 1952, 26 out of 57 cows failed tuberculin tests and had to be sold. Milk was bought for the first time from outside. A new herd, however, was bought later that year. One man told me how he was born and grew up on Cuckoo Farm:

I was born in 1939 at Cuckoo Farm, because Cuckoo Farm is the hospital farm, and I used to belong to the farm, and my grandfather was foreman, and my father worked down there, and my uncle, my grandfather's brother, and I think one of his sons worked on the farm as well. So there were lots of us, quite a few of us, on the farm at one time.

And when we looked out the kitchen window, the horse yard was right next door, and all the horses, because they had horses then, the tractors hadn't come in. And the horses were in the yard just beside us. I can remember them. It's a three-bedroomed house. The big house belonged to the farm manager, or the farm bailiff. My father was there, he must have worked on the hospital farm for over twenty-odd years, until they sold, gradually started selling off the dairy herds and that.

I used to help a lot round the farm, and then I started really, because we left school at 15, and then I started. I wanted to work on the farm, that's all! It was, yeah, well, all the family had been on the farm, and that was all I wanted to do, really, was to work on the farms. The battery hens were already there when I started, and I remember Jean Smith, she was one of the Land Army girls, she was the last of them.

I was chicken boy, then the tractor driver. I had a little Fergie at first, and then when I had to do all the ploughing I had a big P6. Before that there was one horse, Tinker, and I done some rolling when they still used the horses, and I had the last horse on the farm before the actual tractors really took over. I hadn't ploughed with horses, only done rolling and harrowing with horses, which was just up and down.

In 1953 the labour-force on the farms rose from fifty-six to seventy-four, and some thirty-five to forty male patients worked there. The man quoted above grew up with the patients who worked on the farm around him, and he had very fond memories of them:

We had a working gang of patients, because there were about twenty used to come and help on the farm and do a lot of the farm work. I can remember them quite well. They used to play with me. I can remember them playing cricket and all sorts with me. I loved them. Yeah. I got on with them all right. I was brought up with them, weren't I. They was always around. Didn't seem odd at all. No, there was somebody to play cricket with. Or football.

They used to start at nine o'clock, used to come over at nine, and I think they used to finish about four then. So for harvest takers, they used to be later, they used to have to help with the harvest and things like that. Because in them days, you see, we had binders and we still had horses, and bring them in in the sheaves. And there was two attendants used to come out with them. They used to pick them up from the wards, bring them to the farm and then they'd be with them all day. And then they would take them back to the wards.

Ten o'clock tea break they used to have, the patients used to have their cup of cocoa and bread and cheese. And I think they used to get three ounces of Black Juggler tobacco, because it was like their wages for working there. It was really black, strong stuff. I remember, as a boy, when I ran out of fags, they used to give me one of their roll-ups, and that used to make me cough like anything!

They were mostly kept in a gang. When we did the threshing and that the patients used to help on the stacks, and then help cart the corn away from the drum and things like that. They were used on the farm mostly for sort of general tasks, helping. I remember having the horse and tumbril, and the patients would fill it up, then we'd

161

Figure 6.2 Male patients doing farm work, 1950s
Source: North East Essex Mental Health NHS Trust

take the horses down. Some of them were good workers, really good workers.

Some of them, yeah, some knew what they were exactly doing. Some didn't. But some of them did. It was quite hard work in them days, I mean, pitching sheaves of corn all day is pretty, pretty strenuous. I know when they used to go in at four, and we carried on in the evenings, when the cows had been milked and turfed out again, they would come back in the evenings and cart the harvest in, and I would go out and help cart the harvest. I was always out there with them.

Bill Banham, who began working on the gardening staff in 1948 and later rose into senior nursing, remembered taking patients out to work on the farms, and how therapeutic this was for them, given their agricultural backgrounds:

I worked on the gardening staff for a year – looking after flowerbeds, roses, and cutting grass and all the things that are involved with gardening. And, of course, the hospital farm was still going then. We used to take gangs of patients pea-picking, potato-picking, those sort of things. As a gardener I had several patients with me. There's one man who's still a patient there now, I think who was in the Navy with me. Yeah. And you know, I mean I sort of grew up with them. In those days, of course, a lot of the patients we got in were rural community people who had worked on farms and all that, and they enjoyed doing something they'd done all their life. And they came in, most of them ill − when they recovered, you put them back to convalescent, which is doing the things they're used to doing.

In 1954, however, the Regional Board began meeting with the Management Committee to discuss the future of the farms. Over the next two years there was considerable anxiety among farm staff about their future employment as the Regional Board put pressure on to sell the farms, a move which Dr Duncan was strongly against. By 1956 the dairy herd had been mostly sold off, as had the pigs. Farm workers began to be transferred to other jobs on the hospital. It was decided to lease Cuckoo Farm, but to keep the orchards and 130 acres for market gardening. By January 1957 the entire dairy herd had been sold, as had all the pigs, 256 boxes of apples, peas, wheat, beans, leeks. The man quoted earlier, whose family had worked on Cuckoo Farm since the hospital opened, remembered these changes and how they affected him:

When the farms went I come up on to the market garden. We used to market garden the fields around here after the farm went. Then I went into the kitchens, that's when I got married, in the sixties. The kitchen porters were doing six till two and having afternoons off, and I used to go and work for another farm. And then I went to Nayland to help one of the farmers down there, to milk his cows.

I missed the animals. I liked working with animals. The kitchen was different. It was all right. Oh, we were peeling all the potatoes and preparing all the vegetables. I did all the preparation, and then gradually worked up to the cooking. We lived at Mill Road at the time, my grandparents lived in Mill Road and we lived with them at the beginning of our marriage. And then we got, they allocated us a house, hospital house, yes, on Mill Road. And when the farms went, my grandfather was working in the stores.

ADMISSIONS AND ESCAPES

In the period before the Second World War, by far the majority of patients were poor, often without kin to care for them. Elderly farm labourers like Isaac Smith,[5] for instance, were quite typical. Smith was certified in 1953 at the age of 71. Smith's wife had 'made herself conspicuous by her behaviour to other men when he joined the Army' in 1914, and on return from the war he lived with his parents. He worked all his life as a farm labourer and was regarded as 'affectionate, quiet, cheery, kindly, sensitive, conscientious and generous'. In 1953, however, he was having physical treatment at a hospital in Braintree and became concerned that cattle and sheep were coming into the hospital, and that he had to take care of them. He had delusions of receiving phone messages about cattle and sheep. Certified, his mental report diagnosed him as suffering from senile dementia; senile dementia was a common reason for certification for both men and women. He stayed in Severalls six months, without treatment, and was discharged back to his landlady. She, however, found him impossible, and he was readmitted a year later. Again, they discharged him after a few months, but the landlady said she could not tolerate him, and he was admitted once more. Eight months later he died in hospital. Absence of kin and lack of adequate social services were undoubtedly contributing factors to Smith's need for hospitalisation.

General paralysis (or paresis) of the insane, or GPI, which was a form of dementia caused by syphilitic infection of the brain, was a frequent cause of mental illness in men. In 1917 Wagner-Jauregg discovered that mosquitoes infected with malaria could cure GPI. The numbers of men in mental hospital who were suffering GPI declined from then. A secretary remembered malarial mosquitoes being delivered to Severalls as late as the 1940s:

> During the war they used to give malarial treatment. I remember that, because we used to have to write off to Horton Hospital for a supply of malaria. A box about that size would come – there'd be a lot of cotton wool padding and like a flask – you know, the interior of vacuum flasks, the shiny piece – and as soon as it came of course I had to tell the ward and they had to come up immediately to get this. It was for treatment, but I'm not sure if it was for malarial patients. I'm trying to think why they wanted to give a patient malaria! But I quite often had to do it. During the war, I'm sure they'd been in the war. They were mainly male patients, I don't remember anything for the female side.

Two years after Severalls opened, Charles Myers introduced the term 'shell-shock' in *The Lancet* to describe a traumatic condition brought about on the psychological condition of men by the harsh realities of war.[6] It was characterised by loss of memory, disturbance of vision, smell and taste. It was a startling development in many ways, but primarily because it was located in a group of psychoneuroses generally associated with women rather than men. This challenged prevailing ideals of masculinity, especially in connection with war, as brave, strong, courageous and disciplined. By 1918 about 80,000 cases had been identified.[7] Severalls received its first shell-shocked service patients in 1917, and from the end of the First World War there was a group of fifty to sixty of them; some died, a few left, and more came after the Second World War. By 1957 there were twenty-one men left who had come after the First World War and fourteen who were certified following the Second World War. From the start they were issued with 'special suits' and received pocket money at a time when other patients did not. A report in 1957 found they were on a good diet and received excellent training in handicrafts, had good recreational facilities and got 'all modern forms of treatment including shock therapy and leucotomy'.

Alcoholism and delusional insanity related to alcoholism were also common reasons for men being certified. Abraham Edwards,[8] for instance, was a general labourer at Tendring Infirmary and was admitted in 1928 at the age of 43. He had been married for twenty-three years and had ten children. He was diagnosed as suffering from delusional insanity as a result of alcohol and was certified for 'laughing in an idiotic manner, and said he could see the spirits of his children, and spirits of dead people talk to him at night'. The only treatment Edwards ever received was malaria treatment in 1930. After the treatment, case notes state: 'shows no mental improvement. Delusions continue. Hostile.' He worked first on the ward, then for many years in the ward kitchen. By 1950 he was deaf and in 1955 contracted tuberculosis. He died in the hospital after spending twenty-seven years there. Alcoholism remains a serious problem, and, since the mid-1960s, drug addiction and drug-related illnesses have become a major cause of, or contributing factor to, mental illness.

The custodial system that prevailed until 1960 resulted in an accumulation of long-stay patients: in January 1960, 51 per cent of all male patients had been in Severalls for ten years or more, 36 per cent had been there for over twenty years.[9] Men were sometimes certified for quite trivial reasons and ended up effectively incarcerated but not ill. The labelling process was such that *any* behaviour could be read as 'mad' once a person had been certified and confined to hospital. Pleas for release were sometimes, but by no means frequently, acknowledged. The only alternative option for a certified patient was to try and escape. If not found for fourteen days, he – or she – was declared 'discharged by order of the law'. When a patient escaped, however, the attendant in charge was held personally responsible; his job was at risk if escapes were successful. Vigilance was thus rigorous. Nevertheless, many did make bids to escape and a small handful succeeded.

Between 1913 and 1937, 145 male patients escaped (the term was changed to 'wandered away' in the early 1920s), and 30 of these were discharged by order of the law. On one occasion in 1929, 4 escaped together successfully, and two other pairs also made a successful bid for freedom in the 1930s. One died of exhaustion. Another sent a postcard from London to the hospital. During that same period, only 32 female patients 'wandered away' and none gained their freedom. Between 1945 and 1966, the numbers rose, partly perhaps a result of staff shortage, partly a result of a more lax regime and the knowledge – for some – of an impending abolition of the certification process. During these years, 189 male patients wandered away, 10 achieved freedom and 6 were found dead (after the doors were opened and the railings came down, in the early 1960s).[10] Michael Wilson, who came as a 16-year-old cadet nurse in 1954, suggests nurses' attitudes were changing to the old certification laws:

> You're going back now to the days before the Act changed. Because patients that were certified were stuck for life – unless they escaped. If they stayed out fourteen days they were free. I remember old Bob – now, where'd he come from? Clacton? Frinton? A nice man he was, never caused anybody any harm.
>
> He told me that he'd been certified because they said he was a pyromaniac. He said, 'It was a joke! It was to get the insurance!' So I said to him, 'Well, don't let me down Bob, but there is this rule, you know, fourteen days!' And about a week later Bob went and we had to do these searches.
>
> I had a small motorbike and so had a few others, so we had to do the wide search – you know, nobody gives us any money to do it. So the walkers'd do the grounds and the cars'd do the wide search – 'cause there was one big car around, you've heard about that! The big 1938 Packard! It was a nice car! But anyway, Bob went and the fourteen days went and a parcel came back with his clothes!

Once the railings were down and the wards were opened, however, the idea of an escape became effectively an anachronism, as Bill Banham recalled:

> They had one famous patient, Harry. I think he escaped about ten times. He used to take the wood blocks out of the windows, pull it down, and disappear. And he'd wander around all night, and he'd come back and be sitting in the day room in the morning! And when

they decided to put them on tranquillisers, the patients were so much better. And the doors weren't locked, the patients were allowed freedom. And we said to Harry one day, 'Well, why don't you clear off, Harry?' 'What's the point?' he said, 'I can open the door and go out when I want.' I think they accepted it as a challenge.

WARD LIFE AND ROUTINE

Many patients worked in the kitchen, the bakehouse and also in the wards themselves. Both patients and nurses carried out the full range of cleaning duties on the male side – scrubbing, waxing, dusting – through the 1960s. What was always seen as women's work in the outside world was regarded as acceptable for men to carry out in this all-male environment. Not just the wards where attendants worked, but the whole male side of the hospital was cleaned by attendants in charge of male patients, as an attendant who began work in the 1930s explained:

> In my early days all the wards were responsible for different sections of cleaning. You see, there was Number 1 and Number 2 – they were the barmy wards. So nobody, no staff out of there went out on any – outside duties. And Ward 3, they were responsible for the cleaning and the setting out of the recreation hall. Then there was Ward 9 – they were responsible for the general bathroom, the cleaning of that. And then you come to Ward 5 and 11 – they were responsible for the corridors – I've scrubbed every inch of them wards and them corridors!
>
> Oh yeah, the nurses, they used to take the patients with them. Yeah, if you, you know, you'd get a patient, or certain patients, who were good workers – and you could take them with you. Well, eventually, all that stopped because the general bathroom was closed down altogether and all the patients were bathed in the wards.
>
> Well, I was in Ward 5 – well, there was no general ward then, because I think I was put there out of spite. You see, in them days, if you were – what shall I say? If you got on the blacklist – for no reason at all, really – well, sometimes there was a reason – but there were all these things. And I was about the fourth man in 5 and normally I'd be left in, either out in the gardens on duty or else left in with the charge. And I was put out on the corridors, and of course, the charge created, he had a junior man . . . he didn't like that. So eventually it stopped.

And I was put over there, and there was Freddie from Ward 11 – because this was a locked unit – and we took a patient. They used to do the floor, scrub the corridor, concrete floors, which they were, weren't they? They were all concrete and we used to have to scrub the walls. And we used to go to the office and they'd take us to the stores, and we'd get the cleaning stuff, and we used to take what they called brushes that were hearth brushes – remember, this was before the war. I've scrubbed every inch from that square right round to where the theatre was and the dispensary, right down to the centre. And I've scrubbed every inch of them walls. And when we finished, we'd start again.

By the 1960s, domestic staff did some of the cleaning of corridors and wards, yet nurses still had to perform a large amount of domestic drudgery as part of their daily routine. A man who came from Hong Kong to train as a nurse at Severalls described his early experiences in the male admission ward, Firs Villa, in 1964:

Those days anybody who come into hospital, they had to stay in their pyjamas, stay in bed for at least three or four days. And all I was doing was looking after them – in bed – bringing them their food, talk to them, just say hello to them, and take their – all the physical things like take their temperature and blood pressure, all these sorts of things. To be honest, there wasn't very much anything psychiatric about it. It was quite basic.

What was a shock to me is how primitive the surroundings seemed to be. For example, you have to light a proper fire, you had an open fire in each room, and you had polished parquet floors, and it was the job of the nurse, particularly a very junior student nurse those days, to have to do things like clean the fireplace out, light the fire.

There were domestics, but they're only there for a certain time. So the rest of the time the nurses have to do domestic chores. At the weekend we had to do things like get a knife out, scrape the old wax off, strip the old wax, and apply a new film of polish. And then you used the thick bumper, the push-bumper to polish it. Now the domestics were allowed to use the electric polisher, but we are not, because we're deemed to be not – not capable of using the electric equipment! So we just had to push the bumper.

In some of the other wards you actually have to work with a few patients, the more capable ones. And to start off, they told me what

to do! And they did a much better job than I did. And then eventually, when you become a bit more experienced, then you are
supposed to be – quote – 'in charge of them'. But, basically, you
just work with the patients as far as all those domestic chores are
concerned. But nobody had ever given a thought that I come from
a country that you never see a fire alight! And I was told to go and
clean the fireplace out and make a fire. And this was all new to
me. Nobody stopped to think that I might never know how to light
a fire! I had to learn.

Discipline was of the essence, and though undoubtedly this varied slightly
from ward to ward, the regime was strict throughout. Yet such discipline
was typical of the early decades of the century generally; most of the men
who came to Severalls as patients would have been used to harsh, sometimes unjust, disciplinary methods in the family-household, the education
system, the workplace and, indeed, the armed services themselves. A high
proportion of the attendants had been in the armed services, as a man
who worked as a nurse from the 1940s explained:

A lot of these old men in the hospital in those days were ex-Army
and great disciplinarians. Oh yes. And you respected their discipline.
And – I mean there was a lot of discipline as regards the patients
as well. I mean, in those days, patients would sit down for a meal.
Before a patient was allowed to leave the dining table every knife,
fork and spoon had got to be taken, washed, counted and accounted
for and locked away before they were allowed to leave the table.
   And the charge used to – if somebody was being a bit out of
hand at the meal table, he'd tell them to go and sit up the far end
of the dining room or the day room, and they'd say, 'What about
my dinner?' 'If you want it, you'll sit and eat it!' And that was it.
And the man had no dinner. And they were – I mean I know people
will say it was cruel and all that, but what do you do if somebody's
throwing his dinner about or having a go at somebody else?

The overall result seems to have been a regime that was firm, even
severe, but usually fair, although with little overt manifestation of affection
or human kindness. When I asked a man who came to Severalls as an
attendant in 1934 whether he ever grew fond of the patients, he replied:

Well, I wouldn't say you got fond of them. But there were some you
got on with better than others, if you know what I mean. Some were
quite – well, no different to a person you meet outside. Until they really

– as we used to call it – went all the stick, and were a totally different person. They were probably Jekyll and Hyde then, you know.

A man who was certified at the age of 18 in the 1950s, said:

> It was a trauma for me really. I mean, if you think, after having the thing to start with. And people wouldn't talk to you, you couldn't understand what they were talking about. They were all properly gone. It was very, very disciplined. Very disciplined. I wouldn't say they were kind to me. But no, they were never cruel to me, although I did spend one night in a padded cell for no reason at all. It wasn't very nice. No. But everything was done without any explanation. You weren't told *why* you'd got to do it. You were just told you've *got* to do it. That's how it was all the time.

Patients were regarded, both in law and in practice, as both without rights and without the ability to be rational. That was presumably the rationale for not explaining to them why they had been certified or why they were being treated in certain ways.

Male patients who were relatively well and not prone to violence, suicide or bids to escape worked in the gardens, on the farm or in the various workshops. Numbers varied from year to year, but probably about a quarter of all male patients worked outside the wards until the 1950s. The rest did odd jobs or cleaning on the wards or did very little at all, their only exercise the statutory walk round the airing courts morning and afternoon. Whenever possible, however, work always seems to have been encouraged. In 1913, for instance, patients laid 800 feet of 2-inch mains piping for the cricket ground. In 1914 male patients built the bandstand, and, at least during the First World War, patients as well as staff played in the hospital band. Male patients returfed the cricket ground after 3,632 men and officers from the Suffolk Brigade of Territorials left the Severalls grounds in 1915.

It is difficult to assess the extent and severity of violence and cruelty on wards in the past. Patients were often strong, large and violent while in the terror of their own internal landscapes, and fear gives people even more strength. Such men had to be restrained some way or other for their own protection and that of others. Before the major tranquillisers came in, a combination of physical restraint and isolation were the only recourse for attendants. Their actions may have been experienced as cruel by the patients at the time – or not, as the woman patient in the previous chapter made clear. Male patients fought one another – not surprisingly, confined as they were to very limited spaces, their body routines dictated by strict outside restrictions and rules.

It is interesting to note that a man who was certified in 1954 found the nursing staff harsh and lacking in sympathy, but not violent or cruel, whereas a man who was admitted in the late 1960s had a number of memories of being treated violently, both by staff and by patients; the following extract is from the man who was admitted in the 1960s:

My brother-in-law took me in. 'You'll be all right in there,' he said, 'don't worry.' But I didn't know what was going to happen. There were such different ways of doing things. I went to Myland Court West first of all. Yes, because that's part of the Chelmsford lot.[11] My doctor – I couldn't get on with him. He wanted to see me and he asked me to come in – initially – and he spent ages looking at the notes and – various things – and I said, 'Look, Dr Rosenthal, if you've got something to say, say it, or I'm going!' I couldn't bear to wait around while he was fiddling about, though I suppose he needed to. I know he came in one morning to the ward and I felt I'd been treated as inferior by a lot of the staff and doctors and that – and he came in and I said, 'Good morning, Dr Rosenthal,' and he didn't answer me. So I called him a dirty stinking rat! And then I said, 'Why didn't you say good morning to me?' And he said, 'Oh, I did,' and he didn't! He actually never said a thing.

Oh we were treated terribly – some people were treated terribly, you know. Night staff – some of those were bullies. I did the wrong thing really, I tried to hide away from them in the toilets – and they'd beat me up in the toilets. I thought I was gonna die. And they kept giving me medication that wasn't prescribed for me, making me more ill. And then I was gonna have a bath – and I was cleaning it – it was filthy, all the area round the bath was dirty from other patients. And I'd clean and they kept saying, 'Get in the bath! You need a wash!' You were supervised by them, you know? And I got in the bath and they pushed my head under the water and held it there. I managed to get free – but I was frightened – I was terrified a lot of the time. Didn't know what was going to happen to me next.

They'd pinch your clothes – the domestics – I don't know, I suppose it was the domestics – used to steal your clothes and you'd end up with Severalls clothes without buttons and things that didn't fit. It was awful. Nobody to talk to about it – well, whether they'd believe you or not. I don't know that they'd believe you or what. Some things were illness. Some things were drug-induced. So I couldn't even get up sometimes – it'd be days and weeks and weeks – and months – just not knowing what was going to happen to me next. I couldn't get out of me chair – when I did I felt as if I was going to fall into something.

People were violent – this was in Graham Ward – some patients were violent there – they used to pee on the seats and they'd pee all over the toilet and some people talked a load of rubbish – and I was scared out of my wits. Somebody picked on me once, watching television, and said 'We're going to watch *The Battle of Blood River*' and I said, 'Well, we're all watching this.' So he said, 'Would you like to go along to the bedroom?' So I thought he wanted a friendly chat! He got a bottle of orange juice in his hand, smashed it against the door, held it in front of my eyes – like that, and I just stared him in the eyes and he dropped it down. A patient. And he started hitting me with his fist – I was just so weak from medication, I curled up in a ball like that.

Anyway, somebody else told 'em that I'd started it and I was put in a locked room – with shutters on the window – in just my under-pants on a mattress – took all me clothing away and me watch and I never got that back again. The staff would beat me up – beat me up and on that occasion when I resisted going into that locked room – and – it had a little peep-hole where they could look through – and the patients used to look through there. Just a night I think. Just a night.

This man spent a lot of time on a locked ward. These wards generally had the most violent patients, and often the worst conditions. Spatially, side-rooms and padded rooms were used when patients were most violent. But they had to be held and taken there in the first place. The 'old guard' had a range of firm, but not cruel, physical techniques for holding and removing men in such a state. No doubt at times restraint could slip over into cruelty, and be experienced as such. Strength was necessary to restrain and contain men when they were themselves violent with terror and rage. Increasing use of chemical restraints from the mid-1950s meant physical size and strength became rather less important as qualifications for nursing.

To be in charge of eighty or a hundred potentially violent patients must have been a frightening experience to young male nurses. It was for Michael Wilson in the early 1950s:

I can remember night duty being on a ward with a hundred patients alone and all you had on that ward was a desk, and you had to keep the fire lit, a desk in the middle of the ward, and then a green covered light that would come down to the steps and in front of you would probably be about between sixty-five and eighty patients

172

with the beds very close together, each with a chamber-pot under-neath. There would be patients in side-rooms locked up, because there would be hatches put over the windows and their doors would be locked, and there would be so many padded rooms with patients in.

And you would be alone in there and your instructions were, 'If trouble breaks out, run out of the door, lock the – 'cause you had self-locking doors – knock the phone off the hook as you went' – they'd hear it buzzing, and they'd know there was trouble and the patrol would come to you. And the point is – talking about the way this place was – that is how it was run at night – *one person*. And you'd be left there, and I can remember nights of violence. When you've got chamber-pots half full of wee and poo – 'cause they weren't allowed to go to the loo, because you daren't let patients out on their own. I've seen a man standing there – middle of the room – throwing these things against the wall! See? Throwing the pots against the wall. That was Severalls' chronic wards in my time.

SPORT AND MUSIC

Sport was of central importance on the male side, particularly for the staff. To be a sportsman was a prime qualification for employment as an attendant. Application forms asked no questions about knowledge of medicine or experience of care. Their two most important questions were: Do you play sport? Can you play a musical instrument? Sport was an important qualification for male attendants at all mental hospitals, although some, like Severalls, had better facilities and better grounds than others. One man gave this account of how he was recruited as a Severalls attendant in 1934:

I used to play football for the school, and swim for the school, and I think it was the sport part of the school that I liked best. When I left school I still continued to play football for one of the junior teams. Now, when I left school I went and worked at a place in St Peter's Street – Trustlow's – there was an engineering firm, and they run a football team and I played for them. And then I was pretty good at football and I played for Colchester Town – and that's how I got my job. You had to. In those days, you either had to be a bandsman, a cricketer or a footballer.

I went to play for Colchester Town in the Spartan League before they ever went professional. I played outside left. Yep. Played for

Figure 6.3 Severalls staff cricket team, 1928
Source: Gift from Julian Taylor

them until I came up to Severalls in 1934, and that's how, I say, that's how I got my job. There was the inspector of Severalls which was, I mean they've got different names for them now, but it was Mr Hammond, Charlie Hammond and – his son Ike Hammond played football, too, but for Colchester. And he met me one Sunday and asked me if I would like a job. And I was in work at the time, because I've never been out of work, ever. And I said, 'Yes,' and I went up and saw his father on the Sunday and I was started on the Monday.

From 1923 there was a football team of male patients and in the 1950s a cricket league for male patients was set up,[12] although cricket had been played from the earliest days within the hospital grounds. Bowls was also popular with both patients and staff. This man remembered the importance of sports for him while he was a patient at Severalls in the 1960s and 1970s:

I'd do a lot of sport, that's what I love doing – and chess – and concreting one day a week. I played cricket – football, though, I haven't played for a long time – table tennis, badminton – a whole lot of different sports really. Darts, snooker. I've got trophies – I got those in Severalls. I used to play on the teams. The table-tennis

174

Figure 6.4 Male patients' cricket match, 1950s
Source: North East Essex Mental Health NHS Trust

team. Football team. Cricket team. Bowls team. I used to do pretty well.

I was captain of the cricket team at Severalls. Things you take for granted outside become a real nightmare having responsibility when you're under the weather, you know, I was so worried. I disagreed with other people's ideas of who to put into bat and things like that, you always get some people saying where you should do it, you know, 'cause you lose and they say, 'Well, we should have gone to bat first, we should've done this and that, so –'. And I was rather – I felt kind of – aware of these people finding fault, you know? Whereas actually the team was lousy at one time! You know, it was our mistake, we had a *terrible* team. I said, 'We can't win!'

I mean I was a good cricketer, but there were very few others that did well – they just couldn't, you know, they weren't capable of it – whether they just weren't sports-minded anyway, but they did try. But you'd get all sorts of strange things, like someone would

175

Figure 6.5 Male patients playing bowls, *circa* 1960
Source: Russell Barton archive

wander off the field, and someone would be burbling all over the place, some people chattering to themselves, you know, and it was quite – but at the time I couldn't take it as being funny, 'cause I was a good cricketer myself and, you know, I'd put someone to bowl who was hopeless.

We played Warley and Runwell and Shenley. I was in such a bad state. I don't know how I got so well for cricket really, but sometimes I was in a terrible state on the fields – and, yeah, well I thought it was better than – at least I got out and I felt fit. But I couldn't play as well, anywhere near as well, as I'd like to have done.

Bandsmen were highly prized and privileged among attendants. In 1914, for instance, they received five shillings each for playing at the annual dance. In 1946 they got four shillings for every practice or performance when off duty. As Nolan comments:

There was a small number of male staff who entered mental nursing direct from Kneller Hall, the Military College of Music. Advertisements would appear in the College's journal for competent musicians to become mental nurses. Hospital bandsmen were difficult to find and highly valued; these attendants often received special perks . . . [they were] entitled to extra food rations and also had more off-duty hours to allow for practising. On each occasion they played in public, they received a pay bonus. It was considered a great honour to be a member of the hospital band, because the skill of the musicians coupled with their sartorial splendour were an expression of the hospital's pride in itself.[13]

Severalls must have had a number of good musicians in the early days, and Mr Hammond seems to have been an industrious and inspired band-master. In April 1923, for instance, he conducted a full oratorio in the hall with the hospital choir and a full orchestra. The Second World War, however, marked the end of the hospital band, orchestra and choir.

TRAINING AND WORKING AS AN ATTENDANT/MALE NURSE

In the early twentieth century attendants were not seen as playing any kind of therapeutic role with the patients – that was the job of the medical staff alone. Rather, they were seen as custodians more akin to prison wardens than to nurses. This was reflected in their military-style uniforms and caps. A man who was the son of an attendant and was born in Defoe Crescent in 1931, remembered:

I can remember in my very very early days queues of patients accompanied by staff attendants, with their peak caps, their belts, their chains, their whistles – their everything! The chain was, in fact, fixed to a special belt, a thick leather three-inch belt with buckle. On the right-hand side of the belt, by the pocket area, was a large ring, split ring, which divided the belt, and from that split ring was a very heavy chain which went into the pocket, but there was enough to reach into the pocket to bring it up to open doors, and it contained the keys that they were allowed to have. And it contained a whistle – if it was necessary – in case there was an escape.

I used to come across and see my father, if I had a message, because living in Defoe Crescent I was able to climb the boards, as they were called, run across the field – and into Ward 1, and it was surrounded by railings, and all the attendants were dressed in a short-point coat with a long white apron. And I would go to the gates and shout out, and somebody would come and I would say, I can remember saying, 'Can I see my Dad, please?'

Before then attendants who were neither sportsmen nor bandsmen had few privileges. A man who began work as an attendant in the 1930s remembered:

> We used to have ten minutes' break for lunch – this was at nine o'clock time, you know. One hour for dinner and three-quarters of an hour for tea. And we used to do five days a week with two days off. Now you had – the two days you got off – first of all the charges, nearly all the charges had Sunday and Monday, or Saturday and Sunday. And then you come to the footballers – they had Saturdays off for football. So they either had Friday and Saturday, or Saturday and Sunday off. And in the summer you had the cricket. And then the bandsmen. The bandsmen had Wednesday and Thursday, because – there was the band on the Friday and practice on the Tuesday, so they had Wednesday and Thursday. So Monday and Tuesday was left over.
>
> So if you were one of the odd men out – I had Monday and Tuesday for five years running, when I was in Ward 5, that was the epileptic ward. And I went up to see Mr Markland[14] and I said, 'Mr Markland, do you think I could have a change of days?' I said, 'My wife is sick and tired of seeing me wash day and ironing day.' So I had Wednesday and Thursday off for one sheet, which was three or four months. And then I went back to Tuesday and Wednesday. That was the set-up, you see. And there was nothing you could do about it. If you complained in them days – and I've known – I've been told myself, you know, 'If you don't like it, you know where the gate is!' I've been told that. That's the way they used to run it. It was run, you see, when you look back on it, it was run on military lines. Mr Hammond was an ex-marine, and he was the bandmaster. And the way it was run them days was on military lines, similar. Discipline was ever so strict.

There were clearly reasons why certain attendants became blacklisted; unfortunately, this man did not clarify this. Perhaps it was to do with union membership, politics or membership of the Freemasons.

All attendants had to fulfil a six-month probationary period, after which they were either dismissed or made permanent members of staff, although sometimes the probationary period would be extended. The next major hurdle was to pass the preliminary and final parts of the Royal Medico-Psychological Certificate in Psychological Medicine exams.[15] These examinations began in 1885, when the Medico-Psychological Association persuaded the General Medical Council to introduce a qualifying examination for asylum attendants.[16] The 'bible' for these exams was the *Handbook for the Instruction of Attendants on the Insane*, which was first published in 1885 and ran into seven editions, the last of which was published in 1978, when the Royal College of Psychiatrists declared it out of date. Known as 'The Red Handbook' it emphasised the importance of discipline, industry, order, cleanliness and obedience. Basic medical knowledge, rather than specific nursing knowledge, was central to it.[17]

Order, tidiness, cleanliness and deference were, however, key principles taught to mental nurses in the first half of the century (and, of course, before). This man, for example, described his education and training at Severalls in the 1930s:

> Dr Turnbull's deputy, Dr Duncan, used to take us for our exams. He wouldn't let you take notes. But he'd stand at that blackboard, he'd have it on the blackboard both sides – and he'd just have one look and off he went. I used to go afterwards, I used to always take my book and write everything off that board. I used to finish about five to ten. Then when I was off duty I used to rewrite all that out, and that was wonderful to read that – and read that and read. He had everything tabulated. Ooh, that was beautiful.
>
> 'Cause we had very very hard exams when we did ours. We went right into psychology, the lot – not just straightforward – and general, we had the lot combined, although we only got two lectures a week. You were trained on the wards more or less. What you did get was one hour lecture from the sister tutor – first starting with anatomy and physiology and all that, then when you'd got your first exam, you went after your final. Then of course you got the doctor. Then when we went for the main exam, then you got that knowledge, and do you know it was years later before we even really realised what you were being taught.
>
> Later on the sister tutor used to take us down to the theatre and she used to teach us all the instruments an' that, and she used to always lay 'em out in such a way that you gradually got to know 'em parrot fashion. When I was there, there was eighty-eight we had to know. And then I always remember her telling us, when we were goin' to sit for exams, 'Now I'll lay these instruments out the same as I've always laid them out, so remember now, you should remember them.'
>
> The doctor took you for exams, not like they do now. That day we sat there was thirty-one girls and twenty-four men – some men had failed a couple of times, but they played football or they were

bandsmen, and they used to keep 'em. And up on the pass list was one woman and three – they didn't give 'em away then. No. No. Well I mean, you went before the matron and then you had to sit down from nine till twelve paper, and there was two compulsory questions to answer, and then you had to go in the afternoon for half an hour or more with the doctor. And – cor, dear me – but as I said, thank goodness I took all those notes down from Dr Duncan.

Between 1913 and 1929, 109 male attendants passed their preliminary examination, and 73 their final.[18] Results in the early 1930s were even better: in 1932 alone, for instance, 32 men and women passed their preliminaries and 21 their finals, while one male nurse passed the GNC exams that year. Similar results continued until 1936, after which time records were incomplete, but certainly Severalls was getting very good results in training nurses until then.

Until the 1950s, promotion went from probationer to 3rd class attendant to 2nd class attendant and finally to 1st class attendant. The next step up from that was to be appointed a charge nurse, which meant having responsibility for – and a great deal of power over – the whole of a ward. Charge nurses answered to the deputy inspector and the inspector (later called the assistant chief male nurse and the chief male nurse) who were, in turn, responsible to the medical superintendent. While doctors, the medical superintendent and the chief male nurse would visit wards briefly, most of the time it was ruled by the charge nurse. A man who came from Hong Kong as a student nurse commented:

Sometimes I thought we actually exploited the patients. I think the staff were exploited, but the patients were also exploited. I was shocked that the charge nurse, in those days, had so much power over the life of the staff and the patients. They were absolute gods. And sometimes when you stop and think, 'Why he is doing that?' But there's no way you can actually question it, because your place is – not to question their word, your place is there to do what they tell you to do. I was quite shocked, I was quite amazed that in a hospital, where you're supposed to be looking after people, what they did was not actually looking after patients, but making life easy to run a ward.

This account makes it clear that male nurses, when they rose to become charge nurses or deputy chief male nurses, wielded a great deal of power over both junior nurses and the patients. Once a man became a charge nurse and had established his authority and regime within his ward, the tendency was to keep it that way and to discourage newcomers or change, as this man who began as an attendant in the 1930s and rose to become charge nurse pointed out:

> Once you get a nice settled ward, don't make a vacancy, 'cause if you upgrade 'em, sure enough you'll get a bad 'un come in. Charge nurse won't let 'em sit inside, well he wants to sit down and watch TV, don't he? Wants to see the news in peace! You don't want 'em walking up and down when you're watching the news or the horse racing.

Because male attendants tended to stay for most, or all, of their career, waiting to become a Charge Nurse was slow but steady: 'waiting for dead men's shoes'. Union agreements between male nurses and the administration in the 1950s – agreements which defied Regional Hospital Board policy – ensured all promotions were internal. With Dr Duncan a Freemason and also, some claimed, the chief male nurse, it is likely that promotions were influenced by Masonic links.

THE EFFECTS OF WAR AND THE
POST-WAR ERA

During and after the war many new ideas were influencing psychiatry and psychiatric practice. Rehabilitation was increasingly seen as preferable to custodial care, and these ideas preceded the use of neuroleptic drugs. Mental illness was being discussed more openly, attempts were being made to reduce the stigmatisation of it, and enlightened medical superintendents were stressing the importance of treating patients with human dignity and trying to reduce the worst effects of institutionalisation. Yet in actual mental hospitals during the war conditions deteriorated rapidly as a result of food shortages and staff shortages. From the start of the war the labour shortage, already severe, became even more so; temporary and part-time nurses were employed on the male side, many of them unqualified, elderly and incompetent. Staff/patient ratios undoubtedly deteriorated dramatically. Further teaching and training almost certainly was minimal, if not non-existent. Doors closed. Whole wards were closed because of the severe lack of nursing staff. Food was scarce: by 1941 it was impossible to obtain onions, lemons, eggs, slab chocolate, tinned milk or bananas. In 1942, thirty-eight female patients were killed when three bombs were dropped on Severalls.[19]

After the war, demobbed male soldiers who had worked – and qualified – before the war returned to their old jobs. Several applied to get leave for general nursing training. A number of male nurses were released for this from 1949 onwards, thereby furthering their own careers and bringing in a wider range of knowledge to the wards at Severalls. At this time kinship links were arguably at their peak. One man, for example, who began working at Severalls in 1948, was born in Defoe Crescent; his father was head chef in the hospital, his mother, sister and brother all also worked there. Another man was born in Defoe Crescent, the son of an attendant, and, although his father was against him taking up nursing, he left the police force in 1955 to become a student nurse at Severalls. The brother of the man quoted above was also a charge nurse and they shared one ward between them, one doing day shift, the other night shift. Fathers often 'had a word with' the chief male nurse on behalf of their sons. Kinship, like sport and music, was a crucial ticket to work as an attendant at Severalls. Once in, however, training and discipline were strict for everybody.

When the older generation of male nurses appointed in the 1920s began to retire or die, from the early 1950s, a shortage of male staff developed. Only gradually during the 1950s did a new wave of male nurses begin to work – and get qualifications – at Severalls again. Younger nurses like Michael Wilson came to Severalls keen to try and implement some of these new ideas:

> It was an institution – and, oh God, it was dreadful. When you had bath days and if you didn't watch it these old school staff would have them in and out of the same water, but we, the young ones, insisted, no, this doesn't happen, and we changed a lot of these things. We had rows and there were rows with the charge nurses about all sorts of things, we were causing trouble – but we were persistent, we said, 'No, if a patient was having a bath we think that baths should be rinsed out and there should be clean towels and things.' 'But that takes all day!' I said, 'That doesn't matter.'
>
> It was totally bare. And we used to go round the grounds, 'cause there were all these wild flowers growing and we used to put flowers in for them – *we changed the environment*. We asked for a fish tank. We were not the key-swinging lunatic attendants that were there before – that's not being unkind to them, but that's the way they worked then. That's the way they were.
>
> We used to say to the old charge nurse, 'We've got patients, can we take them out?' And I remember having to go to old Cobbold[20] to get permission to take one into town. 'Don't you realise, he's a psychopath?' they all said. 'He's twice your size!' It was the old school, the old charge nurses, they didn't want any change. They

lived at Mill Road or in Defoe Crescent and they used to pedal in on their bikes and to the pub and back. A lot of them were north country lads – and they found a secure job. These houses were built for them! Pension, everything, secure. And they were probably only 55 when we came, but to us they were old! Unfortunately they didn't like too much change.

You either joined the old school or you fought them or you left. In 1956 or '57 there was a gentle influx of feminine people – now they'd be called gay – but these were nice guys, there was nothing rude or crude about them. Quite a few came. I think it was a safe place for them and they were protected and we treated them as normal people of society – and anybody could come here. I don't think we changed it that dramatically as an individual, but as a group it sort of changed.

As discussed earlier, pressure was put on the superintendent and the committee to make internal appointments only in the 1950s. This was apparently mostly a result of union pressure, but, as mentioned earlier, the chief male nurse at this time was allegedly a Freemason, and Dr Duncan was high up in the Masonic order. Masonic Lodges were often a feature of mental hospitals, so the real pressure to defy the Regional Hospital Board on the part of management may have come from Masonic links throughout the male side of the hospital itself.

It is almost impossible to decipher now what the exact network of power relationships was then, but a nurse who came from Hong Kong remembers that the power and influence of what he called the 'internal Mafia' were still strong when he began work in the 1960s. He was ambitious and wanted to train as a general nurse after he qualified as a mental nurse. Many before him had been released by Severalls on paid leave while they did their training. This was refused him. He left as a result and lived in severe hardship while doing his general training. He then reapplied, was reappointed, and was treated with more respect. In the 1960s, nursing staff were often second generation, even third generation, from families who had worked in Severalls since its opening. Kinship, the Freemasons, trade unions were all ways in which a strong network of support and influence were developed on the male side of the hospital. Such networks, this male nurse explains, barely existed on the female side:

At one time, unless you'd been there for so many years, you hadn't got a hell of a hope of getting promotion. And particularly if you've got family working in other parts of the hospital, there was other people who would get there first. They stayed working for Severalls, so they made sure those people get their job. But I think I broke the camel's back by jumping the queue when I became a charge nurse in 1971. There were people sort of calling me names, the other male nurses called me names, but, funnily enough, once I got the job they all changed. Boom! Yes.

Some of them had been here for a long while and – and they had cliques. Yes, those cliques were what I call the 'internal Mafia'. They control your reputation. They feed things back to the people – important people. And they make sure they influence those important people whether you get the job or not. They were fellow charge nurses. Because a charge nurse was very powerful those days. The assistant chief male nurse, assistant matron – those kind of people – and also some very senior staff nurses who themselves are going for promotion – they were allying themselves with these important people. The senior people, you see.

Whether a nurse got everything prepared before the ward round start, was a big recommendation whether you should be a charge nurse or not. But it wasn't unusual those days to see the senior staff nurse or the charge nurse, before the consultant went round, they'd go and change to a clean crispy white coat – make sure they have their shoes polished, comb their hair, have a shave, and make sure the desk is lined up with clean, unused paper and all the pencils are sharpened and lined up. This is for the consultant coming doing a round. Now, if you do all that and make their coffee with milk, and present them with a tray and a cloth – you're in! They think, 'Oh, a good chap there!' you know, 'A good chap, that person.'

They spent all their time worrying about things like that, but when it comes to patients' dignity, they didn't. I wouldn't say they don't give a damn – but the orderliness and the tidiness of the place must come as a first priority. The institutionalisation of the patient has got a lot to do with the staff wanting to keep the institution rigid.

This new wave of young male nurses sometimes clashed with the older generation of nurses who had been recruited and trained in the inter-war period. Michael Wilson, for instance, who came to Severalls in 1954 as a cadet nurse at the age of 16,[21] told me how the charge nurse in his ward knocked him flat on the floor when he challenged the existing procedure for dispensing medicine to patients:

I personally was attacked by a member of staff and – it was all hushed up. I'd actually gone at that time right straight across to

Kniveton, who was the chief male nurse, and nothing ever came of it. In actual fact, I was the one that was criticised at the time – and I was very unhappy about that, but that was just something that happened. But that was hushed up and kept very quiet, you know, and I think it was even the fact that the person himself had been here for some time, therefore the old clique – my name was never put forward for any awards or anything after that occasion.

I'm not too bothered about it, but as far as the patients' situation is concerned I'm sure a lot of things could have been – you know – covered up, because it has to be remembered that we were young people, we'd come into this establishment in the mid-fifties and the first sort of generation of people were retiring then, the second generation had taken over from them, and a lot of the habits or, if you like, institutionalisation, of the staff carried on, and we were the only people I suppose – not because we were anything special – but a lot of us objected to this situation and it would be very easy for the old clique of the people to hide things – because it was a *hole* at the time.

I remember, I was not quite 17, and the deputy chief male nurse's first words to me, he said to me, 'Frighten them before they frighten you! If you get any trouble, Michael, knock 'em to the floor, and lift their head up that high and put it down smartly!' I'd only been here a week! Oh yes, he was serious all right. It's because – they were lunatic attendants, the first approach was – the heavy-handed approach. I think one has to accept the fact that, what did they have to restrain patients? What did they have? They had haustus paraldehyde – it was a mixture – chlorohydrate – and that's about it.

Tony Christie, however, who came as a nurse from Hackney in 1960 because of the superior sports facilities at Severalls, had another perspective on the changes. He felt that it was the old guard who were the 'gentle giants', and that it was the new nurses who caused difficulties:

Then you had the older staff – the charge nurses used to be in charge of the wards. You had two shifts. You quite often had rivalry between the shifts. It wasn't a good thing, sometimes, for the patients, because they were pulled one way with one shift and then the other one wanted it done another way. And so the patients were caught in a little bit of cross-fire. I think it was the young ones, the younger ones like myself, which might have been causing them more problems than anybody else. The old ones, because they were sportsmen and bandsmen – you're talking about healthy minds. And they would translate that into the patient care as good.

You had the odd pocket of unpleasant people, which I didn't like, and that spoilt it. There's no excuse for what they did. Kick patients on the leg. I've witnessed it on – particularly the psychogeriatric ward, St Michael's Ward as it was called then. But the vast majority of the charge nurses and the senior staff were good. They had a way with patients. They were very very clever indeed. And having been sportsmen – footballers, cricketers and that kind of thing – and musicians. And then I think people came into the profession who weren't sportsmen so much, and that probably wasn't such a good thing, in some ways, because – when you're playing sports you're a member of a team, and that's translated into a psychiatric hospital, you got teamwork.

And then you didn't have to be a sportsman and then you had a different kind of person, perhaps, coming in. And then somehow you had these cruel little sods, and I think they probably always were around – there were a few of the old ones a little bit that way.

But the things that I witnessed were total intolerance. Punch. Hit. Knock and bash. And some – one or two charge nurses just turned a blind eye to it. There were a few, a pocketful of people who were out for mischief and would laugh and joke about it off the ward. These were largely younger nurses, my age, who'd joined and they shouldn't have been there. There were one or two older ones who probably were rough-houses, but had matured with age, so I couldn't account for what they did in the past.

But it was very difficult, I think, without drugs. And I think a lot of them were marvellous. Some of them were gentle giants and were excellent. Marvellous. I owe a lot of gratitude towards some of the older nurses, who would take me aside, you know, and try and – they would show me how you do it, in their own way. I think 85–90 per cent of the hospital used to sing along nicely, but there was this nasty little undercurrent, and I think a lot of it, a lot of the cruelty I saw was of the younger generation.

By the mid-1970s almost all the older generation who had been recruited and trained in the early days of Severalls had retired or died. The new generation of nurses who rose to power and influence at this time was a generation who, though largely respecting the 'old guard', incorporated new ideas of rehabilitation into the community, the use of empathy and therapy with patients as well as the use of new drugs and treatments, into their nursing ideals and practice. Bill Banham began work at Severalls in 1948 as a gardener, but soon transferred to train as a nurse. In 1957 he went to Essex County Hospital to do his general training, returned to Severalls the following year, became a charge nurse in 1964, then in 1967 was made an assistant chief male nurse (later called a nursing officer). His career at Severalls spanned from the latter days of the 'old guard' until the 1990s and the last days of Severalls:

When I first started there, let's be honest, you'd got to be a big man and reasonably fit. There were no – no modern tranquillisers, very little sedation and – one ward I was on you had seventy patients, and unless you'd had half a dozen fights before breakfast, you didn't know you were on duty!

And then the modern tranquillisers came in and that did change the whole aspect of mental nursing. Before, there was a lot of restraint. And – there were funny incidents. I mean, I went through the Refractory Ward on one occasion, and there was one famous customer in there, and you always reckoned that he had got to test every nurse that went in. I mean, I'm going back to the old days.

And my job, as a junior nurse, was to take the foul laundry and put it out into the laundry cupboard. So I go down the backs – down to the toilets – put this laundry in this laundry cupboard, locked the door – and there was Sid! 'Right,' he said, 'We'll see who's best!' And I weren't very brave. And they'd got toilet doors only about this height, so you could see who was in the toilet door – what we used to call 'horse boxes'. And he came roaring down. And I opened the door and hid behind it – and he ran straight into it! And the charge nurse said to me, 'You shouldn't have done it.' I said, 'I never touched him!' And that's just one of the types of things that happens to you.

Oh no, you didn't hit the patients. I mean, most of the fights were patient-to-patient, and your job was to separate them without using your fists. You just grabbed them and that was it. I mean, you were taught restraint – and that was it. Well, you gained it from senior nurses. I mean, you'd go in the ward, the old charge nurse would say, 'Don't do this! Don't do that!' and you'd watch the older nurses how they dealt with it, and you'd learn that way.

Although this nurse felt the tranquillisers that came in had an enormous impact on patient care generally and the atmosphere at Severalls specifically, he still thought it was the change in *attitude* at this time that had the greatest effect:

The change was mainly one of attitude. There were the industrial workshops where patients could go and work and earn money. And that gave patients a purpose in life. So their attitude changed. In the old days, of course, they were still always sort of 'them' and 'us'. I suppose, mainly, when it came to patients, instead of *telling* them to do something, you *asked* them to do it. Those sort of things. We had group therapies. Personalised clothing, too, that was another thing that improved. But there again, you see, I remember one patient committing suicide because they closed the ward down. And they moved him. And he said, 'I don't know what I'm going to do.' So we said, 'What do you mean?' He said, 'That's my home! I've lived there for thirty-five years!' he said, 'And they're throwing me out!' That was way back in the seventies.

Perhaps these changes created something of an identity crisis for male nurses. Whereas before their physical size and strength were valued both for team spirit (in the sports teams as well as the wards) and as an important asset for dealing with physically violent patients, these traits became less and less important. Empathy and understanding with patients were becoming increasingly valued, traits usually associated with women. Up until the 1970s, male nurses were still expected to perform a range of domestic drudgery – work perceived as women's work. It seems possible male nurses may have experienced a crisis in their masculine identity between the late 1950s and the early 1970s, a time when nursing as a profession was being redefined in myriad ways and both caring/therapeutic skills and administrative ability offered male nurses new role models. By that time, however, nurses who worked on wards were working with female nurses, many wards were beginning to become mixed-sex, and an increasing number were working as part of a community psychiatric team. By the end of the 1970s the old model, based as it had been on a male-only space and regime, had largely disappeared.

7

THE SPACE AND PACE OF
TREATMENTS

*Lift the hem
of medicine, and you discover torture
and placebo twinned, still there*
(Amy Clampitt,
'An Anatomy of Migraine')

Those who designed Severalls allocated little space for treatments, primarily because there were virtually no effective treatments available at that time. While some patients in the early decades would leave 'relieved' or 'recovered', the assumption when it was built was that it was primarily for custodial care. The certification system, along with the poor-law foundations of public asylums, meant that, certainly at least until 1930, patients came only as a last resort. This meant any hope there might have been initially of helping them towards recovery had generally gone. Well-managed routines, nourishing food, clean clothes, plenty of light and exercise – these were by and large the ideals of care and treatment set by asylum psychiatrists for their patients in the early twentieth century. These were reinforced by regular use of sedatives and hypnotics such as bromides (introduced in the 1850s) and paraldehyde (introduced in the 1880s). In 1912 phenobarbital was first used to control epilepsy. Restraint of patients when violent and severely disturbed was achieved primarily through physical and spatial control: side-rooms, padded rooms, 'strong clothes', physical restraint by nursing staff, and, occasionally, strait-jackets.[1]

The early twentieth century, however, was a time of rapid change and ferment both in medicine and, to a lesser extent, psychiatry. Medicine in the nineteenth century had been weak and often divided by sectarian claims; though its status was rising during this time, it was less highly regarded than, for example, the law, and its practitioners were often thought of as no better than cranks. Yet medicine, the paradigmatic profession that has most successfully defended its privileges, knowledge base, and monopolistic control, established itself at the top of the professional hierarchy in the early years of the twentieth century and has remained there since ... In a culture fascinated with the power of science, and in which science (in the form of electricity, for example) was transforming life in visible and fundamental ways, doctors successfully established themselves as its omniscient exemplars.[2]

While the status of medicine rose, that of psychiatry stagnated or declined. Psychiatry's origins lay in the early nineteenth-century asylums, and psychiatric practice in these was largely confined to institutional management. Various treatments were experimented with, but none showed any promise of cure. In 1913, for example

Leonard Woolf consulted five leading London mental specialists ... about his wife's [Virginia] disturbing condition. Despite their high professional standing, Woolf felt that 'what they knew amounted to practically nothing. They had not the slightest idea of the nature or the cause of Virginia's mental state ... no real or scientific knowledge of how to cure her.' English medical knowledge of insanity in 1913, Woolf concluded, was 'desperately meagre', 'primitive and chaotic' ... What would finally change the direction of English psychiatry was not the fin de siècle epidemic of female nervous disorder, to which Virginia Woolf fell victim, but the experience of the Great War ... Not feminism but shell shock initiated the era of psychiatric modernism.[3]

'Moral treatment' had been the great breakthrough of psychiatric care in the early nineteenth century; a regime of paternal discipline, regular care and control replaced more brutal methods such as chains, whipping, total confinement.[4] But moral treatment was not by any stretch of the imagination *scientific* treatment, and if psychiatry wanted to be regarded as on a par with general medicine – which it did – then it had to find some way of laying claim to scientific status. This quest has been central to psychiatry's search for status and recognition in the twentieth century.

In the late nineteenth century Kraepelin set out to classify psychiatric illnesses, grouping together symptoms into the two distinct categories of *dementia praecox* and manic-depressive insanity.[5] In 1911 Eugen Bleuler labelled *dementia praecox* as *schizophrenia*. In 1915 Myers added shell-shock as a new psychiatric illness. Yet classifications and reclassifications did not offer viable treatments, much less cures:

To psychiatry's critics as well as to some psychiatrists themselves, who routinely denigrated their forebears while staking their own

claims to truth, it seemed that two thousand years of classifica-
tory enthusiasm, from the ancient Greeks to the modern Germans,
had generated one grand nosology after another and an arcane
vocabulary of Latinate neologisms, but precious little else – primitive, even punitive, treatments and no cures.[6]

In the early years of the twentieth century, however, there was one
breakthrough in this impasse. The breakthrough was in the treatment of
syphilis. Syphilis had been rife in Europe since the late fifteenth century;
its traits included impaired locomotion and speech, partial paralysis, delusions of grandeur, and eventual dementia.[7] L.F. Calmeil established a
definitive link between syphilis and what he termed 'general paralysis (or
paresis) of the insane' between 1905 and 1913. He identified the causative
agent of syphilis – *spirochete treponema pallidum* – in the brain tissues
of persons who had died from general paresis. In 1906 the Wasserman
diagnostic test for syphilis was developed and in 1917 Wagner-Jauregg
found that mosquitoes infected with malaria were an effective form of
treatment for syphilis (see Chapter 6). The development of a cure for
dementia caused by syphilis gave psychiatrists enormous hope and enthusiasm for the possibility of making many more scientific discoveries that
could cure insanity. It was a long wait, however, and when new treatments were discovered, psychiatrists tended to leap into immediate
implementation of them with little regard for adequate trials or testing.

EARLY TREATMENTS

In the 1920s and early 1930s, however, there were no major discoveries
made. Paraldehyde, a foul-smelling liquid compared by many to the stench
of rotten apples, remained the most widely used sedative at Severalls.
Sleep therapy, or 'prolonged narcosis' was also increasingly used; the first
use of this is generally attributed to a German psychiatrist, Jakob Klaesi,
in 1922, who developed this as a treatment for men with battle fatigue
in the USA, although 'rest-cures' had been a popular form of treatments,
particularly for middle-class women, from the 1870s.[8] Barbiturates or
opium derivatives were given to patients to keep them asleep for a period
of one or two weeks, even as long as a month. Cures were frequently
reported as 70–80 per cent.[9] One nurse remembered sleep therapy being
used in Severalls in the 1930s:

> Somniphine, that was it. They were asleep for a fortnight. Yes.
> Between the injections they became slightly conscious, so you could
> pick them up and put them on the commode, wash them, change

their clothes and their bed and feed them. Then they were injected again, and off they went to sleep again. It was very good. Looking back, I think they must have been manics. Yes, because it really quietened them, yes, it made a terrific difference.

Sleep therapy was still being given at Severalls in the early 1970s, albeit in a modified form, as a doctor explained:

Another treatment we used to do was called 'modified narcosis', which was a development of the old continuous narcosis treatment. But the way we did it was, somebody who was extremely agitated – from whatever reason, whether it was a psychotic illness or a neurotic illness – if they were terribly restless and agitated, and particularly where there was a lot of sleep deprivation involved, we actually put them to sleep for three to five days. With sedation. Only woke them up for meals and to take them to the toilet. And they just slept for five days, you see. I mean, in a way, their kind of batteries were recharged, and the brain, it had a rejuvenating function within the brain, obviously, and they did wake up feeling refreshed, and feeling – having lost a lot of their agitation and anxiety. But again, it was a bit risky. I mean, their blood pressure could have dropped – you know, their blood pressure was monitored, but it wasn't all that sophisticated. It isn't used any longer.

One woman patient, however, remembers her treatment with modified narcosis as being rather problematic:

In 1970 they gave me deep sleep treatment, the modified narcosis thing. I was supposed to be going on a cycling holiday. And my old uncle who was living with us – it was arranged for him to go into an old people's home for a fortnight. I got all ready and I hopped on my bike to test that it was stable – and I came down the road and somersaulted over the handlebars for no apparent reason – smashed my head and smashed my lower back – somehow got home and was rushed to hospital.

They stitched my scalp up and they couldn't admit me for observation because there were no beds, so they sent me home. The next day this – in my opinion – bad consultant came to see me. The consultant had been told I'd tried to commit suicide on my push-bike – and had me straight into hospital, into Myland Court. And decided to give me modified narcosis. This was concussion!

Two days later my uncle dropped down dead. Because he hadn't been at the old people's home long enough to be under a doctor, they needed to have his body identified. My husband said, 'Well, I can do that.' 'No, you can't. It must be his niece.' So they had to bring me out of narcosis and take me to the mortuary.

Then they put me back in narcosis, and then someone said, 'She's got stitches in her head, they've got to come out!' So they had to bring me out of narcosis to take me back to Essex County Hospital to have the stitches out. And I was slightly pie-eyed, 'There's another stitch in there, there's another stitch!' 'No, there isn't.' They took me back to Myland Court, put me back under narcosis.

They had to bring me out for my uncle's funeral. And again I said 'There's still a stitch in my head.' Finally, they found it. They found it! Put me back in narcosis. And then brought me out finally.

The next week, I said, 'I'm going home, I'm fine.' I was high as a kite! So I – I came home, and six days later my husband said, 'I've had enough!' And they took me back.

I think I was so desperately looking for someone to care for me and make me better that if Old Nick had walked in the door I would have – put my trust in him, because I was absolutely desperate. Well, when I came out of narcosis finally, I was lying in bed and I could see the sun shining through the curtains – and oh, it was bliss! I was so pleased. Well, you know, when you've got hot and sweaty and you have a nice refreshing bath, it was like that – but mentally. And I was convinced I was fit to go home. But I wasn't.

Treatments given in the inter-war period, in addition to paraldehyde and phenobarbital, were mostly related to water therapy and light therapy. Prolonged baths were given at Severalls in the inter-war period as a sedative. These proved so popular that four more 'continuous baths' were built in 1935, and four ordinary baths were altered and adapted for treatment baths in the two hospital villas. The nurse quoted earlier remembers in the late 1930s:

When I worked on the acute block we had to give every patient a prolonged bath every morning to try and soothe them. It rarely worked, in fact, I think it used to stir them up. Many a time we would have a real fight on our hands. One morning I was almost choked.

Ultraviolet ray treatment was also given during this time, and into the early 1950s.[10]

Freud's pioneering work in psychoanalysis had been given increasing credence by the relative success of treating post-traumatic neurosis of shell-shocked soldiers during and after the First World War using psychotherapy. While psychiatrists in the USA incorporated much of Freudian theory into their practice from the 1920s, this was much more uneven in Britain. Dr Duncan offered some outpatients psychotherapy in the new outpatient clinic in Colchester from the late 1920s; it may also have been offered in the clinics in Chelmsford, Braintree and Clacton when they opened in the 1930s and 1940s. At least one consultant at Severalls was trying psychotherapy – as one of several treatments – on inpatients in the early 1950s. Psychotherapy, however, has always been problematic in terms of resources, given that it takes a considerable amount of time; it has never been a 'quick fix' in the way ECT or drugs have been, and so has never been widely used within the framework of public services. Counselling and less intensive psychotherapeutic techniques, however, have been increasingly used by psychiatric nurses in particular since the late 1970s, although heavy investments in terms of finance and time make them difficult to offer on a widespread basis. Psychotherapy and psychoanalysis have also presented a long-standing problem as to how effective they actually are, and as to whether they can be regarded as *scientific*.

There is certainly evidence that Dr Turnbull and his colleagues in the inter-war period sought scientific respectability in conjunction with an essentially custodial policy. Their concern, however, was overwhelmingly with the *physical* state of patients. One of the first spatial alterations to the hospital was the conversion of a waiting room in the mortuary into a pathology laboratory. Post-mortems were carried out here from that date, and in 1928 a full-time pathologist was appointed. In 1929 a special room for pathology was built on the east side of the main entrance corridor, and a licence was granted to the pathologist for the purposes of vivisection at the hospital. Julian Taylor's father, Cyril Bush Taylor, was senior technician in the path lab from 1928 to 1951:

> The path lab was fascinating, in as much as they had a door and in the door was a hatch, and you could knock on the door and somebody would come and let you in. But if there were specimens coming in, you just opened the hatch. At the end of the corridor you walked into a small preparation room, a preparation/cleaning room for test tubes, and there was a – certainly a home-made bottle-washing machine and test-tube washing machine that Father had made, and there was the store cupboard and there was the chemical stores in there. And then you went through an interconnecting door, which was actually the path lab proper.

There were teak benches right the way round and the internal wall had bookcases and then in the centre of the room there were large tables which were arranged as writing desks with, again, books on a bookshelf in the centre of that. On the internal wall was an oven-type machine, which was so that specimens were kept at the correct temperature. Then on the bench overlooking the inside court-yard there were about three microscopes, and two of those were binocular microscopes, and they were under glass domes when not in use.

Looking up over the gardens, there was a sectioning machine to take microscopic sections which were embedded in wax, you know, and that was a hand-operated microtome. Then there was a massive machine which was a centrifuge, and this was a fairly big centrifuge, about 3 foot, yes, 3 foot diameter, and that used to vibrate as it went round. And then there were sinks and various bits of appa-ratus.

Outside there were some gardens which were used for allotment-type gardens, but there was also rabbits and guinea-pigs kept in cages, which were used to test reactions, to find out what people had got, and they'd be injected with certain extracts from sputum, from faeces and other things, so that they could actually do autop-sies on them to find out what people had got, you know. But Father had got a patient whose job was to look after the rabbits and guinea-pigs, and he looked after the gardens.

Taylor caught an infection from one of the specimens he was examining and collapsed in 1951 and had to be rushed to the National Hospital for Nervous Diseases in London. He then returned as a patient in Severalls, where he died in 1956.

SOMATIC TREATMENTS

The first wave of major discoveries for somatic cures (or alleged cures) of psychiatric patients came in the 1930s. Ladislaus Meduna believed that there was a mutual antagonism between epilepsy and schizophrenia, and concluded that inducing convulsions in schizophrenics could cure them. The Austrian psychiatrist Manfred Sakel began using insulin as a treat-ment for morphine addiction in 1927, five years after it was first used as a treatment for diabetes. Insulin coma and Metrazol convulsion therapies (Cardiazol in Britain) were first brought into use in 1933 and 1935, although 'there never was a convincing explanation of how Metrazol convulsions worked. The original belief that schizophrenia and epilepsy do not occur in the same person turned out not to be valid.'[11] As early as 1936, doctors expressed grave concern over both the efficacy of insulin and its safety: 'It ought to be said at the onset that the procedure is complicated, difficult and dangerous. No definite principle of dosage has yet been found, and much of the procedure is still a matter of rule of thumb and intuition. There have already been two deaths in the series.'[12] These treatments, nonetheless, were to become extensively used; a woman who worked as a nurse remembers Cardiazol-convulsive therapy being used at Severalls in the late 1930s:

> Another treatment being tried out at this time was called Cardiazol. We prepared the patient by not allowing her any breakfast and putting her to bed with her head at the foot of the bed. The doctor then gave her an injection and we had to hold her down very firmly while she had an induced epileptic fit. The patients didn't have the injection of relaxants, though, we had to hold them down, because they could break their bones. So we had to hold them down. Many treatments of this nature were given and we found a very marked improvement. The patient would start to take an interest in herself and her surroundings.

Insulin shock therapy was also developed in 1935, and I have found one instance of it being used on a patient as early as 1935, but it was probably not used extensively at Severalls until after the war.[13] In 1938, electroconvulsive therapy (ECT) was first used elsewhere, but was not used until after the war at Severalls. Similarly, leucotomy/lobotomy was first promulgated as a 'miracle cure' in 1936, but was not implemented at Severalls until after the war. Better funding, the enactment of the National Health Service, and a new generation of young psychiatrists eager to prove themselves and their profession as 'scientific' all combined to make the late 1940s and 1950s a time when a whole range of new treatments were tried – if almost never tested – in Severalls as in other mental hospitals at the time. All of these treatments were based on 'faulty-machine' models of bio-medicine, and took no account whatsoever of psychological or sociological models of mental illness, although many psychiatrists were also interested in, and committed to, ideals of social rehabilitation.

On 21 November 1945 treatment by insulin shock for certain forms of schizophrenia began on the male side of Severalls;[14] shortage of trained staff prevented its use on the female side for several years. The Management Committee awarded the deputy medical superintendent £3 2s. 6d. for a visit to Croydon Mental Hospital to study insulin treatment, and in April

1946 Ward 14 was converted into the centre for insulin treatment, under the charge of male nurse Lawson, who was promoted to being a deputy charge nurse there. In December 1948 the medical superintendent persuaded the committee that the insulin unit on Ward 14 could be rearranged to accommodate both male and female patients, but it would necessitate female patients being nursed by male nurses. In January 1949 the Board of Control vetoed this, saying it was contrary to the terms of the Lunacy Act 1890. In 1953 the hospital administration again tried to get permission to give women deep insulin treatment, but the medical superintendent reported 'it is regrettable that lack of nurses makes it impossible to submit female patients to the hazards of deep insulin therapy.'

Patients having insulin treatment often sustained fractures; no muscle relaxants were given either for insulin treatment or for ECT at Severalls until 1956. ECT and insulin were often given together, as a male nurse remembered from the early 1950s:

> They used to give insulin coma therapy with ECT on Ward 14. There were mattresses all along the floor on one side of the ward with alternately one mattress then two on top of each other. This was so the patients couldn't fall or roll about and harm themselves. The ward was also used for ECT and sometimes they had ECT when they were in insulin coma.
>
> There'd be between six and eight in the unit at one time. The ward would be cleared by lunch time and they'd start round about eight o'clock. They'd then start it and by ten-ish people would be well into coma. They went through different stages on the way into coma and were brought out of it with high glucose naso-gastric tube feeding. We'd give them ECT neat – I can remember the introduction of – I suppose it might have been Pentathol – or something to give as a sleep-inducing substance, and then with a mixture of Scoline – that was a muscle relaxant. I remember one time seeing ECT given to a male patient who was standing up struggling with the staff. Oh yeah. I must admit, some of those patients would resist it.

In 1958 the insulin unit was changed to a Largactil unit. By 1960, when Dr Barton came as physician superintendent, only 'modified insulin' treatment was used:

> Well, there were two kinds of insulin treatment. One where you increased the dose until they went into a seizure, and that was the insulin treatment for schizophrenia. There was another called modified insulin, in which you gave the individual about 10, 15 units of

insulin in order to improve their appetite, and you let them go just so far until they were feeling a little woozy and then they had a breakfast of potatoes, bacon and egg. That was modified insulin.

Now the first one, the insulin, the real insulin treatment, which was quite a bugger because it was really like an operation in the Battle of Britain – it was dying out in the sixties and it had been stopped at Severalls when I got there. But, on the other hand, as I used to say to them, if you do all these things to a person, if you're concerned about them, if you're active about them and you talk to them, and you give them *any* form of medical treatment, the fact that you are interested and concerned – they improve tremendously. So it may not be the insulin at all! And this was met with hoots and derisions, because of course the only things that work are drugs in many people's minds. But I think that's how it worked.

It is interesting to note that 'a properly controlled study of the effectiveness of insulin coma therapy was not undertaken until roughly twenty years after the treatment was first introduced, when Ackner, Harris and Oldham demonstrated that insulin was not the effective agent in causing therapeutic change.'[15]

The most long-standing treatment, however, has been ECT. This was first offered at Severalls in the 1940s, and is still in use today. Electricity had, in fact, long been believed to have therapeutic effects on mental disorder. In AD 47 nonconvulsive electrotherapy was used by Scribonius Largus, who treated the headaches of the Roman emperor with an electric eel.[16] Electric catfish were used in sixteenth-century Ethiopia to produce shock and expel devils from the body. Experiments with electricity were carried out in the seventeenth, eighteenth and nineteenth centuries in Europe. It was the Italian psychiatrist Ugo Cerletti, however, who is generally credited with inventing the application of electroshock therapy to the brain. He became interested in the electroshocking of hogs as a means of tranquillising them prior to being butchered and decided to test the method on a human subject. A complete stranger was found wandering in a confused state in Milan, and was brought to Cerletti by the police, supposedly 'for observation'. Instead, Cerletti used him for experiments with electroshock, despite the patient's pleas: 'Not another one! It's deadly!'[17] In 1938, in collaboration with Professor Bini, he devised the first electroshock apparatus.

Initially Severalls had problems with the ECT apparatus, because the hospital generated its own electricity supply which was incompatible with the apparatuses then on the market. Convertors had to be purchased, but certainly from 1945 (and possibly earlier) ECT was being used, usually in conjunction with insulin. Table 7.1, based on records for 1948–56 shows the numbers of patients treated using ECT.

Table 7.1 Numbers of women and men given ECT at Severalls, 1948–1956

Year	Men	Women	Total
1948	43	109	152
1949	71	234	305
1950	66	153	219
1951	119	203	312
1952	140	232	372
1953	138	293	331
1954	90	336	426
1955	116	412	528
1956	114	317	432

Source: Medical superintendent's annual reports to the Board of Control

Table 7.2 Numbers of patients given insulin/modified insulin treatment at Severalls, 1948–1956

Year	Insulin coma		Modified insulin		Total
	Men	Women	Men	Women	
1948	22	0	0	0	22
1949	23	0	0	0	23
1950	30	0	0	10	40
1951	33	0	28	36	97
1952	34	0	n/a	n/a	–
1953	32	0	47	50	129
1954	36	0	30	20	86
1955	32	0	27	22	81
1956	22	17	17	1	57

Source: Medical superintendent's annual reports to the Board of Control

Although there were always more female inpatients than males – generally about a third more females – it is interesting to note the far higher proportions of women who were given ECT, by 1955 almost four times as many women were having this treatment. Table 7.2 shows the number of patients receiving insulin treatment during the same period, numbers which, compared with those receiving ECT, are really quite low. ECT had (and has) the advantage of being quick, cheap and easy to administer, whereas insulin treatment was more labour-intensive, required a special diet and took much longer.

A male nurse who ran the ECT unit at Myland Court remembered the early days of its use at Severalls:

I spent my last eight years running the ECT clinic, because I retired, then I went to work with ECT because the nurse that was there

199

was leaving. When the sister from there went back home to Mauritius or somewhere I took over as a senior staff nurse and ran the unit until I retired in '91. We moved it to The Lakes. But, of course, in the old days there used to be straight ECT. No injections and no nothing. Lay the patient out, hold him, put it on there, press the button – and bang! Oh, it was crude, it was crude. But if you got an acutely depressed patient or an acutely manic patient they'd sometimes have it twice a day – morning and evening. It definitely helped. And, I mean today, I still say that is the quickest treatment for severe depression there is.

Another male nurse, however, also remembered the early days of ECT at Severalls and makes clear that it was by no means always administered with kindness:

Used to do ECT up in Maplehurst, about six at a time, twice a week. There was no anaesthesia – oh no, no, no. It was just sort of the rough way we did it then. They'd lay down, you used to give the injection – a muscle relaxant – 'cause, you see, once they got it on, some of these doctors were cruel. They used to go, 'I'll give him one for luck!' Hold 'em down, you have to hold 'em down, as you know. And of course they kept that jerk up. Then some smart alec just when you sort of relax 'em a bit, 'Oh, you can give him one for luck!' See, you're responsible, that used to be foolish some of them doing that. But some of the young junior doctors they used to love to do it.

Many patients were terrified of ECT, and it is clear that it was some-times used as both threat and punishment by nursing and medical staff. Electricity has often been used as a form of torture, particularly on political prisoners, in the twentieth century, and in the USA, of course, the electric chair has been a central means of execution. Sylvia Plath, in *The Bell Jar*, associated her own ECT treatment with the execution of the Rosenbergs – alleged communists during the McCarthy witch-hunts – in 1953. Confronting needles and electrical apparatus, followed by mental confusion and loss of memory can be a terrifying experience. This woman was a patient off and on at Severalls for years and remembered ECT with dread:

I think ECT was awful. I mean, you had a dreadful headache, you couldn't remember things, you know. Sometimes you got better, but sometimes you got worse and you had to have more and more and more. You did get used to it in the end, you realised what was going to happen. But at the beginning it was quite frightening. Yeah. They gave you a general anaesthetic and – you can feel this rush going through you and it knocked you out.

I didn't have much choice in it at the beginning, but at the very end my family didn't want it. And there was doctor who said, 'Well, yes, we would like you to just have one.' And I said, 'Well, look, I'm against it.' And he said, 'We can just get another doctor's opinion and we can give it to you anyway!' So I had one. I don't know if it made much difference anyway. I think *time* makes the difference. You get better over time.

Dr Russell Barton had ECT administered to himself in the 1950s to see what it was like:

I went into Shenley Hospital and began to see the process there, began to find out that it was a disregard for people's feelings, like giving ECT just by giving Anectine,[18] a muscle relaxant which is very painful and you feel suffocated before the merciful electric shock comes. I'd had it administered in Westminster when they were trying it out. I had no idea how horrifying it was, so from then on I always gave sodium amytal – 200, 250 mg – and then when the patient – I'd make them count backwards and when they'd begin not to count then I would shove in the Anectine and then they'd give the fibrillary twitches – the little movements which tell you that the motor receptors are being knocked out so that you won't get a spasm – and then I would give the shock. We then made it a rule that all treatments should be preceded by a mild anaesthetic and that's the rule now. There's no need – this needless infliction of cruelty is quite unjustified.
Do you think ECT was an effective form of treatment?
Well, not if it were given for punishment. And it was. Not if it were given for schizophrenia. And it was. Not if it were given because you didn't know the diagnosis. But if you had a patient who was really depressed, who was not sleeping, lying awake, and who had lost interest in things, in life, in music, and who had lost any energy to do anything and who felt much better as the day had wore on. And if you put these cardinal factors of insomnia, anhedonia, depression and so forth and gave them ECT, it was magic. And you would see – I used to give two or three a week – in two weeks someone that had come in neglecting themselves, perhaps incontinent, women

with hair all tousled over their head. In two weeks she would be perky, her breasts would be showing, her hair would be – because I always got them hair-dos – and it was so wonderful to see the change.

One patient, who was diagnosed as schizophrenic, far preferred ECT to most of the – many – drugs he was given:

ECT, yeah. That was a lifesaver. If I hadn't have had that I'd be mad and I'd be dead. Yeah, it really made a difference. I used to feel so relieved when I'd had it. It cleared my mind of all thoughts of good and evil and things that happened to me I forgot. I couldn't remember my own parents when they came to visit me. I said to them, 'I know who you are.' But then, I said, 'No, I can't think of who you are.' I'd only seen them the week before! That's what the ECT did. So. It took me years to get me memory back – of some things. But it was worth it.

Administration of ECT has become gentler and more humane, first, by introducing muscle relaxants, second, by giving anaesthetics or sedatives, and in the 1960s in Severalls the electrical apparatus was placed behind a curtain so that patients did not see it when they were brought in for treatment. It remains, however, a controversial treatment and one which still frightens people. Quick, cheap and easy to administer, it is undoubtedly an attractive option in times of financial stringency, and evidence does suggest it often helps severe depression, as this consultant made clear:

The Royal College of Psychiatrists has gone into great depth at investigating and studying the effects of ECT, the indications of ECT, and has come out with a whole document about it. And they have come out with a clear statement, clear guidelines, that if you select the right type of patient, that particular depressed person who is near to a depressive stupor, who is not eating, who is not drinking, whose suicidal drive is so strong that they can't wait for anti-depressants to work, whose psychomotor retardation is so marked that nothing is working, to save their life, ECT is the only treatment really. I think if you select the right patient and you give them ECT, then it works miracles. In the early days it was used – it was overused – and it was used in the wrong sort of patients and I think that's why it got a bad name. By the mid-seventies there were enough anti-depressants on the market for us to decrease the use of ECT, because instead you could select, you see, an anti-depressant.

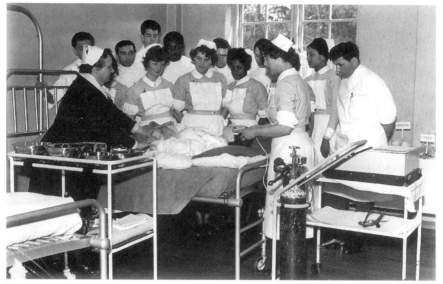

Figure 7.1 Sister tutor teaching student nurses ECT procedure, 1950s
Source: North East Essex Mental Health NHS Trust

LEUCOTOMIES AND EXPERIMENTS

A far more drastic, and indeed, more horrifying, form of treatment which began to be used at Severalls in the 1940s, was leucotomy. Trepanning the skull had been used in the Stone Age, according to recent archaeological evidence; a neolithic site in Alsace, more than 7,000 years old, revealed a man of about 50 years old who had two holes in his head that were apparently surgical operations. There was evidence they had healed.[19] What the general success rate was, however, I do not know. In the 1930s, Moniz began experimenting with a similar technique, the success rate of which may not have been much greater than that of Stone Age neuro-surgeons.

Nonetheless, so great was the general desire for 'scientific' cures for mental illness, Moniz was awarded the Nobel Prize in medicine in 1949: 'lobotomy was promoted by the popular press. Magazines and newspapers, whose readers numbered in the millions, popularised each new "miracle cure" with uncritical enthusiasm, while commonly overlooking its shortcomings and dangers.'[20] Moniz performed the first frontal lobotomy in 1935, but the first British operation did not take place until 1940 (at the Burden Neurological Institute in Bristol). It received widespread acclaim both in medical journals and in the popular press, although there were some who spoke out against it, notably Donald Winnicott in *The Lancet* during the early 1950s.

It seems extraordinary in retrospect to consider how hard-pressed rural mental hospitals such as Severalls were for finances and, indeed, medical staff, and yet how willing they were to invest scarce resources in new techniques for which evidence of success was, at best, scanty. In fact, the tools required for leucotomy were crude and fairly cheap – the 'leucotome' was an instrument not unlike an apple-corer, and, indeed, ice-picks were used for operations by Walter Freeman in the USA; the first investment in surgical instruments for leucotomies at Severalls totalled £19 in 1949, two years later an additional £26 10s was spent on further instruments. An operating theatre, however, was necessary, as was a brain surgeon. Severalls had the former, but not yet the latter.

In April 1949 Dr Duncan reported he had some discussion with a Mr Sherwood, a 'neuro-surgeon' of the London Hospital and had arranged for a regular session for leucotomy operations. Sherwood began at once, and by 1951 had carried out a hundred operations, primarily on women patients. Dr Duncan's report on Sherwood's early work was most enthusiastic:

> It is now possible to report on 100 patients on whom Mr S L Sherwood has performed leucotomy between April 1949 and January 1951. There were no deaths following operation, no cases of haemorrhage, and only one case of complications. For a serious operation known to carry a decided mortality risk this constitutes a very fine achievement. Of these 100 patients 38 have been discharged, and some others are expected to become well enough to leave hospital. Three patients died, at least twelve months after operation and from causes quite dissociated from it. One patient has been transferred elsewhere. Of the 58 patients remaining in hospital, the majority are much improved; many of them had psychiatric conditions in which the most that could be expected was some alleviation of symptoms, and it has been very gratifying to observe the improvement of interest and general enjoyment of life.[21]

Case notes, however, suggest that Sherwood's operations were by no means always as successful as Duncan had first hoped. In 1953 a man was admitted as a voluntary patient to Severalls, aged 51. He had suffered from sleeplessness, depression and paranoia, convinced that his neighbour was persecuting him. Within two weeks his depression had lifted, he was sociable and did well in OT. Discharged after a month in hospital, he was readmitted the following day, insisting his neighbour was still persecuting him. It does seem perplexing that nobody thought of taking this claim seriously; neighbours, of course, can, and do, persecute people.

Again, his depression lifted quickly once in Severalls. Nevertheless, they gave him insulin treatment for twenty-six days, followed by three ECT treatments.

He was then discharged, but back again a month later with the same complaint as before. Between March 1954 and May 1955 he was given sixteen ECT treatments and insulin. By the end of those, he was found to be 'tense and agitated'. In April, they proposed giving him a leucotomy. Some notes were then rubbed out and it is not clear whether he had a leucotomy then or not. The next legible notes say he suffers from constant headaches and is depressed. In July he tried to commit suicide and was given Largactil. His depression continued. In November he tried to kill himself again. He was given a leucotomy. Five days after the operation he had a swinging temperature and was doubly incontinent. Two weeks after that he had difficulty with feeding, his pulse was weak and his bedsores were getting worse. A month after the operation he was unable to cooperate enough to test reflexes or visual fields. Dr Sherwood explored part of his temporal lobe with a needle on 21 January 1956. Afterwards the patient suffered severe pain in the neck and ran a high fever. Ten days later he was dead.

Sherwood received substantial fees for each operation and was also awarded fees by the committee for travel and research abroad. The medical superintendent's reports revealed that between 1949 and 1956 Sherwood carried out 308 leucotomies.[22] Intertwined with these reports, however, is mention of Sherwood's – unspecified – research work and requests for funding, especially for an electroencephalograph, which he had installed in 1953. In the sentence that follows the reported number of leucotomies performed in 1953, is stated 'Intraventricular injections, 82 in all, were given to 10 patients'.[23] In 1954, 222 were given, in 1955 there were 76 intraventricular injections, and in 1956, 224. Other records kept between May 1952 and January 1955, however, claimed 198 intraventricular injections were given to 20 women and 3 men. One woman received 33 of these. Chemicals injected included banthine, adrenaline, 'CHE', atrophine, Pentothal and tyrode. Yvonne Caron, who worked as a nurse at the time, remembered watching Sherwood carry out one of these experiments:

Sherwood said, 'Well I'm going to put this thing in, you know.' Well, it's not that I'm frightened of needles – but this wasn't just a needle! I mean it was something – God knows what he was doing! Some of them, I don't think they got any better. Definitely not. Some of them got worse actually. Not so much violence-wise, but you know, they used to repeat themselves all day long. One lady, she had that done, and they put her in Ward C – I don't think she should have been there – and she sat there all day long saying, 'I don't belong here, you know, nurse, I don't belong here, nurse, I shouldn't be here, nurse.' You know – I remember – I was so sorry. But it wore me out. What that had done to her state of mind I don't know. It was tragic actually. She couldn't have been more than 40, 45.

Russell Barton remembered hearing Sherwood speak about his research in the 1950s:

I met him at the Royal Society of Medicine when he gave a very interesting paper on the work he'd been doing. And before one blasts Sherwood – he shouldn't have done it and it was wrong – one must remember that a distinguished woman consultant in London, who was very well thought of, was putting needles into the livers of newborn babies without their mothers' permission to get hepatic samples. I think that sort of experimentation is dreadful, and Sherwood was doing this.

Admittedly he chose very deteriorated patients, but he would drill a small – it's not very difficult to do – hole, and then insert a cannula, which is a non-reactive metal, down into the mid-ventricle, and then at the top there'd be a little screw with a rubber pad, you know, a piece of rubber, a rubber diaphragm, and he would inject into that various substances to see the reactions.

And this came out and there was a huge scandal and the *News of the World* had it and so forth, and this made the Regional Boards and the ministers and the Ministry of Health and all that very worried about experimentation. He was trying to show that there was absorption of these active chemicals through the third ventricle into the cerebro-spinal fluid, and that it was this that changed mood.

By 1954 Sherwood was conducting six sessions a week for leucotomy operations and his research at Severalls. The Regional Board, however, was by this time less forthcoming with expenses for his travels. They also turned down his application to be upgraded from senior hospital medical officer to a consultant. About this time there was an increased reaction against leucotomies generally. In *The Lancet* the following report appeared: 'On December 17, 1955 questions were raised in Parliament about leucotomies "alleging that in an unnamed hospital in England experiments were being carried out for sheer experimental purposes on these patients" by a Dr Sherwood.' This had come to the notice of certain people and MPs as a result of reports in the press. In spite of this, a report from the Board of Control in May 1957 clearly showed that, despite questions raised in Parliament, Sherwood did continue his work: 'Some investigation is taking place with regard to the treatment of catatonic schizophrenia by intra ventricular injections of Cholinesterase and synthetic endocrines with encouraging results'.

The hospital secretary, who started work a year before Sherwood left, had no recollection of any press reports (which would have been prior to his coming) but when I asked him if he remembered Dr Sherwood, he told me:

I do. What are you going to ask me about him?
Well, I've heard quite a bit about him. I know he was doing research on patients, for instance.
Cutting brains open, yes.
Do you remember, at the time, was anybody on the staff uneasy about what he was doing?
Eventually Dr Duncan. Eventually – you see, he'd encouraged his coming. He'd encouraged his coming because a friend of his at the London Hospital had recommended him, was a doctor. He was a German, of course, his name was Schoenberg, as you probably know, and he experimented on these patients, and eventually one died, and the coroner was very critical, and Duncan decided that was the end.

As far as I know, it got no publicity, not from this end. But I think there was suspicion from the chief doctors on the Board, the Hospital Board, you know, Regional Board, got worried about him. But – you see, they were doing leucotomies in places all over the country, so – it was reckoned that he was experimenting – but this patient who died caused a lot of trouble. I can't remember who was the coroner. But that's what happened, and so Duncan asked the Board to – cancel his contract.

The nursing staff obviously knew some form of experimentation was going on, as this male nurse remembered:

Leucotomies. Yes. Oh yes. It was the worst job you could ever have. I used to work in the operating theatre with a Dr Sherwood, and you'd got to hold this sucker, and you'd got to hold it that close to the brain, and you weren't allowed to touch it while he was doing. Oh, and you were only there a few minutes, but by God, you'd gotta hold it still. So, they used to do leucotomies and undercuts and all various things.

Yet this man was also witness to recoveries from leucotomies which he found impressive:

I can't remember his name – he was very depressed. He was a well-educated man, very depressed, and they gave him a course of ECT and everything, and it didn't help him at all. So they gave him a leucotomy. And within six months he was one of the air controllers at London Airport. It's like everything, isn't it. I mean, fashions change. They go round, I mean, they still do a thing called 'stereotactic leucotomies' and it's very rarely done. And what they do is drill a burr hole, and they put a radium seed into the nerve path, and it's got a life of – or a half a life – of forty-eight hours, so within four days it's burnt the nerve paths, and that relieves the depression. That's the latest thing.

Michael Wilson had rather more mixed feelings about the efficacy of leucotomies:

I must say, I didn't really like the idea of leucotomies. It was just my own personal feelings, but I did see some dramatic changes in people following leucotomies. They were more tranquil, let's put it this way, and possibly led a better life because they weren't having so much stress and anxiety. Well, whether you want somebody that's very agitated all the time, I don't know, but we did see this result. Leucotomies were the vogue at the time. But of course these faded out when the – what we call the chemical leucotomies came in, the Largactils and things like this, which were better because they were adjustable. 'Cause once you'd been Attila the Hun with the leucotomes you couldn't put it right again afterwards. I know it sounds a bit crude, but that is roughly how they were doing it.

Case notes suggest that psychiatrists basically operated on a trial-and-error basis when treating patients. If one treatment didn't work, they tried another. Long-stay patients, particularly from the 1950s, often experienced numerous treatments as a result. One young man, for example, was admitted in 1952 at the age of 21. He had previously worked as a clerk and been in the Navy. His consultant found him 'dull and very retarded' and thought his memory had been impaired by recent events during which he had been picked up by the police in a place far from his own home. He gave him six treatments of ECT with deep insulin on alternate days, but a month later recorded: 'shows no improvement. Talked about a firing squad.'

The patient then made several bids for escape, all of which were unsuccessful. A month after the ECT and insulin treatment, the consultant decided to give him a 'methadone abreaction' session, but was disappointed that only 'a vague schizoid detached argumentative type of ranting is displayed. No clear memory.' So he sent him for a further sixteen ECT sessions ten days later, even though earlier this treatment had had no beneficial effect. No improvement was noted this time either, rather, he seemed more confused. The consultant then decided to give him a series of 'couch sessions', presumably his version of psychoanalysis or psycho-therapy, but he was given methylamphetamines first. Some ten of these couch sessions were given, but the doctor found his emotional displays 'disorganised' with slight bewilderment and lack of clear memory. In fact, the patient *did* reveal how and why he had gone so far away from his home.

The consultant, however, found he was 'getting many repetitive phrases' and decided 'a psychotherapeutic approach will not be fruitful and I am deciding to abandon the attempt.' He had him put back on deep insulin, although earlier insulin treatment had achieved nothing; thirty insulin comas were then recorded. After these 'little change' was recorded, so they tried ECT again. The notes say he was worse after ECT. He was then left without any treatment at all until 1958, when he was given Largactil, made some improvement, and then made no further change at all. There are no further records of what happened to him after that.

Reading this I got the impression that the psychiatrist took almost no note whatsoever of the previous failures of other treatments. Trying insulin, ECT, then methadone, amphetamines, psychotherapy and finally Largactil suggests a trial-and-error approach that had little basis in 'scientific' rigour whereby, presumably, certain treatments would be accepted as appropriate for certain symptoms. While the desire for scientific objectivity was often undoubtedly present, psychiatrists also turned to less scientific treatments, such as psychotherapy, and also hoped that social rehabilitation and occu-pational therapy might help. The persistent lack of clarity as to what exactly mental illnesses were, however, meant that moral judgements frequently determined diagnosis. It is now widely believed, for instance, that some young women who bore illegitimate children not only had their children taken away, but were certified as insane and often given ECT, leucotomies and other treatments for their transgressions, which by the time they were hospitalised became pathologised as illness. Such behaviour has not been labelled as mental illness now for many years. Definitions of what constitutes mental illness come and go, as do treatments.

In the 1950s and 1960s, for instance, an increasing number of homo-sexuals were treated as pathological and in need of psychiatric treatment:

> Aversion therapy, in the Fifties, was psychiatry's new toy. It was intended to eliminate unwanted or dangerous behaviour, from thumb-sucking to paedophilia . . . It worked, said the textbooks, by altering behaviour by the application of an unpleasant or noxious stimulus . . . The administration of a vomit-inducing drug,

such as apromorphine, was one of the noxious stimuli frequently employed. Another aversive stimulus was the use of electric shocks.

The unwanted behaviours originally targeted ranged from overeating to obsessive hand-washing, but homosexuality soon joined the list along with other types of sexual 'deviance' such as exhibitionism and transvestism. Studies suggest that it was administered to many hundreds of homosexual men in Britain, the US and many other countries throughout the Fifties and Sixties. The Royal College of Psychiatrists says it is impossible to know how many men underwent aversion therapy for gender reorientation in the UK, because records have been destroyed or lost during computerisation, and hospitals have been closed down.[24]

Russell Barton was using aversion therapy with paedophiles when he came to Severalls in the early 1960s. He used graphic photographs of older men buggering young boys in conjunction with the self-administration of electric shocks. There was, however, disapproval at the time, as he remarked:

> I remember Dr Sturup from Denmark who came to give a talk. He said, 'we've castrated them, and we've powdered them with every medication known to man. We've given them aversion therapy,' electric shocks – you know, you get a picture of a boy's buttocks that excites them and you then make them flick the epidiascope so the picture comes up, but at the same time it administers shock. Well, if we did it – and we did to start with – then we got accused of torturing. But if they do it to themselves, it's OK. 'Well,' he said, 'I've done all these things, but like Charity in the Bible, it profiteth me nothing.'

A PHARMACOLOGICAL REVOLUTION?

As soon as a new treatment was suggested, psychiatrists tended to dive in head-first in an enthusiastic bid to find the 'miracle cure' for the hundreds of distressed and desperate people they held within their walls. Some treatments were discovered purely by chance, and some worked better than others. Such a discovery was that of chlorpromazine in 1952. Originally thought to have a beneficial effect on morning sickness, it was recognised to have a powerful calming effect on psychosis. The discovery of chlorpromazine – marketed in Britain as Largactil – had an enormous impact on psychiatric treatments. At the time the hope was that this represented, at last, a miracle cure. While many did benefit dramatically, time came to prove that its value lay more as a means of control than as an ultimate cure. Leading from its – important – discovery, however, came a series of other major tranquillisers, known as the neuroleptics.

Like so many other treatments, Largactil was adopted quickly, and often without adequate trial or knowledge. Most mental hospitals in the UK began widespread use in 1954. It seems Severalls also tried Largactil at this time, but then Dr Duncan had it stopped until 1957/8. A man who worked as an electrician at Severalls from the 1940s, was friendly with many of the charge nurses and remembered a discussion he had with one:

> Ward 5 – Jock was the charge nurse, and he said, 'Oh, a doctor said, "I'm going to clear this ward within a month!"' 'Well,' Jock said, 'Well, you're doing all right up to now, five people died last night!' That was when Largactil first came out, do you remember that? They opened that ward for Largactil patients. And they got to a stage when they had what they call 'Big Largactil', which was a massive dose – and five of 'em died during the night.
> *Was it publicised at all?*
> No fear! It didn't even get round the hospital!
> *How did you find out about it?*
> 'Cause I went up the ward and was talkin' to Jock when this doctor came up. It was all hushed up. Very much. Yeah.

One consultant said that in the 1950s[25] Severalls was two years behind other hospitals, and that he had looked at records from the pharmacy and found that a number of patients put on chlorpromazine had died. The doctors, he explained, got frightened and stopped using it. I could find no records from the pharmacy still in existence. It has also been suggested that Dr Duncan was at this time becoming increasingly uneasy about Dr Sherwood's work and research, and decided to play it safe by not carrying out any further experiments – and possible deaths – with Largactil. It was not until late in 1957, after the appointment of Dr Bachner as registrar, that Dr Duncan agreed to try Largactil again. Michael Wilson remembers the effects of the new anti-psychotic drugs as dramatic:

> Round about '57 time they were approached to look at chlorpromazine – and also somebody came through with reserpine, and we tried these out on patients, mainly in the chronic wards was where we tried them. And we would have so many patients on this – probably ten or something, I've forgotten now – and we'd put them on a programme of habit training. It has to be remembered that in the middle fifties we used to have patients who were remnants from

the war, people who'd deteriorated during the war from shell-shock or from prison camps. It was tried on a lot of different patients. Some of the doses were quite high – 800 mgs four times a day, some once or twice 1,000 mgs.

But of course we soon became aware of problems – we had this – I don't know what you call it now – this thing from sunlight, if they went out in the sun their skin would get automatically burned on these high doses. They also had other effects too, with some there'd be a decreased number of white cells. I think it could also be related to the breakdown of the auto-immune system, I'm not sure. And there were a lot of people that had these problems, BUT of the two types of drugs – chlorpromazine and reserpine – reserpine was dropped fairly quickly because it had dreadful effects on blood pressure, but the Largactil was continued and I must admit it proved a boon to society.

Because I can remember patients that had never come out a padded room, that had never been anything but dirty, scruffy people who would defecate and micturate anywhere, who were messy all the time, who wouldn't keep clothes on – and these people we were supposed to feed them with Largactil – we had it in a syrup form as well as in the tablet form – we used to mix it in with their custard and eggs and so on and gradually get them to ingest some of this – chlorpromazine.

And it worked very well. These people came out of their shells, they woke up. And a lot of us wrote letters for them because they would suddenly come up and start talking to us as if they'd come out of – and we had some dreadful shocks for people because this business of – people had withdrawn probably for ten years, twenty years – because all they had up to that time was sedation. And this was an *exciting* time.

And the Largactil syrup was quite good stuff, actually. It was a little bit like a good Bristol Cream Sherry and at Christmas time everybody had parties and things. I can remember one deputy matron being found on the cricket pitch in the morning – we used to mix the Largactil sometimes with the sherry when they came round – 'Oh no, I mustn't drink! I mustn't drink! OK, OK, I'll have just a little sherry – sweet one if you don't mind.' And we used to give her this.

Largactil greatly reduced violence and terror in psychotic patients (and possibly also in deputy matrons). Although it did not turn out to be quite the cure originally hoped, it enabled a more relaxed regime to be put into effect in hospital wards, and it meant that some patients were able to be given far more freedom than before, whether ultimately in the outside community or within the hospital community. Undoubtedly the discovery of chlorpromazine and the neuroleptics facilitated the possibility of gentler, more humane treatment for patients, even if for many this meant needing to stay within the hospital, or coming back and forth on a revolving-door basis. It meant more chronic patients could be responsive to rehabilitation programmes, occupational therapy, physical and social activities than had been the case before. Many were able to enter, or re-enter, the labour force: an option which became increasingly unlikely from the 1980s. It may not have cured them, and many would complain of being overdosed with huge cocktails of drugs in subsequent years, but the impact and the repercussions of the new neuroleptic drugs from the 1950s on patterns of treatment, mental health policy, and, indeed, the demise of psychiatric hospitals generally, have been enormous.

CHANGING ATTITUDES

In the 1950s, however, eminent psychiatrists like Sir Aubrey Lewis thought the new drugs were of secondary importance to other developments in psychiatry such as the advent of the NHS which facilitated better standards of care such as open-door policies, rehabilitation programmes, and an improved career structure for psychiatrists that did not mean promotion was always equivalent to extra administrative duties. When Russell Barton came to Severalls in 1960 he certainly used the new drugs, but as a catalyst to more profound changes. Above all, he aimed to change *attitudes*:

> Well, we were just – we had just introduced the drug treatment for depression – Amitriptyline, and Imipramine and those anti-depressants – we hadn't got very much in the way of sedative for the agitation, so we would usually use one of the phenothiazines like Largactil, which has a sedating effect as well. And then a sleeping pill at night so they would reduce the agitation, elevate the depression, restore the normal sleep rhythm. And usually in two weeks you would see a difference.
>
> But we did have a lot of groups going – chronic groups, too. We had hula-hoop groups for the very chronic – they would all be swinging hula-hoops. And then they would first of all do it – you see in stages – first of all, the nurse would do it on her wrist, then she would hold the patient's hand and they would do it together, and then the nurse – the patient – would do it on her own. Then

Figure 7.2 Chronic women patients help each other with hula-hoops, *circa* 1960
Source: Russell Barton archive

the nurse would do it round her middle and then the patients would try it – it took them a long time to do it. Eventually there were whole wards of people hula-hooping. It was crazy!

Art therapy and music therapy were used increasingly during Dr Barton's early years, as he remembered:

And then drawing. I used to get a sheet of paper and I used to say, 'Now, draw as many lines as you feel is good.' And then, 'Now, pick out shapes you like – mark that in – nice black pen – gorgeous!' And then I'd say to them, 'Paint this bit green and this yellow and

214

then red and it'll look just like Picasso here with the black one there!' So they would pick out the shapes.

At first it was a mess – but eventually it was very satisfying. They all had an easel – made by our factories of course – and they had chlorpromazine tins to dip their brushes in. And they had ordinary pill things to put the different colours in. And then I would do that with them – leading them – and then I'd get the nurse to take over – and I'd go on to, you know, the next group and then we'd draw a face – the lips here and draw the hair in and then the female body – not from a naked lady – and that was dreadful – the Committee came in! I explained, you know, if you take the buttock and you go round and up here, then you've got half of it done, you've just got to put legs in and arms – it's easy. But some of the patients, of course, some of the men did make it look a little rude! And the Committee – you must remember – it was *Essex* – 1960, 1961!

We had a wonderful art and music department and we had Orff instruments – which means you take out the Devil's Interval – that is, the F and the B, so then anything you play isn't out of tune. So you can hit anything and you're in with the music, and they used to love this. That and percussion. Yeah. Creativity gives them the fundamental feeling that what they do is worthwhile, is significant and they're not just on the scrap heap, that they're part of a world in which they have an importance and what they do is important.

Some time around the mid-1950s patients increasingly came to be seen as human beings in distress who could, with help, return to a better way of living in which they could begin to realise more of their potential. Tapping creativity was certainly of enormous importance to some, such as this woman patient who, after innumerable – unsuccessful – treatments of ECT, Largactil, insulin and sleep treatment, was recommended music therapy by her psychiatrist:

I had a dream when I was in hospital, when I was on the general ward after my last suicide attempt. I had this dream which was – accompanied by the sound of tubular bells. And then when I went to music therapy for the first time, Penny got me working with tubular bells, and I suddenly remembered this dream and just collapsed in floods of tears. It was all to do with loss. And I very nearly bashed a hole in the floor of the room, you know. I was trying not to cry – and I was getting angry – and I was thumping the floor. But that was an inspired idea, because the music therapy was the turning-point. I think without that I would still be doing the revolving-door bit. I was very frightened, because music of any kind always arouses very deep emotions, and very violent ones in me.

Both physically and aurally I got some sort of relief, and there was one time, I think I was playing a phrase over and over again, or a rhythm over and over again, and – she often would play the piano while I was playing something else and build up on it, you see – leaving me to lead. But sometimes she would be able to take that phrase and sort of encapsulate it. And then when we were talking afterwards she'd be able to tease out why I kept going to it, you know, 'Did it remind me of something? Did it express something?' And sometimes I was able then to get into words what I'd not been able to get into words for perhaps all my life.

At the same time as more therapies were coming into use, new developments in drugs meant drug use was also increasing. Lithium, for instance, came into widespread use as a treatment for manic-depression in Britain in the 1960s.[26] Its side-effects, however, can be dangerous, as this woman patient explained:

They started putting me on Lithium quite a long time ago and they said, 'Oh, you've got to be on Lithium the rest of your life' and they didn't say 'it's because you're a manic-depressive.' I mean, I never knew I was a manic-depressive till years later. Nobody ever said. It was all sort of post-natal depression. I don't know if Lithium made any difference.

It affected my kidneys. It's a very dangerous thing to have. I was on it for years and then my waterworks just packed up, and they took me off it. My father said to me, 'I think at your age you should be off tablets, doing things like psychotherapy.' Which I've got to wait another year for. This is where they should be putting their money: talking to people and talking through their problems.

Certainly since the 1960s psychiatric treatment, both in Severalls and elsewhere, has become increasingly eclectic and varied. Recently cognitive therapy has been developed and implemented extensively as a quick and apparently easy way of changing patients' negative attitudes and behaviours. A nurse who went into education, however, felt this was not the best solution:

There's been a huge investment in terms of education into cognitive behavioural therapy, which brings about very fast responses. I won't go into the dubious ethics of some of it, but – it is dubious ethically. I don't know a lot about it, but it involves helping people to think differently, and therefore behave differently. What it doesn't appear to address is feelings.

Let me give you an example of someone that was described to me quite recently, someone who actually couldn't go anywhere because she was afraid of a particular word appearing. I can't for the life of me remember what the word is now, but what the therapist said to her was, 'Every time you see that word you need to put an "r" in it, or some other letter, so that it becomes another word.'

And actually, this did allow her to go out, because it worked. It did work for her. She was able to go out and because every time she saw this particular sequence of letters, she put this other letter in with it so that it became something else. Now that changed the way she responded to this. But it didn't at all, ever, at any point, investigate where all this came from. OK, so it can allow you to take control, but to me it's a fairly predictable response to a mone-tarily driven response that they would opt to invest in short-term, sharp-turnover, therapy.

Treatments still include art therapy, music therapy, occupational therapy – all therapies dealt with by professionals other than psychiatrists them-selves. Samson has argued that this has resulted recently in an erosion of the power of the psychiatric profession in Britain.[27] Psychiatric nurses now do much of the work once done by psychiatrists. Psychiatrists, however, retain the important power base of diagnosis and drug prescription. The nurse quoted earlier who works in education commented:

I think psychiatrists have kept us back. I think they've maintained the medical model because it's their power base, and I think one of the things that happens with the move to the community is that they lose a lot of that power. There are a lot of very, very skilled nurses around who are perfectly capable of working autonomously and don't actually need the input of a consultant psychiatrist, except to sign the piece of paper. I mean, I think *they* need to change. *They* need to think about moving on.

For example, a woman came in and she was quite depressed, and this consultant wanted to put her on anti-depressant medication. And she refused. So this consultant said, 'Oh well, there's not much point in you staying here if you're not going to take the medication. I'll discharge you.' And the nurse – fortunately it was a strong nurse

– said, 'Hang on a minute, that isn't all we're here for. This woman is saying, "I know I'm depressed and I'd like to talk about it!"' But of course that made the consultant redundant. 'Cause if they're not prescribing, what are they doing?

I think that had we not become Trusts, their position would have become more shaky. I think that the Trust actually works in their favour, because one of the ways of getting a quick turnover is to pump people full of pills. And only a doctor can prescribe a pill.

The 'pharmacological revolution' has changed beyond recognition both the *pace* and the *place* of psychiatric treatments. Based firmly on a bio-medical model of psychiatry, it has vied for domination with a humanistic, social model of treatment which has emphasised the central importance of listening skills, understanding patients' past pains and traumas and valuing, respecting – and indeed, loving – them as whole people. Both models co-exist, but there is often a tension between them, the outcome of which arguably depends on the economic and political sway of the Trust.

8

CONCLUSION

Severalls was built in the heyday of modernism, the start of what Eric Hobsbawm has called 'the short twentieth century'. Now, at its closure, in the midst of postmodernism at the end of the twentieth century, it stands empty. Postmodernism, like modernism, is notoriously difficult to define, but it can be taken as relating broadly to heterogeneity, fragmentation, indeterminacy, and a new concern for difference and 'the other'. Revolutions in technology, communications and pharmacology, as well as a different political and economic climate, have all contributed to what has become a very different means of providing mental health care than at the beginning of the century. Instead of services and resources being consolidated in one space within a unified group of buildings, they are now provided in a more indeterminate and fragmented spatial framework where networks of community psychiatrists, doctors, psychologists and social workers work on a one-to-one basis with patients dispersed over a wide area.[1]

The Trust coordinates activities between some forty-five different sites using e-mail, bleepers, faxes and telephone answering-machines; it operates from a converted villa[2] on a small patch of land of the old Severalls estate. A few acres of the original 300 have been retained. What was once the medical superintendent's house, and later became doctors' flats, has been converted to a long-stay unit for some half-dozen patients. The material conditions here are comfortable, and each patient has his or her own private room. There is, however, almost nothing for them to do except watch television. There is no work, and now there is little open space left for walks. A resident I spoke to talked of boredom and not having had the choice of co-residents. There is also a secure unit near by, surrounded by fencing, where, again, there is little for patients to do, and where overcrowding and inactivity have become (once again) problems.

Beyond the original estate, however, live hundreds, thousands, of people who have at one time or another lived or been treated in Severalls. Some have found a new life and a greater sense of self-respect and dignity by living in their own homes and pursuing their own interests. Patients have been accorded a new status based on an ideal of the individual, the need for individual space and privacy, and the desirability of individual choice, symbolised by the shift from using the implicitly passive term 'patient' to the more active, consumer-orientated term 'client'. Many, however, are confined by unemployment, poverty and the side-effects of drugs to restricted and isolated lives in bedsits and care homes. Some slip through the net altogether and live on the streets and in cardboard boxes. New acute units and care homes are inevitably well furnished and offer patients space and privacy indoors, something Severalls never did. But these are only available to a small minority of people for a very limited period of time.

As hospitals like Severalls close their doors for ever, so new prisons are being built; in recent months, a prison ship was bought from the USA. People who in earlier times would have almost certainly been labelled mentally ill and sent to mental hospitals, are increasingly being imprisoned, confined without treatment. Suicide rates in prisons have risen. Partly this must be a result of the huge increase in drug problems and both drug-related illnesses and drug-related crimes. Boundaries overlap, and in the process punishment seems to be replacing treatment as a means of dealing with deviance. Arguably society has become less, rather than more, tolerant and 'caring'. Perhaps the recent end of eighteen years of Conservative government will change some of these developments.

There has been a tendency to see the old asylums as isolated, inward-looking institutions that may have benefited staff, but rarely patients, while 'community care' gives patients greater opportunities in the wider world. On closer scrutiny what I have found in this study, as in history – and life – generally, is a great deal of contradiction. In some ways conditions have improved for those suffering mental illness, in other ways they have not. Some people have benefited enormously from changes over the past few decades, others have not. Gender differences seem to have been crucial: many women benefited from the facilities for refuge and peace, and the rare chance of female-only space, which Severalls offered.

The idea of mental hospitals as isolated places is, I think, misleading: the wider world was always there. Economic, political and social relations stretched far beyond the hospital walls and permeated and determined life within them. Governments defined and define mental health policies, and have determined in most instances budgets; they have also acted in appointing inspectors and commissioners. Wars have had enormous impact on staff, patients and the conditions within the hospital. Economic recessions, depressions and booms affected poverty, employment, housing conditions and social policies, which in turn affected, albeit in often oblique ways, people's abilities to cope with horrendously difficult material and personal situations. People are still suffering from severe poverty, unemployment and homelessness – more so now than at any other time since the war.

Definitions of mental illnesses have changed and varied over time quite markedly. Changing definitions have also meant changing patterns of treatment. During the course of the twentieth century, and especially from the late 1930s onwards, many new 'cures' were proclaimed in psychiatry, from shock treatment and leucotomies to tranquillisers and anti-depressants. Arguably such treatments *speeded up* recovery, or at least partial or temporary recovery; mental illness, however, still remains poorly understood and the remedies offered provide control rather than cure. Nevertheless, increasing reliance on drugs has affected the *pace* of treatment and thus entries and exits to hospital, enabling a shift from a very long, often a lifetime's, period of slow recuperation (or not) to a very rapid one of a few weeks, which might well be followed by setbacks or recurrences months or years later. This has meant that increasingly people have gone in and out of hospital for short periods on a 'revolving-door' basis. Yet in recent years even the speed at which the door revolves has increased.

Drugs provide a relatively cheap, and easily administered, solution to controlling violence and acute distress, even if they do not cure. Almost all of the patients I spoke to, however, felt factors such as a beautiful and spacious environment, time, psychotherapy, religious belief and, above all, love, were ultimately what helped them most towards recovery. Management, while acknowledging the importance of most of these, prioritises cost-effective treatments.

Certainly nobody I spoke to who had been a patient in Severalls expressed a desire to return to large, overcrowded wards, and some said how much they appreciated the greater privacy and comfort they now have in the new acute units. Almost all of them, however, said how incredibly important the grounds of Severalls, the time they were able to spend there, the human contact with other patients, with certain nurses, occasionally with doctors, were to them. As one woman patient said:

> There's always a lot of love up there, or there always was. And every time I was in, there was some would give me this extra flush of love. It might be staff, it might be visitors, but there was always someone. Members of staff would give up their free time. Not just for me, but for other people. Certainly towards sort of about '87–'89 – all the taboos about touching seemed to go quite suddenly. Up to that point it would just be a pat on the hand, perhaps, but all of a sudden there would be real body hugs – or stroking of the head or the face. They'd be able to do it so naturally.

Space is not static. The main building that still stands is in the same geographical location as it was when it was built. Yet the social relations and interactions that wove their tapestry of hierarchies, friendships,

Figure 8.1 Empty benches by the sports ground, 1950s
Source: North East Essex Mental Health NHS Trust

enmities, treatments, work, and play within that space have gone for ever. The corridors are void of patients, administrators, nurses and workers. There is no sound of human communication. Kinship ties, friendships, employment networks that for much of the twentieth century linked Severalls with the local communities of Colchester, Mile End, Great Horkesley, Boxted, and beyond, no longer intertwine to create patterns of allegiance and solidarity. Nor, it should be said, do they create and sustain patterns of institutionalisation and regimentation. It was these connections, these intricate webs, that effectively *made* this place, and which people associate in their memories with the place itself. For some, the memories are good, even idyllic, for others they remain bad, even terrifying.

Relationships, services, and treatments have been dispersed. Power is still exercised over them all, but in a new form of hierarchy, a less visible one than before, a hierarchy that operates via e-mail, bleepers, faxes and one-to-one encounters, rather than through daily face-to-face contact with many different, but familiar, people. The medical collectivity, the unions, the collectivities of patients, and the relationships they formed through working, living and interacting together within a concentrated space have been weakened almost beyond recognition. For some this has been disastrous. For others, particularly certain groups of patients, it has meant the possibility of new empowerment, new life chances that were less accessible in the days when Severalls manifested the worst kind of institutionalisation.

Dispersal of this nature has arguably weakened collective action by staff and has thus made resistance to the exercise of power at a managerial level far more difficult. Yet the nursing profession has become far more powerful than it was at the beginning of the century. The irony is that the rhetoric of 'community care' which has informed and justified wide-sweeping changes since the 1960s, has, in its implementation during an era of managerialism and monetarism, effectively destroyed what was for a great many people from all walks of life a vibrant and thriving – if not always trouble-free or entirely benign – community which, over time, offered valuable employment, refuge, asylum, and a sense of cooperation and belonging. And yet, paradoxically, a great deal has been achieved in other ways. Contradictions abound: it is, I think, just as foolish to romanticise Severalls' past as it is to demonise it.

NOTES

INTRODUCTION

1 This stretched into the outskirts of the East End of London, included Canvey Island, and reached across to Bishops Stortford and East Hertfordshire.
2 Harvey 1990: 9.
3 Originally there was, for instance, one farm; another was bought in 1931, but both were sold off in 1957.
4 The effects of institutionalisation were described graphically, first by Russell Barton, Severalls' third and final medical superintendent, in his book *Institutional Neurosis* (1959), and secondly, by Goffman (1961) in *Asylums*.
5 Harvey 1990: 215.
6 Bachelard 1964.
7 Laing 1967.
8 See Kay Jamieson, *The Troubled Mind* (1997), for a similar description of her own experiences of being on another planet. She is an eminent psychiatrist.
9 Harvey 1990: 206.
10 Baruch and Treacher 1978: 60. It is interesting to note that previous to this there was a long history of an ideal of treating physically and mentally ill patients under one roof. Thomas Guy, when he founded his hospital in 1722, insisted that twenty beds should be set aside for lunatics. The later geographical isolation of asylums in rural areas was established by the terms of the County Asylum Act of 1808.
11 The Lunacy Commission was created in 1845 by the Lunacy Act and was a central regulatory body authorised to carry out regular inspections of asylums.
12 The Board of Control was responsible for inspection and review of asylums on a regular, usually annual, basis. It was disbanded by the 1959 Act and its functions were transferred to local health authorities.
13 Taylor 1996: 19.
14 Ibid.
15 *Essex County Standard, West Suffolk Gazette and Eastern Counties Advertiser*, 11 October 1902.
16 The word 'Severalls', according to a report in the *Essex County Standard*, was an ancient, now obsolete, word common in Essex and Suffolk. It referred to enclosed land as opposed to the 'commons' or unenclosed lands. Thomas Fuller's *Worthies* published in 1662 mentions this in relation to 'Suffolk Stiles': 'it is a measuring cast whether this proverb pertaineth to Essex or Suffolk and I believe it belongeth to both, which, being enclosed countries into petty

224

quillets, abound with high stiles, troublesome to be clambered over, but the owners grudge not the pains in climbing them, sensible that such *severals* redound much to their own advantage'. (*Essex County Standard*, 1 February 1913, emphasis mine)

17 This, and all the area known as Mile End, had been mostly woodland in the Middle Ages. In the seventeenth century there are records of a house, or inn, on the Severalls Estate called the 'Half Moon'. Severalls Hall, a farm house, was built in the seventeenth century, and in 1704 there is a record of an inn called 'The Spread Eagle' on the estate (*Victoria County History*, vol. IX). It became part of the Colchester Corporation in the 1850s.

18 That year, 1909, was a particularly hard one in Colchester. Kavanagh's, a footwear industry that made army boots and employed some 1,000 people, collapsed.

19 The foundation contract had begun in 1907, with Chessum & Sons, but they soon ran into difficulties with water. At this time an underground storage tank holding 100,000 gallons of subsoil water was built. Overflow was discharged into the pond in nearby Mill Road. The two miles of subways and creepings for heating, lighting and water supply pipes were also built at this time, and a bore hole some 400 feet deep into chalk was begun. This would provide drinking water.

20 *Essex County Standard, West Suffolk Gazette and Eastern Counties Advertiser*, 6 February 1909.

21 Ibid., 16 September 1909.

22 Taylor 1996: 15.

23 Board of Control reports and reports of the Department of Health.

24 Busfield 1986: 265–6.

25 One line went to Lexden, another to East Gates, and the third to Hythe. These all stopped operating in 1928.

26 Taylor 1996: 17.

27 Busfield 1986.

28 Busfield 1986: 260.

29 Barrett Lennard had served continuously on the County Committee for the Essex Asylum since 1859 and had been chairman of it since 1886.

30 During the Second World War part of the chimney shaft had to be removed because it was considered dangerous for low-flying aircraft flying in and out of the nearby Boxted airfield.

31 With the exception of the bombing of Severalls in 1942.

32 Although, of course, rules are made to be broken. In the early 1950s a woman patient became pregnant by a male patient; they had been making love through the railings.

33 *Essex County Advertiser*, 25 June 1910.

34 Rogers and Pilgrim 1996: 27.

35 See MacKenzie for a full account of the history of Ticehurst. Private asylums declined over the course of the twentieth century: in 1900 there were 116 private asylums, whereas by 1938 there were only 50 (Ramon 1985: 44).

36 Jodelet 1991: 238.

37 Jodelet 1991: 262.

38 It is interesting to compare such fears with those today regarding AIDS, although I can also remember my grandmother's veritable horror of the dangers and polluting potential of using public toilets.

39 This has been studied in depth by Bruce Luske in *Mirrors of Madness*.

40 On Defoe Crescent and Mill Road.

41 Denis Hooton, who was secretary of Severalls in the 1950s, pointed out to

me that one of the main reasons for swelling patient numbers at Severalls in the 1950s, a time when many mental hospitals witnessed a decline, was a result of the rapid expansion of Dagenham, which was part of Severalls' catchment area.

42 Odegard (1964) found the decline in Norwegian psychiatric hospitals preceded the introduction of neuroleptic drugs. Scull (1975), drawing on Marxist theory, argues it was a result of economic factors and, in particular, that institutional costs were considered too high in a context of fiscal crisis. This has been criticised by Busfield (1986), who points out that in the 1950s removing patients from hospitals on a large scale was not considered to be a less costly option because of the need to fund after-care provision. Warner (1985), also drawing on Marxist theory, argued the decline was the result of the changing needs of capitalism, particularly a situation where patients could easily get work outside the hospital in a time of labour scarcity.

43 With regard to bricks and mortar, Ernie Smith, who worked for years as an electrician's mate at Severalls, pointed out to me that all the pointing in the brickwork at Severalls was done *upside down*. Was this a quirk, a mark of the building contractors' or bricklayers' own interpretations of suitable work for 'the mad'?

44 Baruch and Treacher 1978: 55.

45 This concept was used by several scholars, notably Phil Brown in *The Transfer of Care* (1985: 91) to describe the 'mere shifting of people from one facility to another ... whereby the location and some of the phenomena of institutional living change, but the underlying personal control and institutional rigidity remain'.

2 AT THE GATE

1 The new front entrance opened on 26 October 1962. Vehicles now entered in what had been the only entrance but could now leave by a new exit. The new entrance offered greater visibility and enabled buses to stop off the main road. There were, in fact, two gates at Severalls. Originally the back gate was used relatively rarely; it afforded access, for instance, for visitors to cricket matches and football games on the playing fields (who were carefully screened on entry and exit).

2 Goffman used this term in *Asylums* (1961) to refer to any institution, such as a prison or mental hospital, in which a group of people live, work and interact together in the same restricted, hierarchically organised space.

3 Jones 1993: 112.

4 Private patients could be admitted by the petition of a relative with the support of two medical recommendations and an order from the JP. This order lasted for one year and was then renewable for periods of two, three and five years on the order of the medical superintendent. Alternatively, private patients could be admitted under an 'urgency order' with an application from a relative and one medical recommendation without a magistrate's order. This lasted for seven days. If the management of property were involved, an inquisition order could be made for 'chancery lunatics'.

5 Presumably the 1890 Act.

6 This is discussed at greater length in Chapter 6.

7 Jones 1993: 113.

8 Butler 1985: 80.

9 Medical superintendent's report, 24 July 1920.
10 The 1930 Mental Treatment Act also introduced 'temporary' status, and the term 'asylum' was officially replaced with that of 'mental hospital'. Nevertheless, although terminology was to some extent changed, mental health policy still remained defined essentially by the lunacy laws of 1890.
11 Jones 1993: 136.
12 Board of Control Report, 5 May 1959.
13 'An Unnecessary Stigma' in Dodds and Johnson 1957: 32–4.
14 Not their real names.
15 Butler 1985: 98.
16 The idea of 'moral treatment' – of treating patients humanely, as if they were in a (presumably benevolent) family – was first developed by the English reformer Tuke and the French reformer Pinel in the late eighteenth and early nineteenth centuries, and were further developed by John Conolly. Self-control and a well-ordered environment were seen as key aspects of such treatment.
17 First, an observation order, which required two medical certificates and lasted twenty-eight days; second, a treatment order, which also required two medical certificates and lasted for one year in the first instance, and could be extended for three years and then two years; third, an emergency order, which would be applied for by a mental welfare officer or a relative and one medical certificate.
18 An assessment order (section 2) lasted for twenty-eight days, and specifically includes provision for 'treatment' as well as 'observation'. The duration of a treatment order (section 3) was halved from one year, while the emergency order (section 4) was restricted so that it could be used only in genuine emergencies and a petition could be made by an approved social worker or the nearest relative.
19 Rogers and Pilgrim 1996: 90.
20 The acute unit in Clacton.
21 It was, indeed, a traction engine. The first mention of it in the records was in June 1920, when apparently it was being overhauled. Since one of the most serious problems the medical superintendent had during the First World War was obtaining, and having delivered, an adequate coal supply, it seems probable that the traction engine was bought in 1919 or early 1920. In 1927 it was recorded that new steel tyres for the wheels of the two Aveling and Porter traction trucks were being fitted, although there is no record of when the second one was purchased.
22 He later qualified as a psychiatric social worker and worked for the County Council mental health services at Severalls in the 1960s.

3 THE CORRIDOR OF POWER

1 Who was later known simply as the Secretary.
2 There were never any women medical superintendents.
3 Although they in fact existed before this time.
4 David Clark 1996: 66.
5 At the end of September, the Territorials had gone, and male patients were put to work returfing the cricket ground.
6 David Clark discusses this in more detail in relation to Fulbourn Hospital.
7 Jones 1993: 142.
8 Clarke 1996: 72.

9 Ramon 1985: 153.
10 The latter two suggestions were eventually implemented, but this process took longer.
11 Wing and Brown 1970: 4.
12 Ibid.
13 Ibid.: 90–1.
14 Ibid.: 100.
15 Ibid.: 118–19.
16 In fact, it was five.
17 Physician superintendent's report, 15 March 1961.
18 Dr Ramsay was the senior administrative medical officer at the Regional Hospital Board. I have, unfortunately, been unable to discover any records from the Regional Hospital Board pertaining to these years.
19 In addition to his much acclaimed first book, *Institutional Neurosis* (1959) his publications up until 1965 included: 'A Simple Bed Cradle (New Invention)', *The Lancet*, 1960; 'The Institutional Mind and Subnormal Mind', *Journ. Ment. Subnorm.*, 1961; 'Schizophrenia in General Hospitals', *Brit. Med. Journ.*, 1961; 'Social Clubs for the Mentally Disturbed', *Mental Health*, 1961; 'Unrestricted Visiting in a Mental Hospital', *The Lancet*, 1961; 'Unrestricted Visiting', *Nursing Times*, 1962; 'Toxic Side Effects of Drug Usage', *Mental Hospitals* (USA), 1963; 'Science and Psychiatry', *The Lancet*, 1963; and 'Symptoms of Diabetes Insipidus and Obsessional Neurosis', *The Lancet*, 1965. He had also been appointed as consultant psychiatrist to the World Health Organization in Malta in 1964.
20 Foreword to Robb, *Sans Everything* (1967: ix–x).
21 Rosenhan, 1973.
22 Jones 1993: 187.
23 The Cogwheel Report recommended that the post of physician superintendent should be phased out.
24 Phoenix Group Homes was set up by Dr Richard Fox and Janet Jacklin in 1966 with a £3,000 grant from the Gulbenkian Foundation. A day hospital for elderly people was set up and they rented, and occasionally bought, properties which were then made suitable for the rehabilitation of ex-patients from Severalls. Especially in the 1970s they provided an increasing amount of space for rehabilitation, but in recent years, with the demise of hospitalisation of what were once chronic patients, and the more complicated, often drug-related, forms of mental illness, these types of homes have become less suitable and less in demand.
25 Bridge and Walshe 1994.
26 Ibid.: 21.

4 THE GREAT DIVIDE

1 Chesler 1972.
2 Busfield 1996: 98, 101.
3 Kay was the nursing assistant/occupational therapist who worked with the women patients.
4 This was reinforced, particularly during the inter-war period, by deliberate recruitment of nursing staff from areas of high unemployment, areas previously characterised by manufacturing industry and high unionisation.
5 Presumably by the unions rather than by Dr Turnbull!

6 By 1909 the Asylum Officers' Superannuation Act meant attendants received a compulsory, but contributory, pension, which was seen by most as a mixed blessing in that it effectively resulted in a wage reduction (Carpenter 1980: 134).

7 NAWU, November 1929.

8 This alone must have been a substantial impediment to being involved in union activities.

9 *The Lancet*, 1 (19 January 1952).

10 Nolan 1993: 13.

11 Diploma of Psychological Medicine – the principal qualification for psychiatry.

12 Not his real name.

5 ON THE FEMALE SIDE

1 The 'backs' were the toilets.

6 ON THE MALE SIDE

1 Published privately in 1935. I found this among some papers at Severalls. Jerry O'Toole, it states on the cover, was for over eleven years an inmate of the Refractory Ward of a county asylum. It was probably Severalls. I have changed the punctuation slightly.

2 Assuming a part-time nurse was equivalent to half a full-time nurse.

3 Female patients and nurses worked on the farm during the First World War, however.

4 Interestingly, the introduction of battery hens led to a decrease in egg production: 200 eggs were being produced daily from 600 hens in 1952.

5 This is not his real name.

6 Busfield 1996: 213.

7 Ibid.: 214.

8 Not his real name.

9 Annual Report, Severalls Hospital, 1960.

10 Women patients made up for lost time: 176 wandered away, the first one to gain her freedom was in 1952 and another succeeded in 1957. Four were found dead. Many made repeat bids and often went out with friends. Two were picked up by the police in Tiptree cinema.

11 At this time the hospital was divided into four semi-autonomous units, each covering part of the catchment area of the hospital overall, and each directed by one of the consultants.

12 In the 1930s, it is interesting to note, a women's cricket team was set up.

13 Nolan 1993: 91.

14 Mr A. Markland was appointed deputy inspector in March 1935.

15 The Medico-Psychological Association became the *Royal* Medico-Psychological Association in 1926.

16 Nolan 1993: 61.

17 The Nurses' Registration Act of 1919 established a register for general nurses with a supplementary list for mental nurses; they also established their own examination which was similar to that of the MPA (Nolan 1993: 81).

18 The comparable figures for female nurses were 115 and 73.

19 There were altogether 1,093 air raids on the Colchester area during the war. A total of 54 people were killed in Colchester, all but 16 of them from Severalls.
20 Cobbold was the clerk and steward then.
21 This scheme of recruiting young school-leavers as cadet nurses began in 1954 with the appointment of Michael Green, aged 15, who was the son of a male nurse at Severalls. Michael Wilson was the second cadet nurse appointed. It was one attempt to redress the increasing shortage of male nurses at the time.

7 THE SPACE AND PACE OF TREATMENTS

1 A straitjacket was last recorded as used at Severalls in 1929, although 'strong clothing' was used until the early 1950s. The 'bunny suits' described earlier seem to have served a similar purpose to straitjackets.
2 Lunbeck 1994: 27.
3 Showalter 1993: 164.
4 The reforms of asylums are documented in, for instance, Digby's study (1985) of the York Retreat, Busfield (1986) and Foucault (1967).
5 Now called bi-polar disorder.
6 Lunbeck 1994: 115.
7 Ibid.: 49.
8 Charlotte Perkins Gilman gives a classic account of the experience of a rest-cure in The Yellow Wallpaper.
9 Valenstein 1986: 35.
10 It is interesting to note that light therapy has again become an acceptable form of treatment, being used for people suffering from seasonal depression, or 'SAD'.
11 Valenstein 1986: 50.
12 Wortis 1936: 498.
13 This is purely hypothetical, as no records have been found for the war years that relate to treatments.
14 Although I have found one reference to insulin being administered to a patient in 1935, this appears to have been a 'one-off'; the minutes record November 1945 as the start of this treatment.
15 Baruch and Treacher 1978: 40.
16 Roy Frank 1978: 1.
17 Ibid.
18 Succinyl choline.
19 Guardian, 22 May 1997.
20 Valenstein 1986: 5.
21 Medical superintendent's annual report.
22 It is interesting to note that a marked imbalance in the sex ratio existed of those he operated on. In 1949 all 52 leucotomies were on women. In 1950 he carried out leuctomies on 3 men and 42 women (3 of whom died). In 1951, 6 men and 34 women. Although there was a greater ratio of women to men in the hospital overall, it was nothing like this (it generally stood at slightly less than a third more of women). For leucotomies between 1950 and 1952 the ratio of women to men was 128:9.
23 These records, however, conflict with a book that recorded operations during this period.
24 Beverley D'Silva, 'When Gay Meant Mad', Independent on Sunday, 4 August 1996.

25 Dr Richard Fox, in an interview with Rosemary Fitzgerald, 7 January 1993, which is held in the National Sound Archive. Unfortunately Dr Fox was unwilling to be interviewed by me.
26 Dr Barton informed me that a few doctors were using it as early as the 1950s in Britain, although it was not used in the USA until the 1970s.
27 Samson 1995b.

8 CONCLUSION

1 Although, of course, the catchment area of the North East Essex Mental Health NHS Trust is in fact much smaller than that which Severalls covered originally.
2 Originally South Villa, built in the inter-war period for male handicrafts; it has been both a ward and a day hospital.

BIBLIOGRAPHY

PRIMARY SOURCES

The main source material for this book came from sixty-five in-depth interviews I carried out in 1995 and 1996 with people who had lived and worked in Severalls at different points in time. I also made extensive use of Dr Russell Barton's personal archives for the 1960s period (letters, documents, reports), now deposited in the Albert Sloman Library at the University of Essex. Though the bulk of the hospital records were destroyed in bonfires in the early 1980s, the following (unarchived) material remained at the hospital at the time of my research there, and is currently in the possession of North East Essex Mental Health NHS Trust:

Annual Report (1960) Severalls Hospital, Colchester, Essex, North-East Regional Hospital Board.
Annual Reports of Phoenix Group Homes, 1966–1995.
Anon. (1976) 'The Run-down of Mental Illness Hospitals', Revised Report No. 575, February 1976, North East Thames Regional Health Authority Management Services.
Anon. (1977) 'The Future Role of Severalls Hospital', February, no publishing details.
Board of Control Reports, 1920–1959.
Books of newspaper clippings, Severalls Hospital, 1960–1980.
Case notes, Severalls Hospital.
Inspector's Book, Severalls Hospital, 1913–1967.
Matron's Book, Severalls Hospital, 1913–1967.
Minutes of the Management Committee, Severalls Hospital, 1913–1969.
Notices Book, Severalls Hospital, c.1919–1936.
Operations Book, Severalls Hospital, 1952–1958.
Plans and maps of Severalls Hospital, various dates.

SECONDARY SOURCES

Acjner, B., Harris, A. and Oldham, A.J. (1957) 'Insulin Treatment of Schizophrenia – a Controlled Study', *Lancet*, 2: 607–11.
Adam, Barbara (1995) *Timewatch: The Social Analysis of Time*, Polity, Cambridge.
Andrews, C.T. (1978) *The Dark Awakening: A History of St Lawrence's Hospital Bodmin*, Cox & Wyman, London.

Annas, George and Grodin, Michael (eds) (1992) *The Nazi Doctors and the Nuremberg Code: Human Rights in Human Experimentation*, Oxford University Press, Oxford.

Anon. (1969) *Warley Hospital, Brentwood: the First Hundred Years 1853–1953*, privately published.

Ashplant, T.G. (1988) 'Psychoanalysis and History', *History Workshop Journal* 26.

Bachelard, G. (1964) *The Poetics of Space*, Beacon Press, Boston.

Barton, Russell (1959[1966]) *Institutional Neurosis*, 2nd edn, John Wright & Sons, Bristol.

Baruch, Geoff and Treacher, Andrew (1978) *Psychiatry Observed*, Routledge & Kegan Paul, London.

Berrios, G. E. and Freeman, H. (eds) (1991) *150 Years of British Psychiatry, 1841–1991*, Gaskell, London.

Bott, Elizabeth (1976) 'Hospital and Society', *British Journal of Medical Psychology*, 49: 97–140.

Botham, Roy (1976) 'Introduction of a Trayed Meal System for Hospital Villa Patients', North Essex Technical College project.

Bourne, H. (1953) 'The Insulin Myth', *Lancet*, 2: 964–8.

Bridge, Christopher and Walshe, John (1994) 'Management of Mental Health Services in North East Essex 1988–1994: A Personal Perspective', unpublished typescript.

Brown, Phil (1985) *The Transfer of Care: Psychiatric Deinstitutionalization and its Aftermath*, Routledge & Kegan Paul, London.

Busfield, Joan (1986) *Managing Madness: Changing Ideas and Practice*, Hutchinson, London.

—— (1996) *Men, Women and Madness*, Macmillan, Basingstoke.

Butler, Tom (1985) *Mental Health, Social Policy and the Law*, Macmillan, Basingstoke.

Carpenter, Mick (1980) 'Asylum Nursing before 1914: A Chapter in the History of Labour', in C. Davies (ed.) *Rewriting Nursing History*, Croom Helm, London.

Chesler, P. (1972) *Women and Madness*, Aron Books, New York.

Clark, David (1996) *The Story of a Mental Hospital: Fulbourn 1858–1983*, Process Press, London.

Cohen, David (1988) *Forgotten Millions*, Paladin, London.

Commissioners in Lunacy (1856) *Suggestions and Illustrations with Reference to Lunatic Asylums*, HMSO, London, revised 1887, 1898 and 1911.

Conolly, John (1847) *The Construction of Government and Lunatic Asylums*, London.

Cooper, A.B. and Early, D. (1961) 'Evolution in the Mental Hospital', *British Medical Journal*, 1: 1600–3.

Crammer, John (1990) *Asylum History: Buckinghamshire County Pauper Lunatic Asylum – St John's*, London, Gaskell (Royal College of Psychiatrists).

Davies, Celia (ed.) (1980) *Rewriting Nursing History*, Croom Helm, London.

Dawson, Jennifer (1985[1961]) *The Ha-Ha*, Virago, London.

Digby, Anne (1985) *Madness, Morality and Medicine: A Study of the York Retreat 1796–1914*, Cambridge University Press, Cambridge.

Dignam, Irene (1995) 'A Little Piece of Nursing History', unpublished.

Dodds, N. and Johnson, D. (1957) *The Plea for the Silent*, Christopher Johnson, London.

Evangelakis, M.G. (1961) 'De-institutionalization of Patients', *Dis. Nerv. System*, 22: 26–32.

Foucault, Michel (1967) *Madness and Civilization: A History of Insanity in the Age of Reason*, Tavistock, London.

233

—— (1975 [1977]) *Discipline and Punish*, Penguin, London.
Frank, Leonard Roy (ed.) (1978) *The History of Shock Treatment*, privately published, San Francisco.
Game, A. and Pringle, R. (1983) 'Sex and Power in Hospitals: The Division of Labour in the "Health" Industry', in A. Game and R. Pringle, *Gender at Work*, George Allen & Unwin, Hemel Hempstead.
Gilman, Charlotte Perkins (1981) *The Yellow Wallpaper*, Virago, London.
Goffman, E. (1961) *Asylums: Essays on the Social Situation of Mental Patients and Other Inmates*, Penguin, Harmondsworth.
Granshaw, Lindsay and Porter, Roy (eds) (1989) *The Hospital in History*, Routledge, London.
Grygier, P. and Waters, M.A. (1958) 'Chlorpromazine Used with an Intensive Occupational Therapy', *AMA Arch. Neurol. and Psychiatry*, 79: 697–705.
Harrison, A.B.C. (1963) *Severalls Hospital, Colchester, 1913–1963*, privately published.
Harvey, David (1990) *The Condition of Postmodernity*, Blackwell, Oxford.
Hobsbawm, Eric (1995) *Age of Extremes: The Short Twentieth Century 1914–1991*, Abacus, London.
Hordern, A. and Hamilton, M. (1963) 'Drugs and Moral Treatment', *British Journal of Psychiatry*, 109: 500–9.
Hunter, Richard and MacAlpine, Ida (1974) *Psychiatry for the Poor: 1851 Colney Hatch Asylum – Friern Hospital 1973: A Medical and Social History*, Dawson, London.
Jamieson, Kay (1997) *The Troubled Mind*, Macmillan, London.
Jodelet, Denise (1991) *Madness and Social Representation*, Harvester Wheatsheaf, Brighton.
Jones, Kathleen (1993) *Asylums and After: A Revised History of the Mental Health Service from the Early 18th Century to the 1990s*, Athlone Press, London.
Kaplan, Bert (1964) *The Inner World of Mental Illness: A Series of First-person Accounts of What it Was Like*, Harper & Row, New York.
Knight, Stephen (1983) *The Brotherhood*, HarperCollins, London.
Laing, R.D. (1960) *The Divided Self*, Tavistock, London.
—— (1967) *The Politics of Experience*, Penguin, Harmondsworth.
Liggett, Helen and Perry, David (1995) *Spatial Practices: Critical Explorations in Social/Spatial Theory*, Sage, London.
Lomax, Montagu (1921) *The Experiences of an Asylum Doctor*, Allen & Unwin, London.
Lunbeck, Elizabeth (1994) *The Psychiatric Persuasion: Knowledge, Gender and Power in Modern America*, Princeton University Press, Princeton NJ.
Lupton, Deborah (1994) *Medicine as Culture: Illness, Disease and the Body in Western Society*, Sage, London.
Luske, Bruce (1990) *Mirrors of Madness: Patrolling the Psychic Border*, Aldine de Gruyter, New York.
Massey, Doreen (1994) *Space, Place and Gender*, Polity, Cambridge.
MacKenzie, Charlotte (1992) *Psychiatry for the Rich: A History of Ticehurst Private Asylum, 1792–1917*, Routledge, London.
Moore, Henrietta L. (1986) *Space, Text and Gender*, Cambridge University Press, Cambridge.
Nolan, Peter (1993) *A History of Mental Health Nursing*, Chapman and Hall, London.
Odegard, O. (1964) 'Pattern of Discharge from Norwegian Psychiatric Hospitals before and after the Introduction of Psychotropic Drugs', *American Journal of Psychiatry*, 20: 772–8.

O'Toole, Jeremy (1936) *Asylum Life in Verse*, privately printed.

Passerini, Luisa (1983) 'Memory', *History Workshop Journal*, 15, Spring.

Penfold, John B. (1984) *The History of Essex County Hospital, Colchester 1820–1948* Lavenham Press, Lavenham.

Portelli, Alessandro (1981) 'The Peculiarities of Oral History', *History Workshop Journal*, 12, Autumn.

Porter, Roy (1987) *A Social History of Madness: Stories of the Insane*, Weidenfeld & Nicolson, London.

—— (1992) 'Foucault's Great Confinement' in A. Still and I. Velody (eds) *Rewriting the History of Madness*, Routledge, London.

Prior, Lindsay (1993) *The Social Organization of Mental Illness*, Sage, London.

Proctor, Robert (1992) 'Nazi Doctors, Racial Medicine and Human Experimentation' in G. Annas and M. Grodin (eds), *The Nazi Doctors and the Nuremberg Code: Human Rights in Human Experimentation*, Oxford University Press, Oxford.

Ramon, Shulamit (1985) *Psychiatry in Britain: Meaning and Policy*, Gower, London.

Randall, Lou (1993) 'Nursing at Severalls 1935–1990: An Oral History', unpublished M.A. thesis, University of Essex.

Robb, Barbara (1967) *Sans Everything*, Nelson & Sons, London.

Rogers, Anne and Pilgrim, David (1996) *Mental Health Policy in Britain: A Critical Introduction*, Macmillan, Basingstoke.

Rosenhan, S. (1973) 'On Being Sane in Insane Places', *Science* 179: 250–8.

Samson, Colin (1995a) 'Madness and Psychiatry', in B. Turner (ed.) *Medical Power and Social Knowledge*, 2nd edn, Sage, London.

—— (1995b) 'The Fracturing of Medical Dominance in British Psychiatry?', *Sociology of Health and Illness*, 17, 2, March.

Samuel, Raphael and Thompson, Paul (eds) (1990) *The Myths We Live By*, Routledge, London.

Scull, Andrew (1975) 'From Madness to Mental Illness: Medical Men as Entrepreneurs', *Archives Européennes de Sociologies*, 16: 218–61.

—— (1979) *Museums of Madness. The Social Organization of Insanity in Nineteenth-Century England*, Allen Lane, London.

—— (1989) *Social Order/Mental Disorder: Anglo-American Psychiatry in Historical Perspective* Routledge, London.

Showalter, Elaine (1993) *The Female Malady: Women, Madness, and English Culture, 1830–1980*, Virago, London.

Smith, Dilys (1986) *Park Prewett Hospital: The History 1898–1984*, privately published.

Smith, Gertrude (n. d.) *The Old Manor Hospital Salisbury, Wiltshire: Private Madhouse – Licensed Ayslum – Psychiatric Hospital*, privately published.

Sommer, C. and Weinberg, J. (1944) 'Techniques and Factors Reversing the Trend of Population Growth in Illinois State Hospitals', *American Journal of Psychiatry*, 100.

Still, Arthur and Velody, Irving (1992) *Rewriting the History of Madness: Studies in Foucault's 'Histoire de la folie'*, Routledge, London.

Stevenson, John (1977) *Social Conditions in Britain Between the Wars*, Penguin, London.

Szasz, Thomas (1987) *Insanity*, Wiley & Sons, New York.

Taylor, Jeremy (1996) 'The Architectural Image of the Asylum', in *The Victorian Society Annual 1995*, The Victorian Society, London.

Turner, Bryan (1987) *Medical Power and Social Knowledge*, Sage, London.

Valenstein, Elliot S. (1986) *Great and Desperate Cures: The Rise and Decline of Psychosurgery and Other Radical Treatments for Mental Illness*, Basic Books, New York.

Victoria County History: A History of Essex, vol. IX (1994), Oxford University Press, Oxford.

Warner, Richard (1985) *Recovery from Schizophrenia: Psychiatry and Political Economy*, Routledge & Kegan Paul, London.

White, Antonia (1965[1979]) *Beyond the Glass*, Virago, London.

Wing, J.K. and Brown, G.W. (1970) *Institutionalization and Schizophrenia* Cambridge University Press, Cambridge.

Wortis, J. (1936) 'On the Response of Schizophrenic Subjects to Hypoglycaemic Insulin Shock', *Journal of Nervous and Mental Diseases*, 85 (November).

Youngson, R. and Schott, I. (1996) *Medical Blunders*, Robinson, London.

INDEX